JERUSALEM:

THE ENDLESS CRUSADE

BOOKS BY ANDREW SINCLAIR

Nonfiction

Prohibition: The Era of Excess
The Available Man: The Life Behind the Masks of Warren Gamaliel Harding
The Better Half: The Emancipation of the American Woman
The Last of the Best: The Aristocracy of Europe in the Twentieth Century
A Concise History of the United States
Guevara
Dylan Thomas: Poet of His People
Jack: A Biography of Jack London
John Ford: A Biography
Corsair: The Life of J. Pierpont Morgan
The Other Victoria
Sir Walter Raleigh and the Age of Discovery
The Red and the Blue: Intelligence, Treason and the Universities
Spiegel: The Man Behind the Pictures
War Like a Wasp: The Last Decade of the Forties
*The Sword and the Grail: Of the Grail and the Templars and a
True Discovery of America*
Francis Bacon: His Life and Violent Times

Fiction

The Breaking of Bumbo
My Friend Judas
The Hallelujah Bum
The Raker
The Facts in the Case of E. A. Poe
Gog
Magog
King Ludd

Plays

My Friend Judas
Adventures in the Skin Trade
The Blue Angel

Screenplays

Before Winter Comes
Under Milk Wood
Martin Eden

JERUSALEM:

THE ENDLESS
CRUSADE

ANDREW
SINCLAIR

CROWN PUBLISHERS, INC.
NEW YORK

To Sonia, who also took
me to a heavenly city

Published by Crown Publishers, Inc., 201 East 50th Street, New York, New
York 10022. Member of the Crown Publishing Group.

Random House, Inc. New York, Toronto, London, Sydney, Auckland

CROWN is a trademark of Crown Publishers, Inc.

Manufactured in the United States of America

Design by Jennifer Harper

Library of Congress Cataloging-in-Publication Data
Sinclair, Andrew.
Jerusalem : the endless crusade / Andrew Sinclair.
Includes index.
1. Jerusalem—History.   2. Jerusalem in Judaism.   3. Jerusalem in
Christianity.   4. Jerusalem in Islam.   I. Title.
DS109.9.S54   1995
956.94′42—dc20   95-30704
                                                        CIP

ISBN 0-517-59476-5

10 9 8 7 6 5 4 3 2 1

First Edition

CONTENTS

ACKNOWLEDGMENTS

I could not have written this history of Jerusalem in particular without the previous insight and inspiration of Karen Armstrong, Alexander Horne, the King James Bible, Teddy Kollek, Bernard Lewis, Amin Maalouf, Zoé Oldenbourg, Jonathan Riley-Smith, Colin Thubron, A. A. Vasiliev, and Villehardouin. Their works are fully acknowledged in the notes on the text.

I am personally grateful for reproducing maps of Jerusalem and Outremer by kind permission of Sir Steven Runciman, *A History of the Crusades*, copyright © 1966, 1968 by Steven Runciman, and also by permission of Cambridge University Press.

ONE

HEAVEN'S GATE

I give you the end of a golden string
Only wind it into a ball:
It will lead you in at Heaven's gate,
Built in Jerusalem's wall.

—William Blake, *Jerusalem*

Jerusalem is a quest as well as a place. It is a journey to a goal that may never be reached. Its founders hardly saw in it a heavenly city as the Christians were to do, because the ancient Jews believed that heaven was the house of God, while they would finish in *sheol,* a form of mindless Hades or Purgatory, after their time on earth. Although it was built with its Temple as a religious centre, where the tribes of Israel might gather at the three great festivals of worship of the year, the Passover and Pentecost and the Feast of Tabernacles, Jerusalem was a meeting place at the end of a pilgrimage. After Shiloh, it had been created as the resting ground for the Ark of the Covenant, the Law given to Moses in Sinai which governed the tribes of Israel during their long wanderings from slavery in Egypt into the Promised Land. It was a point of return as much as a vision of hope, for the Jews often lost it to conquerors; the Temple was ruined three times and never rebuilt, to become a symbol without stones to the scattered tribes in their Diaspora over the globe and also to hundreds of millions of Christians, who would never catch sight of the object of their prayers. On the rock of the Temple, the Muslims would build a dome to

1

signify the passing on one night of their prophet, Muhammad, on his ride to heaven, and this third religion would recognize along with Christianity that the prophets of Israel were their prophets and that Jerusalem was a holy of holies. For the believer and the dreamer, for the mystic rather than the geographer, Jerusalem was a search for an ideal and a paradise. It transcended that minor spot on the map, where peoples and cultures had been in conflict for millennia in the Middle East. Its fame was its reality and girdled the planet. In the words of William Blake:

> Jerusalem covererd the Atlantic Mountains & the Erythrean,
> From bright Japan & China to Hesperia France & England.
> Mount Zion lifted his head in every Nation under heaven:
> And the Mount of Olives was beheld over the whole Earth:
> The footsteps of the Lamb of God were there: but now no more.

Although it seemed a vision of peace, a kind of urban Eden, the irony of Jerusalem was that it was created from civil war in an unsuitable environment. Lost in arid and stony mountains, without minerals or produce or much water, at no crossroads for the caravans, this little segment of the Jebusites appeared the least likely candidate for the *omphalos,* what the ancient Greeks called the navel of the world. But David's struggle against his father-in-law, Saul, and the splitting of the government of Israel between the southern and the northern tribes about 1000 B.C., made him choose neutral ground for building a capital that could unite the Jews and heal their tribal divisions. It was an act of royal strategy that would presage the founding of Madrid on its dry plateau or St. Petersburg on a marshland.

Perhaps David's great grace in founding his Jerusalem was not to massacre its Jebusite citizens, but to incorporate them. For Moses had already said that the Lord had ordered the annihilation and subjugation of the original inhabitants of Canaan in a holy war. As Deuteronomy stated:

> When the Lord thy God shall bring thee into the land whither thou goest to possess it, and hath cast out many nations before thee, the Hittites, and the Girgashites, and the Amorites, and the Canaanites, and the Perizzites, and the Hivites, and the Jebusites, seven nations greater and mightier than thou;

And when the Lord thy God shall deliver them before thee; thou shalt smite them, and utterly destroy them; thou shalt make no covenant with them, nor shew mercy unto them. . . .

But thus shall ye deal with them; ye shall destroy their altars, and break down their images, and cut down their groves, and burn their graven images with fire.

For thou art an holy people unto the Lord thy God: the Lord thy God has chosen thee to be a special people unto himself, above all people that are upon the face of the earth.

Joshua had particularly practised the policy of what is now called ethnic cleansing, as can still be read in the biblical account of his reign, where he killed all the inhabitants of Ai, men and women together to the number of twelve thousand, and burned the town. "For Joshua drew not his hand back, wherewith he stretched out the spear, until he had utterly destroyed all the inhabitants of Ai. . . . And Joshua burnt Ai, and made it a heap for ever, even a desolation unto this day." He exterminated king after king and tribe after tribe, particularly in Hebron. "And they took it and smote it with the edge of the sword, and the king thereof, and all the cities thereof, and all the souls that were therein; he left none remaining."

The books of the Old Testament showed that the land of Israel was founded by a holy war, in which the invaders were instructed to keep themselves exclusive as members of God's only Chosen People. To centralise the twelve tribes, King David of Judah's act of genius was to transfer the Ark of the Covenant from Joshua's Shiloh, twenty miles to the north of his city. This would provide the focus for religious ritual on the rock of Mount Moriah, where Abraham had nearly sacrificed Isaac to the Lord. The Law given to Moses would be put on a blessed stone and housed in a temple that would attract all the Jews. The possession of the Ark and its temple would consecrate the ruler of Jerusalem. And the rock, on which the Ark was placed, would become the treasure of those faiths that were to be rooted in Judaism, the Christian and the Muslim beliefs.

In Hebrew myth, the site of the Temple of Jerusalem was also supposed to be where the waters of the Flood had gushed out before they had receded into the abyss and had been sealed by the stone of Mount Moriah.

This rock was called Ebhen Shetiyyah, the Stone of Foundation, and it was the first solid thing in Creation, when God had made this earth from the primaeval waters. From it, all life was fed as an unborn baby is fed from a mother's umbilical cord. The waters of the Garden of Eden were also held to have their source near the rock in the Gihon Spring and the Pool of Siloam, where King David may have seen Bathsheba in her washing of herself and stolen her for his wife and had her husband killed. His lethal deeds and personal misdeeds were enough for the Lord God to tell him not to build the Temple, but to leave the task to his son Solomon by Bathsheba, or so the Book of Chronicles stated, making David confess, "But the word of the Lord came to me, saying, Thou has shed blood abundantly, and hast made great wars: thou shalt not build an house unto my name." Beset by rebellious sons of his own such as Absolom and Adonijah, David was also plagued by appetites that turned him into a capricious despot. Yet he did bequeath a coherent kingdom to his chosen son and an alliance with Hiram, king of Tyre, that would make his planned city of Jerusalem the significant symbol of the Western and Near Eastern religious worlds for the next three thousand years.

Except for the Great Pyramid of Egypt and Stonehenge, the Temple of Solomon has excited more sublime mysticism and small sense than any other human construction. Alone of these three places, the Temple does not survive, and there is no proof in archaeology that it ever existed. Where it stood on Mount Moriah, the Dome of the Rock by the Mosque of Omar, now stands over Abraham's altar. The Western Wall, where the Jews still pray, and the caverns of "Solomon's Stables" are traditionally part of the Temple complex, as is Heaven's Gate, through which the Messiah is expected to arrive. But disappearance is the meat of speculation and the drink of theory. The fact that the Temple is no longer there in any part of its three versions allows fancy to take flight. It is held to have been modelled on the Phoenician temples of that time and built as a tall rectangle with a large porch to the east and a dark inner cubicle Devir to enshrine the Ark, based on the plan of the tent or Tabernacle that Moses made for the Ark in Sinai. But in truth, the Temple of Solomon is only the repository of biblical accounts and mystical hypotheses. Perhaps the visionary Blake showed a profound insight when he made his giant Albion speak the words:

Hide thou Jerusalem in impalpable voidness: not to be
Touched by the hand nor seen with the eye: O Jerusalem,
Would thou wert not & that thy place might never be found.

In the biblical books of Kings and Chronicles, Solomon built his Temple with opulence and dignity. David had provided the treasury and the resources and the skilled labour for the mighty construction. Again in the Book of Chronicles, he tells his son:

"Now, behold, in my trouble I have prepared for the house of the Lord an hundred thousand talents of gold, and a thousand thousand talents of silver; and of brass and iron without weight; for it is in abundance: timber also and stone have I prepared; and thou mayest add thereto.

"Moreover there are workmen with thee in abundance, hewers and workers of stone and timber, and all manner of cunning men for every manner of work.

"Of the gold, the silver, and the brass, and the iron, there is no number. Arise therefore, and be doing, and the Lord be with thee."

Arise therefore, and be doing. That was cogent in the accounts of the building of the Temple, both to the Jews and later to the Christians and the Masons. These were *practical* directives for making a home for the Ark of the Covenant and, in the words of the Book of Kings, "an house for the name of the Lord God of Israel." Parts of the Old Testament are almost a builder's manual, while in the Book of Revelation, the inspiration of St. John on the island of Patmos is a surveyor's apocalypse and an architect's apotheosis in the measuring of the Temple with a "reed like a rod." The original Temple of Solomon was described as the work of a multitude of hands in the service of a transcendent vision. Labourer and overseer and prophet were one in a sacred purpose. Thumb and brain served together; matter met with mind. The building of the Temple of Solomon, who was credited with the wisdom as well as the holiness of the Oriental priest-king, was a paradigm for those who wished to unify tribes and clans into a people or a society. In that common and divine work was a harmony between rich and poor, high and low. It was a vision of peace on earth and a heavenly city in a Temple that no longer was and in a Jerusalem that few believers would ever see within its meagre walls and on its stony hills.

A specific artist and architect with a Jewish mother and a Phoenician father, Hiram of Tyre was credited with the design of the Temple. He was, according to the Book of Chronicles, "a cunning man, endued with understanding . . . skilful to work in gold, and in silver, in brass, in iron, in stone, and in timber, in purple, in blue, and in fine linen, and in crimson; also to grave any manner of graving, and to find out every device which shall be put to him." He also was credited with legendary tools like the Excalibur of the later King Arthur, which could pierce stone. For as the Book of Kings stated, the Temple "was built of stone made ready before it was brought thither; so that there was neither hammer nor axe nor any tool of iron heard in the house, while it was in building." The prohibition of the use of tools within the Temple derived from Exodus, when the Lord had directed Moses to make a stone altar without mechanical means, "for if thou lift up thy tool upon it, thou hast polluted it." And so rabbinical tradition ascribed the dovetailing of the prefabricated stones and ornaments of the Temple to the Shamir, a giant worm that could cut stones, a tradition that would fit into Celtic and Norse traditions of the dragon's fire that constructed vitrified forts and Valhalla and Camelot.

The two pillars of the porch of the Temple called Jachin and Boaz, a feature of every future Masonic lodge, were probably modelled on the pair of obelisks that fronted many Egyptian temples or the pillar of pure gold and the pillar of emerald that Herodotus saw at Tyre in front of the Temple of Hercules. For Hiram cast in the plain of Jordan in the Biblical accounts "two pillars of brass of eighteen cubits high apiece. . . . And he made chains, as in the oracle, and put them on the heads of the pillars, and made a hundred pomegranates, and put them on the chains. . . . And four hundred pomegranates on the two wreaths; two rows of pomegranates on each wreath, to cover the two pommels of the chapiters which were upon the pillars." The altar of the Temple was also made of brass, and the Molten Sea beside it was supported by twelve brazen oxen. As in Homer's house of Alcinous and the treasuries at Mycenae and the Etruscan tombs of the Bronze Age, metal plates were used for decoration far more than carved designs in stone. The whole Temple of Solomon glittered with precious and base metals, as if fired in the forges of heaven. And the mystical numbers of its making, particularly the units of two and twelve, were to occupy the visions and arithmetic of the three religions which saw in sacred Jerusalem a holy city.

To the Christian St. John the Divine, a New Jerusalem came down from God, prepared as a bride adorned for her husband. This mystic city shone like jasper and was as clear as crystal. In its great wall, it had twelve gates, which bore the names of twelve angels, which were the names of the twelve tribes of Israel. There were twelve foundations to the wall and in them the names of the twelve apostles of the Lamb of God. Twelve precious stones garnished the foundations and "the twelve gates were twelve pearls; every several gate was of one pearl: and the street of the city was pure gold, as it were transparent glass. . . . And the city lieth foursquare, and the length is as large as the breadth." This was twelve thousand furlongs, as was the height, making a gigantic cube, while the wall was a hundred and forty and four cubits. The measurements of the New Jerusalem were all in units of two or twelve or their multiples, as were the figures given of the Temple by the Books of Kings and Chronicles. There was a counting and a geometry to the sacred numbers that were thought to be the dimensions of the Temple and the city of Solomon.

The square and the cube had been the preferred cosmic shapes used for city planning by the first priest-kings of the Near East, although a circle is shown enclosing the regions of the world on one small clay tablet from Babylon. The first surviving picture of the Third or Herod's Temple on the coins of the Bar Kochba period around A.D. 135 shows a square entrance with four Hellenistic pillars leading to the cube of the Tabernacle enclosing the Ark of the Covenant. That shape was suggested by the Lord God to Moses in the Bible, which is why it recurred in the revelation of the Heavenly City to St. John. The idea of the cosmos as a cube pervaded the thought and planning of ancient India and China and the Near East, which seem to have shared their views on the design of the universe and the mathematical correspondence of its quarters and parts. After ancient Oriental wisdom had bequeathed the square and the cube as the basic pattern of creation to the Jews, so they passed it on to the Christians, who found in the Old Testament the descriptions of the Tabernacle of Moses and the first encampment of the twelve tribes of Israel; these were to be shown in Templo's *Retrato del Tabernaculo de Moseh* of 1654 as a small square surrounded by the twelve larger squares of the tents of the tribes, all contained in one regular field with four equal sides. In mind, if not in fact, the Tabernacle and the Temple were the cubes of symbolic creation.

Not even his kingdom survived the death of Solomon, so wise in his judgement, so pacific in his diplomacy, so voluptuous in his tastes, so prodigal in his works. The northern tribes of Israel revolted, and Jerusalem remained only the capital of Judah, unable to attract pilgrims from outside its borders. The priests and the Levites, however, did congregate in the religious centre of the faith, and the preaching and the prophecies of Elijah and Isaiah lauded and lamented Jerusalem. Disaster fell on the northern tribes when the kingdom of Israel was conquered in 722 B.C. by the Assyrians. Ten of the twelve tribes were deported and forced into apostasy and disappeared from history. The scatterings of them joined Josiah, who again unified the remnants of the Jewish tribes by insisting there was only one Temple which might house the Lord God, and that was the building of Solomon. It was Jeremiah who foresaw the destruction of Jerusalem and the Temple, if Judah did not surrender to the rising power of Nebuchadnezzar, the monarch of Babylon. The survival of the holy places transcended the independence of the Jewish state. But Jeremiah was imprisoned in a cistern, and Jerusalem was besieged and captured and razed, and the Judean people were taken as hostages and slaves to Babylon to sit by its waters and weep for their burned sanctuary.

Yet the deported were not forced by the Babylonians to assimilate, as they had been in Assyria. They were allowed to form what was the first of the ghettos. In exile by the Euphrates, Ezekiel told the Hebrews that they had lost their sacred house because of divine punishment for their sins. But they would go back in glory to rebuild the Temple, if they repented. In the meantime, a local square house of prayer, the synagogue, was to be built to act as a guardian of the faith, as the Tabernacle of Moses had been. Again the people of the tribes of Israel were wandering, the beginning of a cycle of expulsion and return that would mark the eventual Diaspora, or scattering of the Jews over the surface of the globe. Yet as in Babylon, each dispersed community would form a congregation and a synagogue to remember the Temple and to keep the holy law. The rituals and the designs of Jerusalem were carried in words and pictures wherever the Jews were flung by the grabbing hands of history.

The destruction of the First Temple had also been foretold by the death of its architect, Hiram of Tyre, the memory of which was preserved in the literature of the Cabbala. As old as the construction of the ziggurats and the pyramids had been the concept of a foundation sacrifice to ensure the stability of the building. It was fitting that Hebrew tradition would see that sacrificial victim in the human creator of the Temple at Jerusalem. According to the *Jewish Encyclopedia,* a rabbinical legend stated that all the workmen of the Temple were killed so that they should not build another one devoted to idolatry, while Hiram was raised like Enoch to heaven. But the later Masonic tradition was that Hiram was murdered by three fellow master craftsmen, because he would not reveal to them the secrets of how the Temple was made. There are Promethean and Dionysian elements in both the Judaic and the Christian versions of the death of Hiram; yet all saw in the destruction of the Temple the loss of the mysteries of its creator, perhaps in consequence of his own secret knowledge.

When the Persians under Cyrus conquered Babylon fifty years after the destruction of Jerusalem, he permitted the return of those Jewish exiles who wished to rebuild their city. Under Sheshbazzar, the prince of Judah, and his successor, Zerubbabel, first the houses and then the Second Temple were restored. It was built in the size and shape of Solomon's house of the Lord, but in simple stone and with little decoration. As there were yet no walls to defend them, each Temple builder—in the words of their later leader Nehemiah—"with one of his hands wrought in the work, and with the other hand held a weapon." They set an example for the later Christian knights of the Order of the Temple of Solomon, the Templars. That had been a concrete example of the making of the house of God as a Crusade. But at that time, the New Jerusalem was populated by only a few thousand dwellers on rubble, until the prophet Ezra led back another group of exiles to rebuild the city wall in its long lozenge about Mount Moriah. The Torah once again became the law of the land, and Persian tolerance allowed the recrudescence of the Jewish faith in a form that was both more pure and subtle. Pilgrims from beyond the borders of Judah began to return for the three sacred annual festivals in Jerusalem, beginning that long quest for the Holy City that was to inform the practise and the thought and even the conflicts of succeeding ages.

When Alexander of Macedon defeated the Persians and conquered the

Near East, he did not harm Jerusalem. He usually respected the religions of those lands which he occupied, in order to rule them the better. Josephus in his history, *The Antiquities of the Jews,* described the Greek king's awe at the priests in their silk robes and the high priest in purple with a plate of gold on his forehead inscribed with the sacred name of God. The grateful Jews assisted their new ruler in founding the city in Egypt which was called Alexandria after him, and there the second-largest community of Jews in exile after Babylon would establish itself for the benefit of that great port by the Nile. Yet in their prayers and in their synagogues, those who lived abroad still turned in worship towards Jerusalem.

After the death of Alexander, the Ptolemy rulers in Egypt continued to treat their Jewish province with kindness, but when their dynasty was defeated by the Seleucids in Syria, one of them, Antiochus Epiphanes, tried to impose the worship of the Greek gods on Jerusalem, provoking the revolt of those five masters of guerrilla warfare called the Maccabees of the house of Hasmon. They reestablished the independence of Judah and Jerusalem, then the Temple was dedicated once more, a celebration that is still commemorated in the Chanuka, or the Festival of Lights. They played the growing power of the Roman Empire against the decline of the Seleucids and captured some of the old Philistine ports to gain access to the Mediterranean. The gains in territory of the descendants of the house of Hasmon were torn apart by the quarrels between the reactionary and dogmatic Sadducees, who initially controlled the Temple and the council of elders called the Sanhedrin, and the Pharisees, who represented a strict but evolutionary Judaism. Their conflicts split the state and allowed for the invasion of Pompey, the Roman general, who took Jerusalem and the Temple Mount and made Judah into the Roman province of Judea. Except for an incursion by the Parthians and brief rebellions, the Romans would remain sovereign in the Holy City for four hundred years. They chose Herod as king of their province—perhaps the greatest ruler and builder of Jerusalem after David and Solomon, but with the worst of reputations because he was imposed upon the Jews—an Edomite whose family had once had conversion forced upon them by the conquering Israelites. A friend of Rome and Hellenism from an enemy tribe, Herod had to recapture Jerusalem with the help of mercenaries and Roman legions, and then behead the last of the house of Hasmon and the whole Sanhedrin to establish his long authority in a reign of thirty-three years, ending with his death shortly after the birth of Jesus Christ.

As a builder, Herod behaved like a pharaoh. The fortresses of Masada overlooking the Dead Sea and Herodium above Bethlehem and the port city of Caesarea were his creations, as well as the magnificence of a New Jerusalem, which he surrounded with stone blocks in huge walls and watchtowers. He watered his capital with aqueducts and cisterns, he buttressed the Temple Mount and dominated it with the citadel Antonia and his own palace by the Jaffa Gate, and he rebuilt the remains of the Second Temple of Zerubbabel according to the biblical ground plan of the original structure, doubling the height of the gold-plated porch in front of the inner cube, and levelling the top of Mount Moriah into a vast, flat rectangle supported by retaining walls. The Western Wall, also called the Wailing Wall by the Christians, has remained the most sacred place for scattered Jewry for the past nineteen hundred years, and it was built at Herod's command.

His wife Mariamne came from the house of Hasmon, and her intrigues to replace him with their children and her relatives led to his vengeance against the plotters. "Better to be Herod's pig," the Roman emperor Octavian remarked, "than his son." Although three sons still survived to inherit his kingdom, their squabbles led to a revolt by Zealots expecting a new Messiah to rescue them from Roman rule. The answer of the new emperor, Tiberius, was to appoint a procurator, Pontius Pilate, to govern his unruly province. A severe and rapacious man, he punished all rebellion and plundered the Temple revenues, but he wisely held aloof from the internecine religious quarrels between the Pharisees and the Sadducees and the Zealots and other messianic sects that kept the city in turmoil with their visions of liberation and apocalypse.

Among those who went from the village of Galilee on an annual pilgrimage to the Temple was the infant and the child Jesus. "His parents went to Jerusalem," as St. Luke recounts, "every year at the feast of the Passover." He returned there with his disciples on his last pilgrimage, the expected Messiah come to the Holy City in the belief of the later Christians, but not of the Jews. At the Temple, his action reported in the Bible was to drive out the money changers from the house of the Lord. Condemned as a false Messiah by the Pharisees and the Sadducees, and feared by Pilate as a potential leader of another Jewish rebellion, he was crucified for the divisions in the Holy City between the Roman garrison and the fierce rivalry of the Jewish sects. His message of love and brotherhood was lost in political conflict. And the manner of his trial and his execution was to lead to many other destructions and occupations of Jerusalem. The Christians, who later believed that Jesus was the Son of God who died on the cross to save mankind, were to accuse the Jews of being Christ-killers and forgive the Romans, who actually put Jesus to death. It was a further irony that the Catholic Christian church should be founded by St. Peter upon a rock in Rome, making it a second holy city that derived from the example of Jerusalem, where the Jews had merely condemned a fellow Jew named Jesus for not being the true Messiah whom they were expecting. The judicial murder of Christ on Golgotha was to wreak a terrible vengeance on the sacred places of his ritual travels. Because of his believed sacrifice for the sins of humankind, Christian armies would change his pilgrimage into their Crusade, his palm branch into their sword.

Twice more, the Zealots among the Jews rebelled against the Romans; but their second defeat resulted in the laying waste of Jerusalem and Herod's Temple. Under Roman tax gatherers, thousands of other Jews were crucified for their resistance, until in A.D. 66, the Zealots and the Sicarii, an extreme group of Pharisees, rose up, crying, "No god but God, no tax but to the Temple!" The procurator Florus outraged all Judea by looting the Temple and sacking the Upper City of Jerusalem. The Zealots seized the fortress of Masada and the Lower City, while Florus fled to Caesarea and massacred the Jews, a crime which was answered by the destruction of the Roman garrison in the Antonia fortress in Jerusalem. Faced with the loss of Judea, the emperor Nero sent his leading general Vespasian with his son Titus to subdue the province with his legions. On Nero's death, Vespasian became the Roman emperor and left Titus to retake Jerusalem. After many assaults and a siege, the troops of Titus burst into the city and washed the walls of the Temple with Zealot blood and left the holy places in heaps of rubble. A final heroic stand by the Sicarii at Masada, which had been built by Herod as his bastion of last resort, took thirty months of blockade to reduce its thousand defenders to the necessity of mass suicide. "Let us go from the world," their leader, Eleazer, said in the record of Josephus, "together with our children and our wives, in a state of freedom. This is what our laws command us to do."

Sixty years later, in A.D. 130, the rabbi Akiva inspired the last revolt that would obliterate Jerusalem. In the Talmud of Babylon, he is said to have seen with two comrades a jackal run from the fallen stones of the Tabernacle that once housed the lost Ark of the Covenant. He smiled while the others wept, for he knew of the prophets who had foretold the utter destruction of Jerusalem, but also its restoration of glory. As the first prophecy had happened under Titus, so the second would be fulfilled. But an even greater destruction would take place after another war of independence, provoked in part by the rabbi. Led by Bar Kochba, who stamped on his coins the facade of a Fourth Temple which he hoped to build again, the Jews resisted the decrees of the emperor Hadrian that aimed to extirpate all traces of their religion from the Holy City. For three years, this new Maccabee and guerrilla leader defeated the Roman troops and their mercenaries before turning on Jerusalem and destroying the Tenth Legion there. Hadrian himself had to bring out a large army to quell the rebellion, which ended in Bar Kochba and the rabbi Akiva being tortured to death. What was left of the killing streets of Jerusalem was crushed into level ground between its mounts. Only the Western Wall still stood. Upon the broken stones was built a new Roman city named Aelia Capitolina, from which all Jews were barred under penalty of death. Judea was named Palaestina, a name that would replace Israel as the country of the Jews, now in exile or a minority in their homeland with a pitiful Sanhedrin surviving in Galilee. The new Roman city became a side alley in history, while Caesarea dominated the province of Syria Palaestina. The centre of the cosmos founded upon the rock of Mount Moriah appeared to be a speck of sand blown away by the sirocco of time.

Jerusalem was hardly now a place. It was a concept and a faith and a state of mind. Its memory brought sorrow to the Jews. The feast of the Passover was celebrated by laments for the razed Temple, and for the eighteen centuries and a third that would pass before an independent Jewish state again possessed the site of ancient Jerusalem, where little was left except a tradition. Yet the destruction of the Holy City coincided with the long decline of pagan Rome along with Judaism, while only the Christian faith rose until it would overwhelm the old empire in its new guise and citadel on the Bosphorus. Barbarian tribes, even fiercer than those of Israel when they had entered Canaan and taken it from its possessors, would pierce the far frontiers and knock at the gates of Rome and supersede the emperors themselves. And in response, a Second Rome would rise to the east in Byzantium, until its power was greater than the might of its mother. The emperor Constantine reunited the eastern and the western parts of the Roman Empire and called for the first ecumenical council of the Christian church at Nicaea, which was near his capital. There Bishop Macarius from the inconsiderable Aelia Capitolina told Helena, the mother of Constantine, that there was no monument to the death of Jesus in the city where he had been put on the cross. A Temple of Jupiter, indeed, now stood where the Temple of Solomon had been. In A.D. 326, Helena went on a journey to ancient Israel and selected with Macarius the sites of Christ's birth at Bethlehem and at Jerusalem, the adjoining places of his tomb burial and his Crucifixion, where she happened to discover three ancient crosses in a cavern, one of which was called the True Cross.

At Bethlehem in a grotto, a Church of the Nativity was built, an octagonal structure beside the basilica supported by rows of columns. In Jerusalem, the tomb of Christ was enclosed in a huge dome modelled on the Pantheon in Rome, while the rock of Calvary was enclosed in a cloistered court that led to a rectangular basilica, or Martyrium, again supported on massive pillars. In terms of sacred architecture, two new geometries reached the Holy Land—the octagon, which was made from two superimposed squares containing a cross and surrounded by a circle, a design that can still be seen in the Martyrium of Hieropolis in Anatolia; and the dome, which was constructed to top the original cube of the Tabernacle. To the mystical arithmetic of the units of two, eight was added to the number twelve, while the sliced dome of the cosmos or God, seen as a perfect sphere by Greek philosophers such as Parmenides, was now overlaid on the concept of a cubical universe.

It was another irony for the Jews that a sect derived from the monotheistic Hebrew faith should be restoring Jerusalem with its churches and temples, named basilicas. Yet Christianity had other Oriental influences, chiefly Gnostic and Manichean. From the Torah, it took the emphasis on the worth of individual human actions and the acceptance of the failure of man. From Gnosticism, it derived the concept that God was in each person, and that self-knowledge was a way to him. From Zoroaster and Persian Manicheanism, it presumed that the world was evil, and corrupt mankind had to struggle against the flesh to achieve perfection and the good of God. All these strands of belief might be denounced in the future when Christianity was to become a state religion, because they could question the authority of the ruler and his appointed bishops. But in the fourth century, they were the yeast which baked the bread of the Christian churches, still open to a ferment outside the pages of the Bible. And in the apocalyptic and influential Book of Revelation of St. John, the New Jerusalem would be founded after a cosmic war fought between Jesus and Satan that would result in the millennium and the coming of the heavenly city to earth to create a realm of bliss for those resurrected after the Last Judgement.

With two fundamental concepts, St. Augustine was to define the future of Jerusalem in Christian thought. The first was his doctrine of the just war, the second was his vision of the City of God. The pacific teaching of Jesus Christ was not contradicted by Christians taking up arms to repel the pagan barbarians now threatening Augustine himself in his bishopric at Hippo in North Africa. He watched with horror the destruction of the Roman Empire in the West. In A.D. 410, Rome itself was sacked, where St. Paul had founded the Christian church before his martyrdom. Paul had already stamped his religion with much of the authority and strength of Judaism and its Lord God, who was vengeful as well as merciful. He had stressed that the Christians were the fulfillment of Israel and its history of conquest until the making of the Temple at Jerusalem. Abraham and Moses and David had been the precursors of the Christ who had preached peace and love to humanity. Augustine expanded the resistance to Rome stressed by Paul the Martyr into a kind of Christian militance, not only to their persecutors but to all pagans. Later in history, the Crusaders, who would plunder and try to dominate the Holy Land, would quote Augustine in order to find justice in greed and right in might.

In his praise of the City of God, Augustine would further broadcast an ideal of the actual Jerusalem on earth, as if reaching that sacred site would be the human equivalent of attaining Paradise. As he wrote, "There is no question of man's meriting a place in God's City." The heavenly one could only be attained by grace, because of Adam's fall and original sin; but the earthly city of God could be reached by a just war.

Moreover, Augustine equated the dimensions of the celestial New Jerusalem with the cube of the Tabernacle and of Noah's ark, stating that any structure made "all of square wood signifies the unmoved constancy of the Saints; for cast a cube or square body which way you will, it will ever stand firm." In the Christian vision, the destroyed capital of Judea, rebuilt by the Romans and now by the Byzantines, was the City of God attainable by corrupt men during their lives, as far as possible a simulacrum of the New Jerusalem in the skies. The sacred design of the dome and the cube and the square, and the blessed numbers of twelve and eight and the multiples of two, were the geometry and arithmetic which reproduced the Tabernacle of Moses and the utopian city of the Greek philosopher Plato; these two revelations were united by Philo of Alexandria, one of the Jewish community which translated the Hebrew Bible into Greek and carried across the concept of the Logos, the *written* Word of God, into the vision of an urban paradise of divine creation.

St. Augustine used this concept to define his earthly and celestial Jerusalem. Good works or just wars could take a Christian to the actual church of the Holy Sepulchre, where Christ had risen from his death, which had saved man from his sins. Yet only the imponderable gift of God's grace might raise the sinner to the cherubim and the seraphim and the angels of the New Jerusalem. The search for the divine in this world was a long journey to the Temple Mount. It could be achieved by hand and foot. But a place in what St. Paul had described as a free "Jerusalem in the world above, which is the mother of us all," that was out of reach and the power of the will.

TWO

THAT WHICH
STRIKETH

It is evident from the testimony even of heathen witnesses that in Judea there was a city suspended in the sky early every morning for forty days. As the day advanced, the entire figure of the walls would fade gradually, and sometimes it would vanish instantly.

—Tertullian

The Jews in their dispersion joined the Christians in seeing their ruined Jerusalem raised again. They called their vision Yerushalayim shel Ma'alah, "the Jerusalem of the Upper World," where the archangel Michael played the role of the high priest in the razed Temple that had once been on the Mount. Under Byzantine rule, pilgrims from the remaining Jewish communities in Palestine, and from Antioch and Alexandria and the other cities of the Near East, were allowed periodically to pray at the Western Wall. An inscription of the fourth century in Hebrew has been found carved in the stone of a Herodian wall in the city, part of a verse of a chapter of Isaiah: "And when ye see this your heart shall rejoice, and your bones shall flourish like a herb." The hope of regaining the holy places never withered on the vine, however long the drought of the exile.

Yet Christian pilgrims far outnumbered Jewish ones, and Jerusalem became a Christian city. The Roman temples were destroyed, and shrines and churches were erected. The empress Eudocia was exiled from the court at Byzantium, now called Constantinople, and she built a palace near the Damascus Gate, endowed the Church of St. Stephen and another church to the Blessed Virgin at the Pool of Siloam, and extended the city walls to include the original City of David and Mount Zion. Either from respect or fear, no Christian buildings were erected on the Temple Mount. A detailed mosaic on the floor of a church at Madeba in Jordan still depicts the walled city of Jerusalem bristling with Byzantine churches, and those of the Armenians and Ethiopians and Egyptians. Christianity had taken over the Holy City.

Yet it was a religion that was no longer derived as much from Judaism. The influences of Greek philosophy permeated the faith because the Gospels themselves were written in Greek, the language of the Byzantine state. The Christian Father Tertullian might thunder, "What is there in common between Athens and Jerusalem, between the Academe and the Church? . . . We have no need for curiosity, after Jesus Christ, nor for investigation, after the Gospel." But Origen could reply that the text of the Bible needed interpretation and explanation. If the Old Testament was to be taken literally, then God would appear to be worse in his commands than "the most savage and unjust of men." The ancient Jews were not philosophers and did not have the powers of speculation of the Greeks. Philo of Alexandria was their first and last philosopher for a thousand years. There was nobody among them to question why the Old Testament ascribed to the Lord God the disgraceful commands which he was said to have given to Moses and Joshua and other leaders of the Israelites to justify their conquest of Canaan. The Greeks contributed through Platonism and the early Christian Fathers a moral and ethical theory and a conception of the City of God which enlarged the Christian faith. Yet for all that, it remained with Judaism as its foundation. The trust in a sacred text revealed to a Chosen People, as given by the Lord God to Moses, was fundamental to Christianity. The Bible was the bedrock of belief. Rather than Greek inquiry into the nature of the divine or what ethics meant or whether the cosmos was a sphere, Jews and Christians in their doctrinal divisions engaged in a battle of the texts and their interpretation. The holy words were true. The question was only what they meant.

Both Jews and Christians ascribed to God the characteristics and adjectives of human beings. He was wrathful or merciful or righteous, and often he was said to behave rather worse than men, as the Homeric gods had. But later Greek philosophy after Plato had seen God as more of an essence or a spirit, a Being without form, rather as Islam, the third great religion of the Near East, would envision its God. The Christians, however, most particularly saw the Son of God as a man and believed in the Resurrection of the body; by the doctrine of the Trinity, they humanised the Lord God the Father of the Jews, while distinguishing him from the Holy Spirit of the Greek philosophers and the Muslims to come.

The most important link between the founding Hebrew religion and its two derivatives, Christianity and Islam, was the idea of the elect, the Chosen People of God. This idea would be the triumph and tragedy of the three important religions of the Near East. It would lead to their continual conflict and misunderstanding, to the endless crusade of one against another, to the many destructions of Jerusalem. Each was an exclusive religion, based on the holy words given by a Lord God to prophets or a Messiah. Judaism would not recognise that Jesus or Muhammad was the long-awaited Messiah. Both Christianity and Islam acknowledged the Jewish prophets as forerunners of their revelations. But each of the three groups of worshippers believed that they were the unique people chosen by God to play out his will on earth. The tragedy would be that all three saw in Jerusalem, the Holy City founded by the Jews, the same sacred place which they needed to dominate for the satisfaction of their pilgrims and the good of their souls.

The Second Rome of the Byzantine Empire would control Jerusalem no longer than the first Rome had. The resurgent Persians under Chosroes II defeated the emperor Heraclius in 614 and conquered Palestine, although a Byzantine army retook the province for another fourteen years. The Persians fired Jerusalem along with the Church of the Holy Sepulchre, which was rebuilt in a smaller style. Unfortunately, the Jews cooperated with the Persians in order to regain permanent access to the Temple Mount and were butchered by the returning Byzantines as collaborators with the enemy. The Holy City, however, proved how mutable were the occupiers of its sacred rock when the Byzantines and Eastern Christianity were themselves flung from Mount Moriah after a capitulation to a new foe and a new religion, only another ten years after the pagan Persians had been expelled. That emerging faith was Islam, which meant an absolute submission to God's will, and it would hold Jerusalem far longer than the Romans and the Byzantines had.

The rise of Arab civilisation and the spread of Islam were phenomena as remarkable as the rapid success and broadcasting of Christianity with its appeal to the poor and the enslaved and the downtrodden. Muhammad's revelation of a single Being and Creator, all-powerful and all-merciful, with a series of five rules for living, proved more attractive to the wandering Bedouins than Moses had to the tribes of Israel with the Ten Commandments. The first small group of converts to Islam, called Muslims, were initially forced to migrate in the Hegira from the merchant city of Mecca in Arabia to the rival town of Medina in the north; but the Prophet Muhammad planned his return, even raiding caravans to secure a triumphant pilgrimage back to the ceremonies around the Ka'aba at Mecca, the *Hajj* where the Bedouins congregated in procession around the dark tomb of Ishmael and his mother, Hagar, the concubine of Abraham, which had become a shrine to a host of pagan deities. Its shape was also the stone cube of the Tabernacle of the Ark of the Covenant, and it had pieces of a black meteorite embedded in its southeastern wall, black stones fallen from heaven.

Taking over Mecca, Muhammad cleansed the Ka'aba, as the Jewish prophets and Jesus had the Temple from time to time, in order to make it into a pure house of worship to one true God. All that remained were the three columns of teak that supported the roof, rather as the pillars stood before the Temple of Solomon and of Herod. In his "Recitations," which were collected in the Koran, or Qur'an, Muhammad showed a great knowledge of Judaism and Christianity. The name of Jesus, indeed, is mentioned ninety-three times in the Koran by Muhammad. Curiously enough, his first triumphs at Mecca were menaced by invading Nestorian Christian armies from Ethiopia and Nabatea, while his dominance at Medina was threatened by the strong Jewish element there, which he first conciliated and then attacked when he was stronger. Both Judaism and Christianity had a following in pagan Arabia, but Islam was to sweep them aside. The Arabs were to conquer and cohere through the written book of the Word of God, or Allah, the Koran. Their rules of war and peace were set down.

The appeal of the Prophet Muhammad's revelations was through the subtlety of the Arab language with its vehemence and multiple meanings, so much in contrast to the rigor and experience of desert life. One concept of Muhammad, which was to set on fire the Near East to this day, was *jihad,* the battle against evil and the devil and the unbeliever. This was a doctrine which the tribes of Israel had practised in Palestine, also the Byzantine Christians under the name of a just war. But *jihad* had many more meanings than a holy war. It was the endless struggle to achieve virtue and follow God's will. It was the effort to make society more just and to spread Islam through preaching as well as the armed fist. Muslim scholars emphasised that *jihad* might be fulfilled by the heart and the tongue and the hands as well as by the sword. Its object was to spread the Muslim faith over all peoples by persuasion and aggression, discipline and diplomacy, in order to create a perfect community, the *Umma*. And yet, in the words of the Prophet himself, reported in the hundred and first *Surah,* or chapter, *jihad* was an endless mission that could only terminate with the Day of the Last Judgement—so similar to the faith of the later Crusaders:

"That which striketh!
What is that which striketh?
Ah, who will convey to thee what the Striking is?
The day mankind shall become like scattered moths,
And the mountains like tufts of carded wool.
Then those whose scales weigh heavy shall enter Paradise,
And those whose scales are light shall enter the Abyss.
And who shall convey to thee what the Abyss is?
A raging fire!"

Such fear of damnation if they did not strike to spread the faith was an incentive to the Bedouins to extend their raids on the routes of the caravans into a conquest of the merchant cities that were the rivals of Mecca. A trade war could become a sacred mission: The Koran followed the spear. But the most telling element in the doctrine preached by Muhammad was that of the invisible and merciful God, as transparent as the clear heaven that encompassed the nomadic Arabs, who navigated the deserts from oasis to oasis by reading the stars, as did the seamen of the peninsula when they took their *dhows* from port to port. Above them, in the shape and vision of their eyeball, the glittering map of the night skies appeared as the great dome of God, his presence pervading all space, yet without a face or a person, the immanent Almighty, the enveloping Allah. To the cube of the ancient cosmos of the East, Islam would add the dome of the Greeks and the Byzantines, seeing in their universe the vast transparent tent of Being that overset the desert land.

Because of his proximity to the Hebrew faith, Muhammad considered Jerusalem also to be a Holy City. His first revelations had come from the angel Gabriel, who had appeared to him in a dream on Mount Hira near Mecca, telling him that he was the messenger of Allah. Some years later, Gabriel had also appeared leading a white charger called Lightning, or el-Burak. With Gabriel beside him, Muhammad had ridden through space to the sacred rock on the top of Mount Moriah. There he had climbed a ladder of light to the seventh heaven to be preferred to the prophets of the Old Testament, particularly Abraham and Solomon, and received into the presence of Allah. The journey through the skies was recorded in the seventeenth *Surah,* which was "The Children of Israel." It stated: "Glorified be he who carried His servant by night from the Inviolable Place of Worship [Mecca] to the Far Distant Place of Worship [Jerusalem] the neighbourhood of which We have blessed, that We might show him of Our tokens. Lo! He, only He, is the Hearer, the Seer."

When Caliph Omar came to Jerusalem in 638, six years after the death of the Prophet Muhammad, he came to another holy city of Islam that did not yet know Islam. The Christians in the city capitulated to his mercy, and Omar did not abuse it. He entered alone on a camel and was taken by the patriarch Sophronius to the Church of the Holy Sepulchre, where he was asked to pray. He refused, knowing that the church would be destroyed to make a mosque if he knelt and turned towards Mecca in that Christian holy place. Accordingly, he prayed outside, and indeed, on the site of his act of worship arose the Mosque of Omar. He also asked to be taken to the Temple Mount, which the Christians had converted into a refuse dump. Sophronius was made to crawl through the debris on his hands and knees as an act of penitence for desecrating the holy rock; then Omar built a wooden mosque on the corner, later to become the second Muslim site of worship in the city, the al-Aqsa mosque. With the wise toleration that the Islamic Empire showed after its conquests, both

Christians and Jews were allowed to practise their religions in Jerusalem, on payment of a poll tax.

With the heirs of Muhammad, the Ummayads, establishing their capital at Damascus, they were determined to make Jerusalem a place of pilgrimage for the faithful almost as important as Mecca and Medina, which were now controlled by a rival caliph. For that purpose, they used Byzantine and Greek and Egyptian architects and craftsmen to build the Dome of the Rock over the sacred stone on Mount Moriah, from where Muhammad had ascended to the seventh heaven. Its shape was the holy octagon with twelve inner pillars and four square supports holding up a golden cupola, the sacred shapes and numbers of Eastern religion. Four doors inlaid with gold were set at north and west and south and east to give entrance to the noble building, which wore its gleaming cap over the city. The smaller al-Aqsa mosque at the southern end of the Temple platform was given a silver dome and doors of gold and silver. These two blessed structures were magnets to the faithful, who now outnumbered the Christians in their visits to their holy sites, commemorated by Bishop Arculf's account, later abridged by the Venerable Bede, the first British guidebook to the Promised Land. Arculf testified to the small Muslim presence and the great tolerance in Jerusalem. The Western emperor Charlemagne, indeed, had even been given by the caliph of Baghdad the title of Protector of Jerusalem, and Christians there became predominant. As late as 985, the Muslim traveller Mukaddasi could complain: "Everywhere the Christians and the Jews have the upper hand; and the mosque is void, of either congregation or assembly of learned men." But the Dome of the Rock was glorious. "At dawn, when the light of the sun first strikes on the Cupola, and the Drum catches the rays; then this edifice is a marvellous sight to behold, and in all Islam I have never seen its equal."

Soon after the visit of this Muslim pilgrim, the Church of the Holy Sepulchre was destroyed by order of the new rulers of Palestine, the Egyptian Fatimids, who claimed their descent from Muhammad's daughter, Fatima. This act was anathema to the early Christian Crusaders, who considered it a sacrilege even worse than the Greeks had seen in the destruction of the great library of Alexandria, when Egypt had first fallen under Muslim rule. The Fatimids under the caliph al-Hakim had pursued a policy of the forced conversion of all infidels, but in the early eleventh century, the old tolerance of other faiths was resumed, and the Church of the Holy Sepulchre was rebuilt in new splendour, capable of holding a congregation of eight thousand people within its walls of coloured marble, festooned with icons and Byzantine brocade. For Byzantium had resisted and contained the Arab advance, and three great civilisations now were to contend for mastery of the New East and its venerated ground, while the nomadic populations from the other leading areas of Asia would also enter the fray for control of the Levant.

Byzantium was now rivalled in culture and learning by the Islamic cities, from Bukhara and Baghdad in the east to Fez and Córdoba in the west. Although the Muslim armies did not extend their hold on Europe beyond the south of Spain, they set up an administration and culture that was the envy of its time. So powerful were they that their cities were usually unfortified and organised around one or more mosques; a *souk,* or market; and a centre of government where the Ulama of notables administered the five pillars of the faith and the Shari'a, the sacred law of Islam. "There is no God but Allah and Muhammad is his Prophet" was the first pillar of the exclusive creed. The other four pillars insisted on all Muslims praying five times a day while facing towards the Ka'aba in Mecca, where they also had to make a pilgrimage. They must fast during the period of Ramadan, the time when Muhammad had fasted on the Mountain outside Mecca and had received his revelations. They must give alms to the poor and perform acts of charity in the name of Islam. The Shari'a was the roof of the five pillars, a civil and religious law based on the *hadiths,* the traditions of various *imams* and religious jurists, reporting on what Muhammad had said to his family and entourage. Its authority was similar to early canon law, which was based on the authority of the gospels and the explanations of the Christian Fathers. In Judaism and Christianity and Islam, the guidance of divine revelation was important in the running of the state.

Just as Greek philosophy and science had instructed Rome, so Hellenism taught the flowering urban culture of Islam, which would pass back an enriched classical practise to a Europe struggling out of the Dark Ages that succeeded the collapse of the Roman Empire. For four hundred years after the eighth century, Arab thinkers would enrich Greek studies of botany and medicine. In the Eastern caliphate of the Abbasids—now dominant in Persia under the retreating Ummayads—Rhazes, Avicenna, and

Haly Abbas, a Zoroastrian and Manichean experimenter on animals, would add to learning and influence medieval Christianity. St. Thomas Aquinas was to refer to the wisdom of Avicenna more than two hundred and fifty times. The Western caliphate of the Ummayads at Córdoba would benefit from the studies of Albucasis and Algalzel and Avenzoar and Moses Maimonides, the Jewish philosopher and physician. Jewish doctors, who had studied Islamic medicine, were to develop the first secular European medical school at Salerno. When the Normans would conquer Sicily in the eleventh century and Constantinus Africanus would translate Greek and Arabic texts into Latin from the cloisters of Monte Cassino, Hellenic and Islamic lore would illuminate the ignorance of early Christian Europe. Ironically, as scientific salvation was arriving from the Near East, so the Crusades of Christianity would begin against the sources of this new education. The sword would spring from the progress of the mind.

Before it fragmented, the Islamic Empire brought Asian trade to the Mediterranean and Europe and Scandinavia, where tens of thousands of Muslim coins have been excavated to testify to this far-flung commerce across the Black Sea and up to the Baltic. The ninth-century geographer Ibn Khurradadhbeh affirmed the success of Jewish merchants within a tolerant Islamic world. They spoke many languages, Arabic and Persian, Greek and Spanish, Frankish and Slavonic dialects. "They travel from west to east and east to west, by land and by sea." From the West, they brought eunuchs and boys and girls as slaves, also brocade and sable and other furs, and swords. From China through India and Arabia, they brought back musk and aloes, camphor and cinnamon, more spices and silks. "Some sail with their goods to Constantinople, and sell them to the Greeks, and some take them to the king of the Franks and sell them there."

The accommodation of people of other faiths, the Zoroastrians of Persia and the Jews and the Christians, and the prosperity and profit which they were permitted to achieve within the Islamic Empire, were a testament to a Muslim enlightenment that was unusual in the tenth century and was superior in that regard to Byzantine politics, so often racked by religious civil war. In Jerusalem itself, the Christians and the Jews rather preferred Muslim rule. After all, the very word *Islam* was derived from the same Arabic root as *peace,* and peace did descend on the Holy City for centuries. In many ways, the authority of the caliphs was more tolerable than that of the Byzantine emperors. A Jewish apocalyptic writer of the time made an angel say to a rabbi and prophet: "The Creator, blessed be He, has only brought the Kingdom of Ishmael in order to save you from this wickedness [Byzantium]." And a later Christian historian from Syria affirmed the message with the words: "Therefore the God of vengeance delivered us out of the hand of the Romans by means of the Arabs. . . . It did us some good to be saved from the cruelty of the Romans and their bitter hatred towards us."

Yet the Arabs themselves were to be split by religious and civil wars, as the Byzantines were and the Christians would be, for Rome and Byzantium were already at cross-purposes over the extent of the authority of the pope and the eastern patriarchs. In the Islamic community, the original shift of the Ummayads from Mecca to Damascus had provoked a revolt from the followers of Ali, a rival descendant of the Prophet and claimant of the caliphate. His adherents called themselves the Shi'ites, members of the party of Ali, as opposed to the Sunnis, the backers of the orthodox Muslim state and faith. Among them had emerged the concept of the Mahdi, a messianic leader against the establishment. One Mahdi would even lead a slave revolt that sacked Basra. Eventually, Arab tribal divisions and Shi'ite beliefs had led to the collapse of sole Ummayad control, and the division of the Islamic Empire into three main areas of domination with buffer provinces and states on their borders under different tribal sheikhs. When the Ummayads were restricted to Spain, the Fatimids controlled most of North Africa and Egypt, while the Abbasids were dominant in the Near East, until wars between the sons of the caliph in Baghdad and resurgent Persian nationalists splintered the area into the pieces controlled by quarrelling warlords—an advantage to the Christians, when they would attack the Levant in the eleventh century. A further religious war created the Isma'ili sect with different Imams, who introduced neo-Platonic ideas and secret interpretations of the Koran into the conventions of the traditional faith. The tradition of individual judgement of the sacred texts, the *itjihad,* fell under the dominance of the religious leaders, the *imams* and *mullahs.* Although Islam remained coherent as a culture, its political and religious organisation shattered like a clay pot dropped on a stone.

To the northeast of both the Byzantine and Islamic Empires lay the nomadic cultures of the horsemen of the steppes, where the Seljuk Turks now threatened. By the middle of the eleventh century, they conquered Iraq and northern Syria. Although fervent Muslims, they were still a primitive people as set against the Abbasid caliphs of Baghdad. They pressed against Christian Armenia and the borders of Byzantine Anatolia. At Manzikert in 1071, the Greek armies with their mercenaries under the emperor Romanus IV were totally destroyed, and the Turks rode into Asia Minor and reached the Aegean Sea, where they established the sultanate of Rum. It was the victory of the warriors from the wilderness against the urban civilisation that derived from Greece and Rome. Most of the remaining conquests of Alexander the Great were lost. Unless there was Christian help from the West, Byzantium itself appeared to be doomed.

The incursion of mounted tribesmen also disturbed the city culture of the Fatimids. The Bedouins of the desert, who had begun the Islamic Empire with their raids on their camels, now captured Upper Egypt and Libya and Tunisia. And the Tuaregs, led by the Berber tribesmen called the Almoravids, overran Morocco and eastern Algeria and set up their capital in Marrakesh. The Almoravids further crossed over to Muslim Andalusia, already under heavy pressure from the Christian assaults from northern Spain that were the precursors of the Crusades. There they took over all of Muslim Spain except for Saragossa and a few border sheikhdoms under the control of the Arab warlords named *taifas*. The Almoravids and the Seljuk Turks with their new empires blocked Christian advance in the western and eastern Mediterranean.

Yet they did not hold the sea. That was increasingly the watery province of the Italian cities of Amalfi and Pisa, Genoa and Venice, which had itself begun to conquer territories along the Adriatic coast. And the Viking explosion overseas of the previous two centuries had resulted in the conquest of Normandy and the emergence of a Frankish-Norman people who would conquer the British Isles and then spread down in their formidable dragon ships and merchantmen, called *knorrs*, through the Straits of Gibraltar into their first kingdoms in southern Italy and Sicily and Malta. These French-Scandinavian knights and mariners were the most formidable amphibious fighting machine that had yet reached the inland sea, which lapped Europe and Asia and Africa and led the way to Jerusalem. Across the middle of the waters between the three continents, the Christian kingdom of the Two Sicilies thrust its spear between the Almoravids in North Africa and the Seljuk Turks who pressed against Byzantium. It was the weapon that made for the stab of the First Crusade to recapture the Holy Land of Palestine.

There had already been running wars between Christians and Muslims in the Near East for four centuries, ever since the armies of Islam had captured Jerusalem and Syria from the Byzantine emperors. But then, the following centuries of accommodation had taken place with the Italian trading vessels serving as a necessary link between the caravan traders across Asia and the horse-drawn cart or riverboat routes across Europe. But the concept of a *jihad,* or holy war, was revived by the warrior tribes of the Seljuk Turks and the Almoravids. When the Turks captured Jerusalem after the battle of Manzikert, there was a slaughter, the destruction of churches, the repression of the surviving Jews and Christians, and a ban on all pilgrims who were not Muslim believers. Although the Fatimids re-captured Jerusalem after some years and resumed their tolerant rule, the damage had already been done in the ears of the newly militant Christians of Western Europe. Islam seemed bigoted and murderous. The distinction between the primitive Turk and the sophisticated Egyptian was unknown. Both were followers of the Prophet Muhammad. In a way, the incursion of the Turks followed by other nomadic tribes from steppe and desert, culminating in the destructive genius of the Mongols, would destroy an urban Muslim culture superior to any in Europe and degrade a flowering civilisation into the backwaters of provincial history.

So the stage was set for the expansion of Western Europe into the Near East. A religious revival was taking place alongside the new militarism of the mounted knights, whose small numbers could conquer large territories with their cavalry charges and invulnerable armour. The monastic reform that spread from Cluny was allied to the growing influence of those literate clerics, who ran most of the rising nation-states and wanted the control of "the Peace of God" over the savage tactics of the medieval barons. The Holy Roman Empire based on the German lords and bishoprics was also trying to reform the clergy, even the popes of Rome. Pilgrimages were encouraged more and more—to Iona and St. Olaf's at

Trondheim; to St. Adalbert's at Gneizno and to Santiago de Compostela, where the knights prayed before joining the attack of el Cid on the Moors in southern Spain; and to Rome and especially to the Holy Land of Palestine, if this was not prevented by the Turks. These religious influences whetted the swords of adventurers to the east with the stone of faith. To strike at Jerusalem was to be sanctified by the blood of the Lamb.

THREE

THE ROCK OF
PARADISE

I would build that dome in air,
That sunny dome! those caves of ice!
And all who heard should see them there,
And all should cry, Beware! Beware!
His flashing eyes, his floating hair!
Weave a circle round him thrice,
And close your eyes with holy dread,
For he on honey-dew hath fed,
And drunk the milk of Paradise.

—Samuel Taylor Coleridge, *Kubla Khan*

J erusalem was always more of a vision than a fact, a dream that could
only lead to a sad awakening. It was held to be the site of the primal
stone and the first paradise and the Flood. There was the original Garden of Eden, which was related to the Hebrew word *gan-eden,* which
meant a garden of sweetness and delight. The first translators of the word
into Greek called it *paradeisos,* a word that Xenophon had put into the
mouth of Socrates: In the end, it became our word *paradise.* In fact, it only
meant a "walled garden" or "game park" and derived from the Persian *pairi,*
or "around," and *daeza,* or "wall." From Greek, it was translated into Latin
as *paradisus* and first appeared in Middle English in 1175 as a sentence in

the Bible, "God ha hine brohte into paradis." By the time that Chaucer was to write the *Franklin's Tale,* the term was generally used to describe a flowering garden:

> *May hadde peynted with his softe showers*
> *This gardyn full of leves and of flowres;*
> *And craft of manne's hand so curiously*
> *Arrayed hadde this garden trewely*
> *That never was ther gardyn of swich prys,*
> *But if it were the verray Paradys.*

Outside medieval churches, paradises were constructed—enclosed green spaces for prayer and meditation. In the Cistercian order, each white monk was given his little paradise or garden plot to cultivate. Of course, the Christians confused this new word *paradise* with the Garden of Eden, just as the Muslims confused it with the Garden of Allah, into which the Koran promised a way for all those who died fighting for the faith. "There shall be two other gardens: of a dark green. In each of them shall be two fountains pouring forth much water. In each of them shall be fruits and palm trees and pomegranates. And there shall be agreeable and beautiful maidens." And because of the Song of Solomon, which rejoiced in the description of the king's gardens and orchards and the beautiful women in them, both Christians and Muslims often thought that Paradise was located in Jerusalem.

In prehistory, the idea of a Garden of Paradise had dated back to the first city-state in Mesopotamia, the Sumerian state of Uruk with its *Epic of Gilgamesh,* who wandered in the immortal Garden of the Gods, where

> *stands the Tree,*
> *With trunk of gold, and beautiful to see.*

In their captivity in Babylon, with its famous hanging gardens, the Jews had also learned of the Garden of Paradise, or Eden, and had given it the Hebrew name *pordes.* Rabbinic tradition believed that the Garden was the blessed part of *sheol* where the just awaited the Resurrection, while the olive branch brought by the dove to Noah on his ark was plucked from Eden, which had survived the Flood. The Jews also held Mount

Moriah in Jerusalem as a sacred area on which the Temple of Solomon was built, just as the Babylonians held their stepped ziggurats to be holy and the Christians venerated "the high places" of the Bible—the peaks of a possible hanging garden of Paradise.

Indeed, all the leading religions that derived from the Middle East believed in a divine garden. It contained the tree of life and the tree of knowledge of good and evil. It also held the Mountain of Paradise and Salvation as well as the four rivers that divided the earth into quarters, the Tigris, the Pishon, the Gihon, and the Euphrates. St. Augustine even called Christ the tree of life, while the other saints were fruit trees, and the four Gospels were the four rivers of Eden.

The Bible and the Koran, however, differed in their descriptions of the Garden of Paradise and the Sin, which caused the expulsion of mankind. The Book of Genesis described two trees in Eden, the tree of life and the tree of knowledge of good and evil. The fall of Eve and Adam was because the serpent persuaded them to eat the fruit of the tree of knowledge. Yet the Koran only identified a single tree of life, "the tree of immortality and an everlasting kingdom," and the eating of the fruit of that tree led to the loss of Paradise. Curiously, in his *Divine Comedy,* Dante was only to mention one tree in Eden, and although it instigated Original Sin and the Fall, he did not say whether it was the tree of life or of knowledge of good and evil. But his very work seemed split between two visions of the pilgrim's journey—the quest for an earthly Paradise which, as in Islam, might be reached through a sacred cause or empire, or for a heavenly Paradise which could only be reached through faith and the Church. He even put the great retaker of Jerusalem from the Christians, Saladin, in a divine garden or Elysian Fields just within the gates of the Inferno, where the virtuous pagans lived for all eternity.

The original earthly Garden of Paradise had been designed by Cyrus the Great at Pasargadae in Persia, and his model had been widely copied in the Near East. When Alexander the Great had conquered the Persian Empire, he had visited the tomb of Cyrus in its grove and had mourned his epitaph:

O man, I am Cyrus
Who acquired the Empire for the Persians

33

And was King of Asia:
Do not grudge me, then, my monument.

His true monument was his garden of paradise, and the flowers and fruits and herbs he grew there. Aristotle, the tutor of Alexander the Great, had arranged for another pupil, Theophrastus, to write about the new specimens brought back from the East. Theophrastus had inherited Aristotle's herb gardens, and the two works he wrote about them were the first botanical guides, *On the Causes of Plants* and *On the History of Plants*. These books were of supreme importance to the scholars of the Middle Ages.

Actually, the first Herbal had been carved in relief of the Temple of Amun more than a thousand years before. This original record of a botanical garden depicted blue cornflower and red poppy and mandrake with its yellow fruits, the three most popular Egyptian plants, along with lotus and papyrus. Its trees showed date palms and vines and figs, while the oldest temple garden at Deir-el-Bahari revealed three rows of seven sycamore and tamarisk trees planted in avenues. Recent excavations of a rubbish dump at Saqqâra have also revealed a physic garden in ancient Egypt connected with the priests of the temple. Among the medicines in use were acacia, aloes, aniseed, apricots, caraway seeds, the castor-oil plant, cedar, chicory, chrysanthemum, convolvulus, coriander, flax, hemp, henbane, mint, myrtle, myrrh, olive, onions, poppy, squills, wormwood, and camomile oil, which was distilled to embalm the pharaohs—its secret would be passed on by the Christian Copts to the Crusaders for their preservation of their dead.

Yet these sacred and medicinal gardens of the pharaohs were unknown to the ancient Greeks, who had divided their gardens of paradise into Arcadia for the living and the Elysian Fields for the dead. They had chiefly valued two of the Alexandrian imports from Asia—saffron, from the wild crocus, and the rose. But many other imports were to follow, the spices and the herbs that were to become the drugs and medicines of the Middle Ages. In the Islamic gardens of paradise, the trees and fruit and flowers had a figurative meaning as well as a medical use—the almond meant the eye, the quince and the apple were the chin, the pomegranate and the lemon were the breasts, the rose was the cheek, the plane-tree leaf was the hand, the date palm was the figure, and the mandrake was the down on the skin. It had been the same in the Song of Solomon in its more erotic verses, which compared the beloved to a paradise or walled garden in Jerusalem:

A garden inclosed is my sister, my spouse; a spring shut up, a fountain sealed.

Thy plants are an orchard of pomegranates, with pleasant fruits; camphire with spikenard.

Spikenard and saffron; calamus and cinnamon, with all trees of frankincense; myrrh and aloes, with all the chief spices:

A fountain of gardens, a well of living waters, and streams from Lebanon.

Awake, O north wind; and come, thou south; blow upon my garden, that the spices thereof may flow out. Let my beloved come into his garden, and eat his pleasant fruits.

The desire to reach the enclosed garden of the Song of Solomon and the earthly paradise of Jerusalem could only be satisfied by entering through the gates of the city, which were themselves more vision than truth. The dust from which Adam was formed was held to have been taken from the site of the Temple of Solomon on Mount Moriah. After the angel with fiery sword had driven him from Eden, he was sent to his place of creation on nearby Mount Moriah because it was beside the gates to a heavenly paradise and to hell—a legend again used by Dante in his *Divine Comedy*. Jewish tradition stated that one of the three gates of hell was in Jerusalem, because of a verse of the prophet Isaiah, warning of the wrath of the Lord God, "whose fire is in Zion, and his furnace in Jerusalem." The Muslims also believed in this biblical tradition, holding that the two entrances to the earthly paradise and to the raging fire of the abyss were also to be found in Jerusalem. The way into Paradise, indeed, was within the al-Aqsa mosque, where one holy man had come back with a single leaf from the tree of life.

"I have asked the Prophet which is the most radiant city in the world," said a companion of Muhammad, "and He answered 'Jerusalem,'" and the Shi'ite hero Ali claimed that the city lay nearer to heaven than anywhere else in the world, a fragment from Paradise. The friends and soldiers of

Muhammad were entombed round the walls where Adam and Abraham were believed to have been buried. Here Jesus had spoken in his cradle and Mary had lived "a virgin unknown to mortal man." Whoever died there would be assured of salvation. When the angel Israfil blew the trumpet of resurrection from the rock, Yom-el-gyama—the Day of Judgement— would be proclaimed from the Mount of Olives by Jesus Christ, a leader among the prophets to Jew and Muslim as well as the Messiah of the Christian faith.

Furthermore, to the Christians in Europe, Jerusalem was literally the axis of the circle of the cosmos. In legend, Adam was buried on Golgotha, where Jesus, the Son of God, had died on the cross. To Jews, Jerusalem was also the centre of Israel and the world, and the focus of the Holy City was the foundation stone of the Temple of Solomon, before which lay the Ark of the Covenant. The Christians had an alternative navel stone for the universe, the *omphalos* under the dome of the Church of the Holy Sepulchre, where the True Cross had been sometimes kept. It was a pillar of marble two feet high, on which was set a vessel containing a stone, which would serve as another source of inspiration for the Grail romances and the Gnostics and the alchemists, one of whom would claim, "Make a round circle and you will have the Stone of the Philosopher." The Grail Castle itself would be based on the idea of the heavenly and perfect Jerusalem, an orb that was the heart of faith and existence. To the Crusaders, Jerusalem was both an actual and a visionary city, a walled place in Palestine and a paradise in the Holy Land.

One of the influences on German descriptions of the Grail Castle would be historical as well as Oriental. In the medieval romance *The Young Titurel,* the Temple of the Grail stood on an onyx Mount of Salvation. It was built in the round beneath a golden dome on which jewelled constellations blazed above a mechanical gold sun and silver moon. In the early seventh century, the Persian king Chosroes II had built a similar palace on the holy mountain of Shîz, where there was a previous circular sanctuary of Sacred Fire in memory of the seer Zoroaster, whose Manichean beliefs influenced Gnostics and alchemists. This circular palace of precious metals and stones showed the heavens, which were rotated by teams of horses pulling ropes from sunken pits below. Mineral deposits from a crater lake made the mountain gleam like onyx. The early planetarium was called the

Throne of Arches, the Takt-i-Taqdis; twenty-two ornate arches surrounded the central round, the same number of lesser temples that would encircle the main hall of the Grail Castle in *The Young Titurel*. Unfortunately, the Byzantine emperor Heraclius had defeated Chosroes and torn down the Takt and taken back the True Cross, which Chosroes had removed there after his seizure of Jerusalem. This early Crusade to recapture the True Cross was well-known in medieval Europe and often inspired the songs of troubadours.

Supremely significant in the geography of Jerusalem was the location of the Temple of Solomon and then the Dome of the Rock, which many credulous Christian pilgrims believed to be the original edifice of the early king of Israel. For it was built on a *lapis,* or stone or rock, at the centre of the world. It had contained the Ark of the Covenant, the fount of the Christian faith. The cornerstone "which the builders refused" in Psalms was another symbol of Christ. And it was also upon this *lapis,* or rock, that the Christian church was founded.

Furthermore, there was a legendary treasure of Solomon, which was said to have been taken to Rome after the fall of Jerusalem, then seized by the Western Goths. When Muslim armies had captured Toledo, they asked after Solomon's Table, which was meant to be able to feed all who sat down to eat and to be made from a gigantic emerald, the sacred green stone of the alchemists. The table was said to be hidden away in the mountains of Spain in a Grail Castle, and was a motive behind the early holy wars against Islam in the Spain of the Almoravid dynasty. Charlemagne was also said to have copied the Table of Solomon by having the universe made as three circles in jewels and precious metals, then set on legs of gold as another version of King Arthur's Round Table for himself and twelve knights. The Koran itself referred to another table brought down from Heaven by Jesus to feed him and the Apostles, but this divine gift disappeared again because of the sins of mankind.

Such legends and myths and beliefs were among the inspirations of the just or holy wars that Christian Europe would now pursue against the Muslims. In a way, the attack of Islam on Europe had defined Europe itself. Just as the collapse of the Roman Empire had allowed the rise of the Byzantine emperors, then of the Prophet Muhammad and the armies of his faith, so they had permitted the ascendancy of the first Holy Roman Emperor of Europe, Charlemagne. He had treated with the caliph in Baghdad, who had granted him the title of the Protector of Jerusalem; he had led a counterattack into Spain, from which the most famous of the *chansons de geste* would arise, the *Song of Roland,* that early model for the later Crusades. Although his empire soon split into warring kingdoms and duchies, Charlemagne's biographers liked to write of his capital at Aachen as the New Jerusalem. His throne had been designed to the mystic measurements of the seat of King Solomon, whom he was said to match as a builder with the wisdom of Moses and the courage of Joshua and the statesmanship of King David, who had united the tribes of Israel as Charlemagne had briefly the principalities and peoples of Europe. The Franks in particular had begun to view themselves as another Chosen People in a struggle against the infidel, and this belief they passed on to the Normans in their conquests from the north seas.

Messianic dreams and perceptions of the Apocalypse were also troubling the minds of the Europeans in the eleventh century. There had been mass pilgrimages to Jerusalem in 1033, a thousand years after the death of Jesus Christ, although the Second Coming had not then occurred, but only a terrible famine, more mass deaths without the Resurrection. Thirty years later, another seven thousand pilgrims left on an exodus for the Holy Land, under the influence of fervid preachers. Discontent among the poor and the serfs at the rule of the knights and the barons was expressed in the urge to march towards an earthly salvation in the actual city of Jerusalem as well as a journey to the heavenly bliss of a New Jerusalem. Faith was the catalyst between place and myth. In a backward society where the rising new churches of the Peace of God and Cluny were miracles of strength and aspiration with their buttresses and towers set above the squalid huts and hovels around them, the confusion between stone buildings and imaginary sky domes was general.

This confusion had almost been a tenet of the faith since the time of St. Augustine. He had tried to divide the rule of law from the rule of God, as Christ had done when he directed his followers to render to Caesar what was Caesar's, and to God what was God's. He had used the parallel of the two cities, one on earth and one in heaven, to demonstrate his case. Plato had also made a similar distinction in his *Republic* and *Laws* as well as in the dialogues of the *Timaeus* and the *Critias.* With his doctrine that the soul was immortal, Plato had created the idea of a city of spirits in contrast with the mortal and declining *polis* of the Greeks. St. Augustine made his tale of two cities a Christian one, with Jesus the Redeemer from Jerusalem as the gate through which the pilgrim might rise from the alleys of the flesh to the avenues of the soul. But to simpler minds, neither Plato nor Augustine made an absolute division between the walls of the earthly and the heavenly city. Just as the body contained the spirit during life, so the obscure Jerusalem on the hills of far Palestine appeared to include the glittering domes and spires of God's empire in the skies, where the faithful would dwell after death.

This vision of the right way to the old and to the New Jerusalem differed between the poor and the rich, the villeins and the lords of Europe. Yet a web of obligations bound them together. Since the Frankish invention of the charge of the massed armoured knight, the *blitzkrieg* of its time, which had brought success against the Islamic invasion of Europe, political methods were found to bind the villagers to the baron in his castle. They provided the food, while he gave them protection. And if his few men-at-arms were not enough to guard against a foreign or pagan incursion, he was obliged himself to serve in the army of the state under his duke or king. In return, the ruler would protect the districts of the countryside from invasion. These nets of oaths culminated in the service to God's cause, whatever the priests held that to be. For pledges of loyalty could only be hallowed—and so enforced—by swearing to God, and the punishment of excommunication from the Christian faith had terrible penalties on earth outside the threat of hellfire—the loss of all lands, the rupture of all temporal bonds, the reduction of the potentate to the outcast. In the early feudal system of Europe before the rise of the nation-state, the Church was the glue of contract and the anathema of the forsworn. To the club of authority, it added the curse of divinity.

In one of the more piercing texts of the later Middle Ages, *Piers Plowman,* the understanding between knight and peasant was strictly maintained. The knight offered to help Piers in his work, but the ploughman knew that societies were as divided as the furrows were. The knight did not know how to handle the team of horses, but by Christ, if he was taught, he said he would try. Piers refused, saying that by St. Paul, he had been made a good offer. He would sweat and sow for both of them, and labour all his life for the love of the knight, in the trust that the knight would keep the Holy Church and himself from the wicked people who were destroying the world. Courteously, the knight replied:

"As I have power, Piers, I give you my word
That I will fulfill this, even if I must fight.
As long as I live, I will protect you."

This was an idealised version of feudal obligation, in which so often the barons oppressed the peasants. Already by the twelfth century, a complaint by Peter de Blois was vehement. The knights of old had bound themselves to serve the ruler and the Church, not to flee from battle, and to put the good of others before their own lives. But all had gone awry. The moment the knights received their belts, they rose against the Lord's anointed and raged against the patrimony of the crucified. "They rob and despoil Christ's poor, afflicting the wretched miserably and without mercy, that from other men's pains they may gratify their unlawful appetites and wanton pleasures." Those who should have fought Christ's enemies fought themselves when they were drunk and idle. "They dishonour the name and office of knighthood by their degenerate lives."

Between the ideal of chivalry and the facts of getting a living, the knight existed. His trade was war, he was often illiterate, he depended on the Church for legitimacy and administration. He was superstitious as much as pious, and his wish for God's mercy rarely tempered his chosen brutality. In the twelfth-century *chanson de geste* of Ralph of Cambrai, the hero burned down a convent with all its nuns, and then asked for meat to eat. It was Good Friday and his knights were dismayed. If he ate the meat, he would slay their souls. So he turned to fish, not wishing to offend God, and not thinking that God might be more offended by the loss of the nuns in their convent.

Versions of the *Song of Roland*, indeed, were being sung at the time of the First Crusade, and gave the best contemporary insight into the barbaric and fearful and proud temperament of the European knight. Recalling a defeat by Charlemagne in his campaign against the Ummayads in Spain, the destruction of his rear guard at Roncesvalles in a Basque ambush was translated into a heroic slaughter of the Muslim hordes and the martyr's sacrifice of a hero through betrayal. This legendary epic was shot through with the silk and blood of the period. It was a declaration of a holy war against Islam, in which chivalry was restricted to the knights on both sides, while there was no mercy for the rest of humanity. Those who died in Charlemagne's cause would enter the gates of Paradise, as the sanguinary Archbishop Turpin promised. "Infidels are wrong and Christians are in the right," Count Roland proclaimed. "I will set no bad example." Killing a few hundred infidels with his sword Durandal, which could split rock like the Shamir that built the Temple of Solomon and like King Arthur's Excalibur, Roland thought a good example, even though he condemned himself and his twenty thousand men to death by refusing to summon help from Charlemagne with his horn. The sacred relics in the hilt of Durandal made it more murderous, while the count's arrogance and the butchery of the enemy turned strategic folly into sacred romance.

The *Song of Roland* presaged the disaster that would befall the later Christian Kingdom of Jerusalem born in the confused ideal of a Crusade, condemned by the pride and treachery of the actual rulers of the expeditionary force that was to occupy Palestine. In the *Song of Roland*, the Franks were the Chosen People of God, and their enemies were doomed to hell or the sword unless they accepted conversion. When Charlemagne in the *chanson* took Córdoba and razed its walls, the poet took it as a matter of course that "all infidels in the city had been slain / Or else converted to the Christian faith." The Holy Roman Emperor himself held court in the great garden or paradise there, created by the Moorish king, "the foe of God, who served Muhammad and to Apollyon prayed." The massacre of the unbelievers who resisted a forced conversion to Christianity was advocated as a habitual strategy in the counterattack of Europe on Islam. To die in such a holy war would be to enter the heavenly gates with warrior angels as a guide. When Count Roland prayed for remission of his sins with his dying words, he offered up the mailed right glove on his fist to God, and St. Gabriel took it from his hand. And so he died:

> To him God sent angels and Cherubim
> Along with Saint Michael of the Peril;
> And with them came down Saint Gabriel
> To carry the Count's soul up to paradise.

In the epic poem, Roland's death provoked a form of apocalypse, an announcement of the Second Coming. There was an earthquake, stone walls trembled and tumbled, a great darkness descended at noon, the heavens split, and there was universal terror:

And many said: "This is the very end;
The Judgement Day is surely now at hand."

This prevalent millenarianism was always a stimulant behind the preaching of the Crusades against Islam, which had already begun in Spain and Norman Italy. In 1063, the pope gave a papal banner to the leader of an expedition against the Muslims in Spain, William de Montreuil, called by an Islamic historian Captain of the Cavalry of Rome. The expedition ended in the massacre of the infidel prisoners at Barbastro. Three years later, Cardinal Hildebrand, later Pope Gregory VII, gave William the Conqueror a papal banner to carry at the Battle of Hastings. And when he sat on the papal throne and reduced the Holy Roman Emperor Henry IV to humiliation at Canossa, the prospect of imperial revenge made him call on the Norman freebooter and lord of southern Italy, Robert Guiscard, to join him in defending Rome from a German attack as well as thrusting at the rival authority of the Second Rome of Byzantium. It was an irony at this time of internecine war between the Christians before the official First Crusade against the Muslims, that Rome itself should have been captured and sacked as a prophecy to the fate of Jerusalem. Robert Guiscard, indeed, had conquered Illyria and held Constantinople at the point of his sword, when he was recalled by Pope Gregory to save him from the antipope installed by the German emperor in Rome. Guiscard's Normans treated Rome as brutally as the Huns had, pillaging and burning and even selling many of the citizens into Muslim slavery. Yet the Norman replacement of Gregory as the pope by force excused the crime. The rape of the second sacred Christian city after Jerusalem was forgiven because of the motive for the deed.

It was a bad precedent, which was confirmed by the increasing successes of the *reconquista* in Spain. The idea of a holy war was promoted at the Court of King Alfonso VI of Castile and Leon by the papacy and Frankish mercenaries and Cluniac monks. The frontier rolled southwards to the banks of the Duero River through skirmish and ambush, feint and battle.

Behind the armoured knights, the fortress builders and the masons followed, and the settlements of Sepulveda and Avila and Segovia and Salamanca rose as forward bastions in the Estremaduras. As one historian noted, war became an industry which afforded a living, either directly or indirectly, to most of the Christian population of the region.

The death of Robert Guiscard in Corfu removed the threat to Byzantium, while the death of Pope Gregory opened the way to the First Crusade against Jerusalem. The new pope, Urban II, had met the most charismatic preacher of the time, Peter the Hermit, at Bari on his return from a pilgrimage to Palestine. Peter had been a French monk from Amiens and was said to look like his donkey; but his sermons and his visions were compelling. He swore to Pope Urban that he would "rouse the martial nations of Europe" in the holy cause of aiding Byzantium against the Turks and retaking the Christian shrines of the Holy City from Islam. The pope held a council at Piacenza in 1095, where the Byzantine emperor Alexius Comnenus sent envoys to plead for help. He followed it with a second synod at Clermont in south central France, where his chances of attracting the support of the Frankish warlords would be greater, and where the masses inspired by Peter the Hermit and his fellow preachers might congregate to hear the call.

In advocating an expedition to the East to reconquer the holy places, Pope Urban had a hidden motive. The first was to liberate Palestine, although he did not want Jerusalem to become too much a rival of Rome as another focus of the Christian faith. The second was to reduce the power of the Second Rome of Byzantium, which had asked for help, but which rivalled St. Peter's authority with its Eastern patriarchate. The actual attack overland on the Levant would have to pass through wealthy Constantinople into Asia Minor. There was no knowing what the crusading armies might do on the way, plundering in the name of a just cause. Only the sea route lay directly from Italy across the Mediterranean to the Near East. But by preaching the Crusade to recapture the Church of the Holy Sepulchre and the place of Christ's martyrdom, Pope Urban could amalgamate all the disparate reasons and visions of the poor knights and the peasants, who sought an earthly quest as the first steps on the road to heaven.

An aristocrat from the court of Champagne as well as a Cluniac monk,

Urban believed in sacred wars fought by his old countrymen. And his proclamation of a divine mission to aid Byzantium and seize back Jerusalem was pitched to the ears of his audience. The Eastern adventure combined strategy and hope of salvation, greed and penitence, risk and absolution. Urban used the words of Jesus from the text of St. Matthew: "And every one that hath forsaken houses, or brethen, or sisters, or father, or mother, or wife, or children, or lands, for my name's sake, shall receive an hundredfold, and shall inherit everlasting life." This verse was used habitually for the induction of monks, but now it was used to recruit soldiers who were expected to behave as monks with swords, and who would not do so, believing that the hundredfold they would receive could be measured in rewards on earth.

As soon as Pope Urban had finished his address, the crowd shouted, *"Deus hoc vult!"* (God wills this!) It was unanimous approval for the expansion of Europe in the name of the religion that united it in spite of its schisms, a search for the mystical city where the founder of the Faith had died and risen to heaven. Jerusalem was the focus of creed and of spiritual quest; it was set in the words of the prophet Ezekiel "in the midst of the nations and countries that are around her." It was the magnet for the scattered tribes of Israel and Christian pilgrims, too. As Isaiah had declared of Jerusalem, "The mountain of the Lord's house shall be established in the top of the mountains, and shall be exalted above the hills; and all nations shall flow unto it." When the words of the Bible were a matter of literal belief, the call for a Crusade to Jerusalem was an exaltation as well as a battle cry. This was the opportunity to forsake a brutish life in medieval Europe for the place where God came down to his Chosen People on earth, where the Resurrection might be provoked after the reign of the infidel Anti-Christ, where the Saviour and the prophets of the Holy Book were buried, and where the gates of the heavenly city and Paradise awaited their opening.

The poor left for Jerusalem before the rich, who took longer to organise themselves, knowing some of the dangers that lay ahead and not trusting wholly in divine intervention. Peter the Hermit worked with his fellow preachers to assemble a gathering of some twenty thousand soldiers and pilgrims with a few nobles at Cologne on Holy Saturday in 1096. One of the questions asked by the crusading priests equated a family feud with the Crusade to Palestine. "If an outsider were to strike down any of your kin, would you not avenge your blood relative? How much more ought you to avenge your God, your father, your brother, whom you see reviled, banished from his estates, crucified; whom you hear calling for aid?"

The mob led by Peter committed atrocities in Hungary on the way to Constantinople, where the emperor Alexius Comnenus shipped them over the Bosphorus to be massacred by the Turks in Asia Minor. Peter himself survived the disaster to play a further sacred role in the First Crusade. Other German Crusaders in three parties, led by Peter's disciple Gottschalk and the obscure Volkmar and Emich, decided to attack and plunder the Jews in their homeland before setting off for the East. These early pogroms appeared an easy way of financing the journey as well as avenging the blood of Christ. Although the Christian bishops of Speyer and Worms, also the archbishop of Mainz, tried to protect the Jewish communities, they did not succeed and dozens of ghettos were attacked. Even in Prague, Volkmar had all the Jews massacred that he could find. All three German bands of fanatics and bigots were in turn destroyed by the Christian king of Hungary and his forces, who could not tolerate such an armed rabble within their territory. To a prelude in the Norman sack of Rome, the First Crusade added a popular wave of anti-Semitism and the persecutions of the first builders of Jerusalem.

It took a year after the council at Clermont for the four professional armies that marched on the First Crusade to be recruited and armed and set on the road. Their leaders had to make wise sacrifices to fulfil the papal dream. Godfrey de Bouillon, duke of Lower Lorraine, mortgaged his estates to equip his force of ten thousand men, and the aged Raymond, count of Toulouse, swore that he would die in the Holy Land. The two Roberts, the duke of Normandy and the count of Flanders, were never to lay claim to any of the cities or lands conquered in the Near East, although that was not true of Godfrey de Bouillon and his brother Baldwin of Lorraine, nor of many of the Norman warlords such as Bohemond and Tancred, who were already carving out Mediterranean principalities based on the kingdoms of Sicily and Naples. Without religious faith, few if any of the leading Crusaders would have set out, nor could they have recruited their barons and their knights and their foot soldiers without a fervent common conviction in their mission. Their task was in the service of God. The red cross sewn onto each surcoat and tunic was proof of divine protection as well as a mark for the Muslim enemy. This was to be the Army of Christ, with the Messiah riding in the heavens in front of the celestial hosts. He was ready to descend again once the reign of the Anti-Christ had been ended and the holy places restored to his worship. To the Crusaders, *Deus hoc vult*. The will of God would oversee their way.

FOUR

THE CROSS OVER JERUSALEM

"Deus hoc vult!" (God wills this)

—The Christian crowd shouting to Pope
Urban II, announcing the
First Crusade to take Jerusalem.

Although the divisions between the Muslim emirs and potentates allowed the First Crusade to reach the Near East, the breach between Western and Eastern Christianity, between Rome and Constantinople, should have destroyed the invasion from Europe before it ever left Asia Minor. The pope's reason for stimulating the Crusade was ambiguous, and the Byzantine emperor knew that. Who was the true foe? Was it the Christian patriarch in Constantinople or the infidel *imam* in Jerusalem? This uncertainty was to bedevil all the Crusades and lead to the conquest of both cities. Holy war held a double-edged sword. The heretic and the rival might be more dangerous than the pagan and the blasphemer.

Certainly, the first coherent crusading army which reached Byzantium proved that the mistrust of Alexius Comnenus was not misplaced. Godfrey de Bouillon and his brother Baldwin had negotiated their way across Hungary with their followers, who did not run riot until they reached the Sea of Marmora. There the Byzantine emperor victualled the army and arranged its transport across the Bosphorus. But he demanded that all the territories that might be taken by the Crusaders would recognise his sovereignty. Godfrey de Bouillon demurred and made a sortie against Constantinople itself. The imperial guard, some of whom descended from the Anglo-Saxon thanes defeated at the Battle of Hastings, easily drove off the attackers, who had ignored Holy Week to press their assault. The Crusaders acknowledged the emperor's power, and then they were supplied and shipped immediately to Asia Minor. Unwilling guests to unwelcome hosts, they were the heralds of the later Crusades.

Bohemond of Taranto and his nephew Tancred followed with their Norman army, recruited from those who had already established their power in southern Italy and Sicily. They crossed the Adriatic to march through Macedonia and Thrace to Constantinople. Bohemond asked Alexius Comnenus to serve as the commander in chief of all the imperial forces in Asia; but he was refused and transported with his forces to join the previous Crusaders across the Bosphorus. So was Raymond, count of Toulouse, with his following, which had fought its way through Dalmatia to the borders of the Byzantine Empire. The fourth major group of Crusaders, led by the eldest son of William the Conqueror, Robert, duke of Normandy, along with the counts of Blois and Flanders, was also processed through imperial hospitality to join the previous Christian expeditions. The emperor could feel safe again and even hopeful. His fellow Christian armies were on the far side of the straits across from his capital. Unless they turned back in defeat, Jerusalem should be their objective.

To the Muslims, the incursion of the people they called the Franj soon became a disaster. The local emir, Kilij Arslan, was defeated at Nicaea and the city captured. "He began to recruit troops and enrol volunteers," recorded the contemporary Arab historian Ibn al-Qalanisi, "and proclaimed *Jihad.*" But his summons to a holy war against the infidel was hardly heeded by the bickering emirs of the Near East. An ambush was set for the Franj armies, now marching southeast through the mountains towards Palestine. Yet the attack of the light Turkish cavalry on the heavy armour of the Christian knights proved ineffective, and the Turks themselves were caught in a pincer movement by a Franj rear guard. The Turks were cut to pieces and the survivors were enslaved. "When this shameful event for Islam became known," Ibn al-Qalanisi wrote from Damascus, "there was absolute panic. Fear and anxiety swelled beyond all bounds." And the anonymous author of the *Gesta Francorum* declared that if the Turks had only been Christians, no stronger or braver soldiers would ever be found. Those who died fighting them were martyrs.

At the rear of the victories of the first Crusaders, the Byzantine Empire was taking back its lost provinces with its fleets in the Aegean. The Greeks were trying to use the Franks and Latins to reconquer their old territories in Asia Minor, while the Crusaders thought that the Greeks should only be helping them to recover the Holy Land. Both the Eastern and the Western Christians had a low view of each other. There was mistrust in the family of the Faith. The Greeks feared treachery from the Latins, who were also considered uncivilised and inconstant and voluble. The Franks in their turn found the Byzantines wily and deceitful, effeminate and luxurious. Above all, the Greeks appeared to be poor soldiers and had to hire mercenaries to fight for them. They lacked the moral fibre needed to weave a Crusade.

That was the irreconcilable difference between the two areas of the Christian faith. The Westerners believed in a holy war, the Easterners in a just one. Both fought under Christian banners and gave thanks to God for their victories. But for the Byzantines, war was a necessity and a sin, unless it was justified, which was a rare occasion. The soldiers who returned from fighting were denied the Sacraments because of the blood on their hands. But since the popes of Rome had begun to grant indulgences to Crusaders in Spain and Italy and now the Near East, there was absolution available before the crime of killing. Bishops and archbishops fought in the front ranks of the Crusaders, or even in the Norman conquest of England, hardly a mission against a pagan country. There was no conflict in the Latin mind between the warrior and the believer, who joined in the Crusader. The Greek ideal separated the man of war from the man at prayer. It was a greater logic.

Nearly starving as they defiled through the passes of the mountains of Anatolia, harassed by guerilla attacks and separated by skirmishes and freebooting expeditions, the main force of the Crusaders reached in the autumn of 1097 the walls of the city of Antioch, six miles long with four hundred guardian towers. Their chances of taking the fortifications were small, although the fleets of Genoa were bringing them supplies. But their faith that they would take the city was great, almost as much as in the capture of Jerusalem. St. Peter had been the first bishop of Antioch, and now his church was converted into a mosque. Here, indeed, the believers in Jesus had first been called Christians. And with the help of a fortunate miracle, the faith of the Crusaders would carry them over the battlements into their prize.

The winter months brought pain and despair to the Christian army and the accompanying pilgrims. They were threatened with encirclement in their turn by the emirs of northern Syria. They felt minimal in a subcontinent of Muslim domination. But their bishops told them not to despair, for they were the army of Christ. "We do not trust in any multitude nor in power nor in any presumption," the letter of the bishops to the crusaders read, "but in the shield of Christ and justice, under the protection of Saint George and Theodore and Demetrius and Blaise, soldiers of Christ truly accompanying us." Suffering turned pride back to true humility. And with the discovery of the Holy Lance itself, which had pierced the side of Jesus on the cross, the actual sight of a sacred relic would produce a surge of morale and aggression.

The Christians of Antioch had been expelled from the city at the beginning of the siege for fear that they might become traitors. But because of their long cooperation with the Muslim authorities, they were suspected by the Crusaders and condemned to double jeopardy. They had to join the ranks of the extraordinary Tafurs, a group of poor marauders led by a penniless knight, who terrorised the surrounding Muslim communities and were accused of every atrocity, including cannibalism. At Ma'arra, even the Frankish chronicler Albert of Aix agreed with the Arab horror stories, writing: "Not only did our troops not shrink from eating dead Turks and Saracens; they also ate dogs."

The privations of the siege of Antioch led to a strange bond between the feudal lords and their impoverished followers. It was a common faith and purpose, although hardly a communion. Peter the Hermit himself was so discouraged that he fled; but he was brought back to pray another day. Yet the interminable siege was broken by the inspiration of another poor servant of the Lord, Peter Bartholomew, who had a vision of St. Andrew, who showed him that the Holy Lance was buried within the cathedral of Antioch. If the city were taken, the Christian army would have an invincible weapon that would lead them on to Jerusalem. And the city had to be taken, for the emir of Mosul had united the princes of Syria in a confederation against the Franj. A Christian converted to Islam betrayed a way into the Tower of the Two Sisters. Crying *"Deus hoc vult!"* the Crusaders took Antioch two days before the Syrian army arrived to invest them. The nutcracker was now the nut.

Exhausted and starving, the Crusaders were doomed without a miracle. And it was produced, a piece of iron from a pit dug in the cathedral, pronounced to be the Holy Lance foreseen by Peter Bartholomew. To the Arab historians, it was a trick; to the dispirited Christians, a visitation of God. With the Holy Lance in the vanguard, the Crusaders attacked the Muslims outside the walls. In a mass hallucination, they saw Saints George and Demetrius and Mercury fighting in the heavens and lowering their standards to the sacred relic below. The desperation and the fanaticism of the Christian knights and soldiers were such that the numerous Muslim forces under their various commanders disintegrated and fled. The Christians did seem to be fighting a holy war against Muslim petty princes, who would no longer be united by the cry of *jihad.* Divine intervention seemed on one side only.

The power of sacred relics was unique to medieval Christianity. It was based on the articles of the faith. At the Last Supper, Jesus had broken bread and given it to his disciples and said that it was his body. He had offered them wine and said that it was his blood. At the ceremony of the Communion, the Crusaders literally believed that the consecrated bread and wine was changed into the Body and Blood of Christ. The Christians also believed that their own bodies would be resurrected at the Second Coming. No such corporeal faith lay in the Jewish or the Muslim religion. But it allowed the Christians of the Middle Ages to become obsessed with bones and vials of blood and objects that were said to derive from the tombs of the saints and the martyrs. These even sanctified the weapons of war. In Roland's lament for his blade Durendal at his death, he recalled the sacred treasures in his sword:

"Ah, Durendal, you are holy and fair.
Many are the relics in your gilded hilt:
Saint Peter's tooth, some of Saint Basil's blood,

Hairs from the head of lordly Saint Denis.
Part of a robe that blessed Mary wore.
It would be wrong for infidels to hold you:
To wield you is for Christian men alone."

The problem of success in war is the division of the spoils. Baldwin had already carved out for himself a principality in Edessa, which had delayed the relieving Muslim army on its march towards defeat at Antioch; but that great Greek city Bohemond was determined to keep and not hand over to Byzantium, which was offering so little help to the Crusaders. His rival leader, Raymond, count of Toulouse, was persuaded by the Tafurs and the pilgrims to continue the march to Jerusalem, although the army was being decimated by disease and desertion. Dressed in sackcloth and carrying a cross in his hands as if he were the poorest of pilgrims, the wealthy count set off for the Holy Land at the head of the remaining Crusaders, who had proved true to their original mission. He took with him the Holy Lance and its awesome power that should protect their dangerous journey. For there were no more than a thousand knights and five thousand foot soldiers left, and a rabble of priests and monks and camp followers.

If the emirs of Syria had combined, they could easily have destroyed this small column of armed vagabonds. But the terrible reputation of the Christian soldiers as invincible cannibals ran ahead of their real strength. "All those who were well-informed about the Franj," wrote the chronicler Usamah Ibn Munqidh, "saw them as beasts superior in courage and fighting powers but in nothing else, just as animals are superior in strength and aggression." Although Robert of Normandy and Tancred, Godfrey de Bouillon and Robert of Flanders later joined the little army, and the fleets of Genoa and Pisa provided supplies and reinforcements, the Crusaders made progress more on reputation and fear than on the application of force. They failed to take the small city of Arqa as a preliminary to seizing the riches of Tripoli; its emir bought off the invaders with food and gold and horses and guides towards Palestine. And once the Crusaders crossed the Dog River, they left the Sunnis and the Turks behind them to fight now against the Shi'ites and the Fatimids of Egypt, who had tacitly approved of the attack of the Franj on their northern "heretic" cousins, but now found themselves under assault in their province of Palestine, which they had just

retaken from the Sunnis. Although the garrison of Jerusalem was reinforced, the port cities of Beirut and Sidon and Tyre and Acre were left
largely defenceless and ready to surrender to the new invaders. The divisions of the infidels allowed an easy Christian passage to the Promised
Land.

There was doubt now among the Crusaders as well as faith. Peter
Bartholomew was asked to prove the truth of the Holy Lance in a trial by
fire. Running between two lines of flaming faggots, clutching the sacred
iron to his breast, he was horribly burned and died in agony. Yet Raymond
and many of the pilgrims still believed in the blessed relic that would take
them to Jerusalem. It was encrusted in gold and jewels. And when the
Crusaders reached Ramleh, the administrative capital of Palestine, and the
Muslims fled at their approach, they gained not only a base in the Holy
Land, but the tomb of the warrior St. George, who would certainly lead
the soldiers of Christ on to their final goal.

Although the places of the Bible were truly there, Galilee and Caesarea, Bethlehem and Hebron, the actual terrain was a grave disappointment. On the dry plateau before Jerusalem, heat and thirst were the order
of the day. But there were Eastern Christians here, who welcomed the
Crusaders as if they were the advent of the Second Coming and showed
them a treasury of relics ranging from pieces of wood from Noah's ark to
the wooden manger in which Christ had lain as a baby. And when finally
the Crusaders saw before them the walls of Jerusalem, vision met action.
They were transported into a paroxysm of rage and anticipation. For over
the Holy City sat the mosque of the Dome of the Rock on Mount Moriah,
its golden cap set beside the minaret of the al-Aqsa mosque on the sacred
rock at the centre of the world. A howl of execration and a cry of exulta-
tion shook the crusading forces. The Muslim response was the cry of the
muezzin to summon the faithful to prayer, a pious response that was a terrible affront. The knights and soldiers and pilgrims fell on their knees and
burst into tears. And in that blurred vision of an imaginary city that was
the gateway to heaven and now lay in the grip of the infidel, a holy fury
was born.

"Now more than ever the army believed it was fighting for Christ," affirmed a historian of the Crusades, Zoé Oldenbourg. "Its object was to defend Christ, to avenge Christ, and to win Christ, and Christ seemed to

them as much present as if he had been reincarnated in fact. Simply to be in the very country, in the very place where the Passion of Jesus Christ had taken place was, to some extent, to relive the mystery of the Incarnation. Whatever might be said of the future conduct of this army of God, it would be unjust to underestimate the grandeur of this experience and the sincerity of those who lived through it."

Yet worship outside the walls was futile. The city had to be seized. And the Christians were provoked by the minarets of Muslim occupation. The infidel was translated into the devil, because he was polluting the holy places with pagan temples and presence. No more than the Muslims could have tolerated a cathedral beside the Ka'aba at Mecca could the Crusaders accept the sight of a minaret beside the Dome of the Rock crowning Jerusalem. A sudden fervour and fanaticism inspired the Christian host to an extraordinary assault on a complacent enemy, which had not yet seen that it was engaged in a *jihad* not of its choosing.

The siege of the Holy City lasted for forty days, the period that Christ had spent in the wilderness. The Crusaders followed the example of the Israelites before the walls of Jericho. The army went in procession seven times around Jerusalem. The soldiers walked with bare feet and sang hymns. They halted at the holy places outside the city; at Mount Zion, where Jesus had eaten the Last Supper and given his Body and Blood to his disciples; at the Garden of Gethsemane, where he had prayed for the cup to be taken from him; and on the Mount of Olives, from where he had risen to heaven. There Peter the Hermit or other priests preached the deliverance of the Church of the Holy Sepulchre. Two siege towers had been prepared to back the sermons. The Christians launched themselves against the fortifications and were repulsed. Holy rituals and observances were not enough to win Jerusalem. Its walls had not tumbled down like those of Jericho at the blast of the psalms and the trumpets.

Stupidly, the Sudanese and Egyptian garrison had answered the Christian ceremonies with boorish insults, desecrating crosses stolen from churches and shouting obscenities against the infidels outside. This inflamed the fervour of the Crusaders. As William of Tyre wrote: "Their hearts swelled with desire to avenge this shame done to Jesus Christ." They advanced their wooden siege towers, lined with flayed hides soaked in vinegar to protect them from the defensive mixture of oil and sulphur called Greek fire, which had been prepared by the Fatimid commander Iftikhar. Reinforcements from Egypt were on their way. The Crusaders had to take the city or be destroyed, as at Antioch. In the words of the Arab historian Ibn al-Athir:

> Of the two siege towers constructed by the Franj, one was on the side of Mount Zion to the south, while the other was to the north. The Muslims succeeded in burning the first one, killing all those who were inside. But they had only just finished destroying it when a messenger came asking for help. The city had been breached on the opposite side. In truth, it was taken from the north, one Friday morning, seven days before the end of Sha'ban [in July 1099].

Iftikhar with his picked troops had established his command post in the octagonal Tower of David, the hinge of the fortifications. The Christians led by Godfrey de Bouillon had crossed from their mobile tower near Herod's Gate. Flemish and Walloon soldiers occupied the northern walls, and then poured into the interior of the city, driving back the demoralised defenders before them. The Muslims fell back towards the al-Aqsa mosque, which they trusted for protection from this barbarous onslaught. And now in the south, the troops of the count of Flanders and the duke of Normandy, of Tancred and of Baldwin, broke through and continued the slaughter of the Egyptians and the Sudanese. Their remnants retired to the Tower of David, where their commander Iftikhar saw that the Holy City was lost. He surrendered to Raymond, count of Toulouse, in return for a safe conduct for him and his men. "The Franj kept their word," Ibn al-Athir noted with surprise, "and let them leave by night for the port of Ascalon, where they set up camp."

Such wise mercy was the prelude to an orgy of destruction that shamed Christendom and led to a *jihad* against the Crusaders as well as confirming the pogroms in Germany. There was a slaughter of the Muslims who had taken refuge in the al-Aqsa mosque, "more than seventy thousand of them," according to Ibn al-Qalanisi, although he exaggerated the numbers of the victims. And all the Jews that crowded into their synagogue were burned alive inside. Mistaking the al-Aqsa mosque for the Temple of Solomon, Raymond of Aguilers wrote a notorious account of what he had observed:

Wonderful sights were to be seen. Some of our men (and this was more merciful) cut off the heads of their enemies; others shot them with arrows, so that they fell from the towers; others tortured them longer by casting them into the flames. Piles of heads, hands and feet were to be seen in the streets of the city. It was necessary to pick one's way over the bodies of men and horses. But these were small matters compared to what happened at the Temple of Solomon, a place where religious services are normally chanted. What happened there? If I tell the truth it will exceed your powers of belief. So let it be enough to say this much, at least, that in the Temple and porch of Solomon, men rode in blood up to their knees and bridle reins. Indeed it was a just and splendid judgement of God that this place should be filled with the blood of the unbelievers since it had suffered so long from their blasphemies.

Another historian of the Crusade, William of Tyre, did show disquiet, writing that "the city offered such a spectacle of the massacre of enemies, such a deluge of bloodshed, that the victors themselves could not help but be struck with horror and disgust." Certainly, the Crusaders tried to kill all the Muslims and Jews in the Holy City, although enough did escape to found a suburb in Damascus. And in this religious cleansing of Jerusalem, the Crusaders did not feel too much horror and disgust, but mainly thankfulness. Albert of Aix spoke of the joy of the victors at their success, which they saw as the triumph of God. The Holy City would be exclusively Christian. Those of other faiths were eliminated and would be excluded.

Indeed, sacredness is a form of exclusion. From the beginning, biblical Jerusalem and the Temple itself had been divided into areas of greater and lesser holiness, where the degree of holiness was reflected in the taboos applying to each area. The Temple Mount was holier than the rest of Jerusalem. No one who was ritually defiled could enter it—including persons suffering from venereal discharge, or women who had recently given birth or were menstruating. The Temple court was yet holier, and heathens were forbidden to enter it. The outer hall of the Temple was holier still, reserved for the priestly caste. Finally, the Holy of Holies, the inner part of the Temple, could only be entered by the high priest, and only on Yom Kippur, the Day of Atonement.

The concept of holiness as the exclusion of the defiled had a histori-cal significance. People who were alien had been gradually included in the category of the defiled. The presence of an outsider in the city, especially near the Temple, was "anathema" in the literal sense of the word. The au-thor of the Psalms said, "O God, heathens have entered Your domain, de-filed Your holy temple." The Crusaders, who besieged and took Jerusalem in 1099, massacred the Jews and Muslims, who they believed were defil-ing *their* Temple of the Lord. Their greatest slaughter was in what they called the Temple of Solomon, but it was actually in a mosque built by Muslims, who had taken sanctuary there.

The war between Islam and Christianity at the time of the Crusades defined Jerusalem as a Holy City whose conquerors could claim that their own religion was chosen by God. During the Byzantine period, Chris-tianity had spoken more of holy places than of a Holy City. The idea of the Holy Land, and to some degree of the Holy City as well, came from the Crusaders. Their triumph relieved Christianity of its ambivalence toward Jerusalem. Spirituality can be a matter of geography. When the earthly Jerusalem is within reach, its value rises; when one is far away from the earthly Jerusalem, the heavenly one gains more importance. The Cru-saders saw themselves as vassals coming to liberate the domain of their Lord Jesus; and with respect to Judaism, they presented themselves as the spiritual, and therefore the true, Israel—that is, the legitimate heir to Jerusalem.

Actually, the Crusaders were using the same texts that the tribes of Israel had used. In Exodus, God was said to say: "If thou wilt indeed obey, then I will be an enemy unto thine enemies and an adversary unto thine adversaries." The Psalms echoed these divine and hostile messages. In the Koran, which also derived from some biblical texts, the enemies of God were the infidels and were doomed to hellfire. All the three monotheistic religions from the Near East, Judaism and Christianity and Islam, called on God to help them against their enemies, who might indeed be calling on a similar, but exclusive, God. When these three faiths were influenced, as they now were, by Persian Manicheanism, the idea of the cosmic strug-gle between God and Satan, good and evil, then the concept of one intol-erant faith enforced by the sword was born. For if the soldiers of Christ were fighting the soldiers of Muhammad, and if each singular Messiah or

Prophet led his host, both were engaged in a holy war where victory over the enemy proved the right God was on the right side. To the infidel, no quarter: to the pagan, no mercy. For these were the enemies of God.

After the mass killings in Jerusalem, the Crusaders sought absolution and the hope of salvation. Their commanders led a procession to the Church of the Holy Sepulchre. There they believed that Jesus had literally risen from the dead and had ensured their own resurrection, if his commands were followed. That day was the day of the Dispersal of the Apostles, who had left Jerusalem to take the gospel to the rest of the world. The Crusaders believed that they were new apostles, and by seizing the holy places, they would spread Christianity across the unbelievers and the far nations. "This day, I say," Raymond of Aguilers testified, "marks the justification of all Christianity, the humiliation of paganism, the renewal of our faith." And William of Tyre said that the Crusaders prostrating themselves in front of the Holy Sepulchre "saw the body of Jesus Christ still lying there, all dead. . . . They felt as if they had entered into paradise."

They did not spare even the buildings of the infidels. The Mosque of Omar was sacked, although he had spared the Church of the Holy Sepulchre. And in a significant action, the Greek priests were expelled from that place of the Saviour's tomb, and Latin priests were installed. At first, the Greeks refused to tell the Crusaders where the True Cross was hidden, but iron persuasion changed their minds. To the Holy Lance, the Crusaders now added the True Cross, the relics which confirmed the worth of their long armed pilgrimage.

A fortnight after the Crusaders had taken the Holy City, their instigator, Pope Urban, died in Rome. He would have been pleased if he had known that the Greek patriarch of Jerusalem had also died, and that the Crusaders intended to found a Latin and Frankish Kingdom of Jerusalem with a patriarch, subject to Rome. That had been a prime object of the mission. Godfrey de Bouillon, elected to be that first king, would not take the title, declaring that he could not wear a golden crown in the place where Jesus Christ had worn a crown of thorns. This humble and politic decision resulted in his assumption of control under the title of the Advocate of the Holy Sepulchre. He moved immediately to rid himself of all rivals and took the Tower of David off Raymond of Toulouse, who withdrew in fury with his men after a pilgrimage to the river Jordan. Godfrey then repelled the counterattack of an Egyptian army at Ascalon. Supported by Tancred, he became the master of most of the holy places of Palestine. According to William of Tyre, only three hundred knights and two thousand foot soldiers now held the captured sacred lands of Christendom.

It had been an extraordinary adventure and an unlikely victory. The First Crusade would not have achieved its goals if it had not been for the vision of Jerusalem, half on earth and half in heaven. For the Crusade was an extension of the pilgrimage, with a sword in the hand instead of a staff. The word *crusade* did not yet exist. The quest for the Near East was called an *expeditio,* an "expedition"; a *peregrinatio,* a "pilgrimage"; or *iter in terram sanctam,* "to go to the Holy Land." The journey was all, the reaching of the divine and the door to Paradise upon earth. The trials and tribulations of the route, the sufferings and the dangers, even the massacres and the slavery, these were the tests which God put upon his Chosen People, who sought to restore his worship to the Holy of Holies. Yet the possession of Jerusalem was only the beginning of more perils, and the divisions of the infidels would preserve the new Christian kingdom far more than any crusading zeal.

FIVE

SURVIVAL BY
DISUNION

Our feet shall stand within thy gates, O Jerusalem.

—Psalm CXXII, Verse Two

Although the Jews and the Muslims were massacred when the Christians captured Jerusalem, there was no torch set to wisdom, as at the Library of Alexandria. Learning had its value. Eight Torah rolls and three hundred and thirty Hebrew manuscripts were sold at a high price to the Jewish settlement at Ascalon, still under Muslim control and toleration. It was, indeed, the mark of the civilisation of Islam in the late eleventh century that its rulers held out an alternative to the Greek and Roman verdict on the conquered—slavery or death. Islam now offered other alternatives. Conversion would lead to full civil rights, while submission would mean that there would be no persecution. After the bloody cleansing of Jerusalem, the Crusaders began to learn from the more merciful policies of their enemies. When Caesarea fell to the Christians, the chronicler Fulcher of Chartres noted that some of the Muslim males were spared along with many of the females, who were needed to work at grinding corn and spinning. Both ransom and concubines were stimulants towards a limited clemency.

Although the Crusaders who returned to their homes in Europe had only reached the earthly site of the meagre city of Jerusalem, they were treated as if they had made the heavenly journey to the seat of God. They were venerated, for they had followed Christ to the places of his martyrdom. Robert of Flanders was called by the Latin name of Hierosolemitanus, "the man who came from Jerusalem." They had been pilgrims as well as warriors in a war of the liberation of the Holy City. The three historians of the First Crusade, Baldric of Bourgueil and Guibert of Nogent and Robert the Monk, wrote of the Western expedition as if Moses were leading the tribes of Israel to the Promised Land. Robert the Monk even compared in importance the capture of Jerusalem to the Creation of the world and the Crucifixion. There was no question that a Crusader achieved salvation as well as anything temporal that might fall to him in the Near East.

The motives for the Crusaders who joined the next disastrous invasion parties of 1101, two years after Jerusalem was taken, were made clear in the charters which they signed before their departure. "I, Stephen of Neublens, have decided to go to Jerusalem, where God was seen as man and had dealings with men and to adore his feet in the place where they trod. . . . " "Bernard Veredun, going to Jerusalem moved by the example of those wishing to save their souls. . . . " For these mailed pilgrims with lances and swords, the Church provided a blessing of a guarantee of salvation. The abbot of Cluny himself put the cross on the back of Stephen of Neublens and a sacred ring on his finger. Absolution lay on the completion of the long road east. "Wishing to show God more painful satisfaction for his sins," the testament of Welf of Bavaria declared, "he took the road to Jerusalem."

The Holy Land, however, was not the only direction for Crusaders. Their goal was preferably Jerusalem; but their motive was to attack paganism or heresy anywhere as the fists of the Church of Rome. Duke William of Normandy had procured papal blessing as a Crusader when he invaded England across the Channel and established his dynasty there after the Battle of Hastings. The many frontier wars of the Christians of northern Spain against the Muslim south were called crusades, and absolution was promised to the knights who fought there. Indeed, a crusade was to become indistinguishable from territorial expansion. When the Saxon princes would be called upon to march to Jerusalem on a Second

Crusade in 1147, they declared that they would rather proceed against the Wends—a Slavic people who lived to the northeast of the Holy Roman Empire. In a notorious letter, St. Bernard of Clairvaux was to proclaim that the goal of the Wendish expedition should be conversion or death, while the pope would grant the Saxon crusaders the same material and spiritual blessings that were granted to Crusaders to the Holy Land. The rising fervour of religious aggression also made plundering raids on the Jewish communities of Germany and Central Europe almost a necessary prelude to a foreign expedition in the name of God. A pogrom provided the gold that began a Crusade.

The European reinforcements called up by the pope to bolster the defences of the Kingdom of Jerusalem in the new century all met with disaster. A first wave of Lombards and Germans reached Constantinople, but were broken by the Turks in Anatolia. The same fate happened to a second army led by William of Nevers, and to a third army under William of Aquitaine and Welf of Bavaria. The triple triumphs of the Turks did not prevent two further smaller Crusades in the next decade by Bohemond and King Sigurd of Norway. These spectacular losses merely underlined the miraculous success of the First Crusade; for Jerusalem was still Christian. Failure to reach the Holy City was held to be a punishment for pride and sin. "God chastised them because of their insolence," Baldric of Bourgueil wrote, "in case their minds should be inflamed with pride on account of their many victories." Had not the tribes of Israel often been chastised by God, who allowed their defeat by their enemies because they had broken his Commandments? The judgement of the Almighty could go against his Chosen Peoples for their wrongdoings.

Fatimid attempts from Egypt to reconquer Palestine demonstrated the precarious hold that the Kingdom of Jerusalem kept on the Holy Land. A few hundred rotating knights were meant to defend an entire hinterland. Disease was common, death was often too early. If the kingdom was to survive, it needed strongholds and manpower. The chains of border fortresses built by the Franks in Syria and Lebanon and Jordan were to become the glories of military architecture and the despair of the Muslims. The mighty Krak des Chevaliers and the citadels at Tortosa, Sahyun, and Saphet were impregnable fortresses of stone that enabled minimal garrisons to dominate large territories and withstand long sieges. These castles and towers were the blocks of the Christian church in the Near East, particularly when the military orders appeared and gave them permanent defenders.

Although the Knights Hospitaller of St. John were founded before the First Crusade and were based in a hostel in Jerusalem in order to care for poor pilgrims, the formation in 1118 of the Knights Templar, or Knights of the Temple of Solomon, in Jerusalem was to provide a dedicated catalyst of monasticism and chivalry, a white monk with a sword in his hand. These two military orders, along with the later Teutonic Knights, owed direct allegiance to the pope and would prove worthy rivals of the enemy ascetic religious warriors, the Sufis and the Isma'ilis—a sect of these Muslim fighters later known as the Assassins. Because of geography and proximity, a curious correspondence would even grow between the Templars and the Assassins. The focus of both faiths was the Dome of the Rock in Jerusalem, which the Templars were sworn to guard. On that sacred rock, indeed, the nine original founders of the military order took their sacred oath to serve as pure knights protecting pilgrims to the holy places. Small wonder that those pilgrims thought the Dome was the actual Temple of Solomon. It was called Templum Domini and its likeness was set on the seal of the first Christian grand master of the order. The al-Aqsa mosque was changed by the Knights Templar into their headquarters. They built a chapel there modelled on the Church of the Holy Sepulchre, guarded below their citadel by the Knights Hospitaller of St. John, who defended the site of the tomb of Christ.

The Knights Templar took in a great deal of contemporary Arab philosophy and science and building techniques, which had derived from classical Greek thought. They had many masons and builders in their order, and they used the Temple and building tools in their symbolism and their designs and their ceremonies. They were neo-Platonists. They believed in one God, the architect of the world, in whom the members of all religions, Christian and Muslim and Jew, might believe. This was central to their beliefs and led to later charges of heresy. The Templars were also the conduit from the Near East of hermetic and cabbalistic knowledge.

The Templars adopted from Oriental mysticism the secret knowledge, the *gnosis*. Its sacred geometry was the octagon contained within the circle. It was interesting that the octagonal green glass Roman cup which fell into Genoese hands in 1101 in Palestine was thought to be the Sacro Catino, or Holy Grail. The Dome of the Rock, which contained a holy stone, was built by Islamic architects as eight equal walls holding up a golden dome. Guarded by the Templars during the period of the Christian Kingdom of Jerusalem, its shape influenced all Templar architecture. Octagonal chapels were built in many Templar presbyteries, particularly at their centre in Portugal at Tomar, and in the chapter houses of the Gothic cathedrals. In a real way, the Templars would transfer sacred geometry and hermetic wisdom to Europe.

But initially, the Templars were very much the armour of the Cistercians, the white monks. St. Bernard of Clairvaux had much to do with the papal recognition of both orders, one to make holy war and one to pray. His description of the Templar knights was salutary.

> They come and go at a sign from their commander; they wear the clothes which he gives them, seeking neither other garments nor other food. They are wary of all excess in food or clothing, desiring only what is needful. They live all together, without women or children. . . . Insolent words, vain acts, immoderate laughter, complaints and murmurs, when they are perceived, do not go unpunished. They hate chess and dice, and they have a horror of hunting; they do not find the usual pleasure in the ridiculous pursuit of birds. They shun and abominate mimes, magicians, and *jongleurs,* light songs and foolishness. They crop their hair close because the Gospels tell them it is a shame for a man to tend his hair. They are never seen combed and rarely washed, their beards are matted, they reek of dust and bear the stains of the heat and their harness.

Although the Templars would never desert their monkish discipline, they would become the bankers of the Kingdom of Jerusalem during its century of survival, also its diplomats with the Muslim world. Only when unschooled grand masters would prefer confrontation would the kingdom fall. One story told by the emir Usamah Ibn Munqidh, a diplomat and writer from Damascus, showed how far the Templars had learned tolerance from their Muslim neighbours. When he visited Jerusalem, he wished to pray at the al-Aqsa mosque, which was now converted into a Christian church. The Templars placed a small chapel beside it at his disposal. When the emir began his prayers, a knight, newly come from Europe, turned him forcibly towards the east, saying, "We pray that way." The Templars took the newcomer away, but when the emir resumed his prayers towards Mecca, the knight repeated his outrage. This time he was ejected by the Templars, who apologised to the emir with the words, "He is a foreigner. He has just arrived from Europe and has never seen anyone pray without turning to face east." The emir ceased from his prayers, but forgave his Templar friends. Among the Crusaders, he explained, "We find some people who have come to settle among us and who have cultivated the society of the Muslims. They are far superior to those who have freshly joined them in the territories they now occupy."

European pilgrims to Jerusalem saw only a Christian city. Inside the Dome of the Rock, by now very much the Temple Church, John of Wurzburg recorded the numerous inscriptions on walls and columns of New Testament incidents at the Jewish Temple in which Jesus had figured. He also mentioned "a stone, which is treated with great veneration—it having been trodden on and bearing the mark of the Lord's foot." (When the Muslims recaptured Jerusalem, the Christian "Mark of the Lord's Foot" was said to be the "Footprint of Muhammad"—and it still is.) He had this observation on the Muslim reaction to the use now made of their building: "The figure of the Holy Cross has been placed by the Christians on the top of the dome, which is very offensive to the Saracens, and many of them would be willing to expend much gold to have it taken away."

In the east wall of the Temple compound, which was the east wall of the city, was "the Golden Gate, through which our Lord on the fifth day before His passion rode in triumph . . . and was greeted with palm branches . . .," and John of Wurzburg added that the gate "was never opened to anyone except on Palm Sunday." This magnificent double-arched Golden Gate which the Christian pilgrim saw was a Byzantine structure which stands to this day, associated with the traditions of all three faiths. An early Jewish tradition held that it was through this gate that the Messiah would enter Jerusalem. For Christians it was the way Jesus came into the city. Muslims thought it to be the gate of judgement referred to in the Koran, "its inner side contains mercy, while the outer side is toward doom." Although it may still be entered from the Temple compound, the Golden Gate is now blocked from the outside, having been sealed by the

Muslims almost certainly for security reasons as well as faith. This exclusion would prevent the entry of any liberating Jewish Messiah, and also ensure that the gate would have no "outer side . . . toward doom" on Judgement Day.

John of Wurzburg then wrote that at the southern end of the Temple compound was "the palace which Solomon is said to have built"—the site of the al-Aqsa mosque—"where is a wondrous stable of such size that it is able to contain more than two thousand horses or fifteen hundred camels. Close to this palace the Knights Templar have many spacious and connected buildings, and also the fountains of a new and large church which is not yet finished." Another pilgrim, Theoderich, had a better description of "Solomon's Stables," calling it, correctly, "a wondrous and intricate building resting on piers and containing an endless complication of arches and vaults." Both accepted the popular assumption that it was built by King Solomon when he constructed his palace on this site.

Although dependent on new recruits and income from their presbyteries in Europe, the Templars were a permanent standing army in the Holy Land, a few hundred knights holding the Holy City and a broken necklace of castles across Palestine. Their existence depended on playing off one Arab ruler or warlord against another. Any combination of all the Muslim states against them would have been their end in a *jihad,* or holy war. They were particularly influenced by the rival Muslim warrior Shi'ite and Isma'ili sect of the Assassins, who held castles and lands in the mountains near the Caspian Sea and in Syria, and were supporters of the Fatimid caliphs of Egypt. Their founder and first grand master, Hassan Ibn al-Sabbah, was a poet and a scientist and the inventor of modern terrorism. He indoctrinated fanatical young men to go out and murder his enemies, usually at the cost of their own lives. From these suicide squads derived the word *fida'is* or *fedayeen,* still used of Palestinian guerrillas. The Assassins found the Templars to be willing allies in the disintegration of the orthodox Sunni rulers of Syria and other Arab states, as well as converts to some of the secrets of their organisation and doctrines.

Marco Polo, who travelled through Persia on his way to China, confirmed in Europe the legend of the Assassins. He wrote that, in a fortified valley between two mountains, the sheikh or "Old Man" of the Assassins had planted a beautiful garden that grew every fruit in the world. The garden was watered with streams of wine, milk, and honey. Like the Prophet Muhammad's paradise, on which it was modelled, it held gilded palaces, *houris,* dancers, musicians, and singers. And it was seen only by those who were to be Assassins. Young men who had been trained in arms at the Old Man's court were drugged, taken to the hidden garden, and initiated into its delights. They lived there in luxury for a few days, convinced that their leader had transported them to Paradise. When they were suddenly drugged again and taken back to his court, they were eager to risk their lives for him in order to return. "Away they went," concluded Polo, "and did all that they were commanded. Thus it happened that no man ever escaped when the Sheikh of the Mountain desired his death."

The medieval story of a castle and a paradise on earth akin to the Grail Castle of the Fisher King was true in that respect. There is little doubt that the Assassins were drug takers, for their name was derived from the Arabic word *Hashshashin,* meaning "users of hashish." The tale of the garden paradise possibly had its origin in the hallucination produced by the drug. But Oriental legend had already created an Eden out of the fertile valley near the chief Assassin stronghold at Alamut, south of the Caspian Sea. Stories about the sect may have been confused with this tradition and with the legend of King Shedad, who tried to equal Allah's paradise by building his own.

Missionaries trained in the Grand Lodge of the Isma'ilis in Cairo preached a doctrine that negated many of orthodox Islamic beliefs. They held that Muslim law and scriptures contained an inner meaning that was known only to the *imams.* They taught that there were only seven prophets: Adam, Noah, Abraham, Moses, Jesus, Muhammad, and the *imam* Ismail. In the order of Creation, the prophets stood at the level of Universal Reason, second only to God. Last in the sevenfold chain of Creation stood man. Though God himself was unknowable, a man could work through these grades as far as Universal Reason, and a new aspect of the teaching would be revealed to him at each level. Because such views were heretical, every Isma'ili initiate was required to conceal his beliefs in accordance with the Shi'ite demand of secrecy and to conform, outwardly, with the state religion. In Isma'ili writings, there was usually a frenzied wanderer like a Perceval in quest of a Grail. He sought truth through trial and suffering until he was at last accepted into the faith by an *imam,* who revealed to him the true meaning of Muslim law and scriptures.

Such a quest was described by Hassan Ibn al-Sabbah in his own memoirs. He pursued spiritual power through political power and changed the role of the Isma'ili initiate to the role of Assassin. At the same time, he modified the grades of initiation. The only descriptions of these grades, and of the mysteries revealed to initiates, were written by European scholars who saw the Isma'ili hierarchy itself as a mere brainwashing system. According to their accounts, the teaching given at each level negated everything that had been taught before. The innermost secret of the Assassins was that heaven and hell were the same, all actions were indifferent, and there was no good or evil except the virtue of obeying the *imam.* Nothing is absolutely known of the Assassins' secrets, because their books of doctrine and ritual were burned by the Mongols in 1256 with their library at Alamut. Hassan emphasized the Shi'ite doctrine of obedience to the *imam* and made changes in the Isma'ili hierarchy. Persian tradition had it that below Hassan, the chief *da'i,* or grand master, came the senior *da'is;* the ordinary *da'is;* the *rafiqs,* or companions; the *lasiqs,* or laymen; and the *fida'is* (devotees), who did the murders. The division of the Templars under their grand master into grand priors, priors, knights, esquires, and lay brothers was closely to follow the hierarchy of the Assassins.

In his asceticism and singleness of purpose, Hassan was an ideal revolutionary leader and conspirator. He is said to have remained continuously within his home in his fortress for more than thirty years, only going out twice and appearing twice more on his roof. His invisibility increased his power. From his seclusion he strengthened the defences of Alamut, purged the ranks of his followers (even putting to death two of his own sons), continued with his strategy of seizing hill positions as centres of local subversion, and irrigated surrounding ground to create his versions of Paradise. He elevated his authority to tyranny over life and soul. The will of the Old Man was the will of his *imam,* the caliph, and thus the will of God. By winning over garrisons and assassinating local governors, he occupied strongpoints and terrorised the Sunnis, Persians, and Turks alike. The conspiracy of the determined few, as usual, was hardly opposed by the fearful many. On the model of Muhammad himself, who had fled to Medina to rally support and reconquer Mecca and all Arabia, Hassan hoped to take over the whole caliphate of Baghdad and launch a terminal crusade against the infidel.

By the authority of his rank and by the use of drugs, Hassan trained *fida'is* in such blind obedience that, like the Japanese suicide pilots of the Second World War, they welcomed death during an attempt at assassination. They preferred the dagger as a weapon, and the court or the mosque as a place of execution. They scorned the use of poison and backstairs intrigue, for their code was more that of soldiers than of harem murderers. Legend tells of one *fida'i*'s mother who rejoiced when she heard that her son had died in an attempt on a ruler's life, then put on mourning when he returned alive. Similar legends grew up around other loyal *fida'is* who stabbed themselves or dashed out their brains on the rocks below the battlements to prove their obedience to the Old Man's command.

Rather like the Mafia of later times, the Assassins operated from their strongholds a protection racket under threat of death. Their techniques helped to undermine the Turkish Empire and to fragment even more the fragmented Arab world. Suspicion ran riot, and murder was a normal method of princely government. Thus the Crusaders, coming to the Holy Land, found only a divided enemy, disorganised by the Assassins. Hassan may not have intended to aid the Christian invaders; but he did help the Crusaders to entrench themselves in the Levant.

The founder of the Templars, Hugh de Payens, knew of the Assassins when he formed his organisation. The Christian and Muslim military orders were aware of each other in Syria before 1128, when the Templar Rule was written. Even the colours worn by the knights, red crosses on a white ground, were the same as those of the Assassin *rafiqs,* who wore red caps and belts and white tunics. Some claim that the Templars only adopted the Asssassin "hues of innocence and blood, and of pure devotion and murder" because the rival Knights Hospitaller wore black. However that may be, the function of the Templars was virtually the same as that of the Assassins—to serve as an independent power on the side of their religious faith.

Modern Isma'ili scholarship discounts the medieval Christian version of the Assassins as a misunderstanding based on orthodox Sunni black propaganda against the breakaway Islamic cult. Three Persian historians of the thirteenth century spread the charges against the mountain Isma'ili fiefdoms, which the Christians were only too glad to accept, including the name Hashshashin, or Assassins. To later Isma'ilis, the believers at Alamut were part of a highly disciplined community which stretched in scattered villages and fortresses from Syria to eastern Persia, yet maintained a cohesive and centralised state under their *imam,* Hassan Ibn al-Sabbah. They acknowledged the exclusivity of the cult, which collectively introduced its members into paradise on earth, while the rest of mankind was made irrelevant. They could not deny the policy of assassination to preserve the mountain state by the balance of terror—two attempts were even made to kill the great Islamic unifier and holy warrior Saladin—but they did repudiate the legend of drug taking and the false paradise garden of Alamut. The devotion of the *fida'is* was a matter of faith, just as the Templars obeyed their grand master without drug or favour. The Assassins were the ultimate loyalists, faithful unto death to their creed.

Yet the *jihad,* or holy war, was becoming a danger to the balance of politics in the Levant. Just as the Assassins and the Templars reached a working arrangement, so the Kingdom of Jerusalem—which was now known as Outremer, the place beyond the sea—and other Christian duchies in the Near East used diplomacy rather than war in order to survive. They only existed on Muslim divisions. The attempts to call a *jihad* after the fall of Jerusalem had failed. There was even a riot in the sultan's mosque in Baghdad in 1111, when *imams* and Sufis attacked the preacher in his *minbar,* or pulpit, which they smashed. "They then began to cry out," Ibn al-Qalanisi wrote, "to bewail the evils that had befallen Islam because of the Franj who were killing men and enslaving women and children. Since they were preventing the faithful from saying their prayers, the officials present made various promises, in the name of the sultan, in an effort to pacify them: armies would be sent to defend Islam against the Franj and all the infidels."

Although the sultan pardoned the actions of the protestors and ordered the emirs to return to their provinces and prepare a *jihad* against the enemies of God, little was accomplished. Baghdad was at odds with Damascus, and both powers with Cairo. Between these three Muslim capital cities in the Near East, there was a host of quarrelling groups and sects,

Sunnis set against Shi'as ranged against Isma'ilis, all faithful to their *imams*, each the true descendant of the prophet Muhammad. Not that the Christian states acted in harmony or unity. On sea, Venice and Genoa and Pisa fought battles to corner the trade to the Levant, while the Latin leaders of the northeast, the princes of Antioch and the counts of Edessa and Tripoli, could ally themselves with Muslim emirs and atabegs against their Christian relatives, while they were still officially under the suzerainty of the king of Jerusalem. Struggles to stay in power bespoke a religious tolerance that was threatened by every call to a general holy war. When the Turkish sultan Muhammad, indeed, proclaimed a *jihad* against the Franks and marched on Syria in 1115, he found himself not only opposed by all the local Christian armies, but also by those of Aleppo and Damascus, which stood side by side with the infidels for fear of what the Turks might do to their Muslim cities.

In a famous passage, Fulcher of Chartres drew a line between the settlers in Jerusalem and in its near territories that divided them from the influx of temporary Crusaders from Europe. "We who had been Westerners have become Orientals," he declared from the Holy City, where he was now living. "The man who was a Roman or a Frank has here become a man from Galilee or Palestine. And the man who used to live in Rheims or Chartres now finds himself a citizen of Tyre and Antioch. We have already forgotten the places where we were born; already many of us do not know them, or at any rate, no longer hear them mentioned. Some among us already possess in this country houses and servants which belong to them as a hereditary right. Another has married a wife who is not his compatriot—a Syrian or an Armenian woman perhaps, or even a Saracen who has received the grace of baptism. . . . He who was once a stranger here is now a native. Every day our dependants and our relatives follow us, leaving behind, unwillingly perhaps, all their belongings. For he who was poor there now finds that God has made him rich here. He who had little money now possesses countless besants. He who did not hold even a village over there now enjoys a town which God has given him. Why should anyone return to the West who has found an Orient like this?"

Christian immigration was actively encouraged by the Frankish rulers, who offered houses and land for nothing to fill up the Jerusalem that they had depopulated. The Jewish Quarter was occupied by Syrian Christians and Jacobites, also by Copts from Egypt and Ethiopia. On Mount Zion, an Armenian enclave built the Cathedral of St. James. The area near the Zion Gate attracted incomers from Provence, while the Damascus Gate was protected by a Spanish group of settlers. Near the New Gate the Hungarians made their home beside the old Christian Quarter, while the Georgians from the Caucasus congregated outside the city around the venerated Monastery of the Cross. The last of the Jews were allowed to set up their dye-works by the Jaffa Gate, where they were visited by the rabbi Benjamin of Tudela and the philosopher Moses Maimonides. And Muslim diplomatic missions and traders were increasingly allowed into the Holy City, which only remained in Christian hands because of the divisions of its neighbours.

Godfrey de Bouillon had refused to become king of Jerusalem, preferring the title of Defender of the Holy Sepulchre. His successor was his brother Baldwin, who took the crown and campaigned so vigorously that he literally split the Muslim south from the north by taking Transjordan and allowing the extension of the string of Crusader castles to the Red Sea. His style of life became Oriental, as he sat in his palace in David's Tower or the Citadel, dressed in silk, lying on embroidered cushions and Persian carpets. He began the rebuilding of Jerusalem in the medieval image, concentrating first on the massive city walls and towers; then he started work on the churches, particularly that of the Holy Sepulchre, which grew into a domed cathedral with high choir and unequal transepts, and the fortress-shrine of St. Anne, the mother of the Virgin Mary; then he looked to the bazaars and trading centres, called the Streets of Herbs and Barbers and even Bad Cookery; and finally he thought of the distinctive small domed houses, which would house the citizens in the manner of the Near East. This ambitious building programme was funded by money and materials shipped from European ecclesiastical sources, which were smothered with endowments from those penitents who had not made the Crusade to capture the Holy City.

During its existence, the Kingdom of Jerusalem bore a strange similarity to the present State of Israel. Both states were founded because of a religious idea that looked to the same place for its fulfillment. Both fought for their lives against the divided Muslim powers that surrounded them. Both depended on immigration and imported resources and weaponry. The Crusaders drew their replenishments from the whole of Western

Europe, particularly from the French, with their connections to the dynasty now installed in Jerusalem, and from the sea powers of the Italian cities, which had gained an ascendancy over the Byzantine and Turkish and Egyptian navies by the beginning of the twelfth century. The modern State of Israel found its reserves in the scattered Jewish communities of the Diaspora and the genetic and spiritual tug back to the mother country. The vision of both was of a Jerusalem that crowned the Holy Land, of a city and a territory that was both ideal and temporal. The conquest of the sacred city gave the power to the rulers to rebuild a New Jerusalem and translate a dream of heaven to the rock of earth. It was the urban temple, which all pilgrims might visit for their worship. It was also a sacred site that Jew and Christian and Muslim would always seek to occupy and die for, a simple sacrifice for an everlasting realm.

King Baldwin I of Jerusalem lived the last of his eighteen years of rule like the Fisher King in the Grail Castle, slowly dying of a lance wound in the groin. His successor on the throne also bore the name of Baldwin and came from the same Frankish aristocracy. But he was already wise to the ways of the Levant. Baldwin II was count of Edessa and was preferred by the barons of Jerusalem because of his military experience. He won immense popularity with the citizens by suspending all taxes and levies and customs duties. After the killing of Roger, prince of Antioch, at the notable defeat of the Ager Sanguinis, the Field of Blood, King Baldwin had to hurry north to save the city from Muslim vengeance, but he could not save the execution by beheading and torture of the captured Frankish chivalry in Aleppo, where Sufis competed with lynch mobs for the benefit of revenging themselves on the infidels responsible for the massacre at Jerusalem. Islamic clemency was drowned in bloodlust and even the huge ransom offered by a leper knight could not procure mercy.

Yet during the thirteen years of his reign, Baldwin II balanced the seesaw of power in the Near East. Even when he was captured for the second time on an expedition to rescue the imprisoned Joscelin, count of Edessa, he had left behind him enough loyalty and deputies for the Kingdom of Jerusalem to survive his forced leave of absence. He was in gaol, indeed, when his subordinates, with the help of the Venetian fleet, succeeded in taking Tyre, the last great Muslim port on the coast of Palestine except for Ascalon. Command of the sea was vital for the maintenance of the

Crusader state, more and more dependent on the various Italian navies for its resources.

The release of Baldwin II showed how intertwined the politics of Muslim and Christian had become. The dozen petty states of the Levant needed their shifting alliances and mutable foes to exist. "I am the enemy you killed, my friend," Wilfred Owen was to write in "Strange Meeting" just before his death in the First World War. It could have been an epitaph on the continual killings and pardonings, raids and counterattacks, confrontations and sieges that created *chansons* for troubadours out of the rest of the reign of Baldwin II and of his successors. When the garrison of Tyre surrendered, there was no mass slaughter as at Jerusalem. The safe-conduct granted to the very Muslim troops who had tortured and killed the Frankish knights at Aleppo was honoured. A certain respect and code of war had arisen between the religious enemies. Only a *jihad* could threaten that new accommodation.

Imad al-Din Zangi, a member of the Turkish aristocracy and the new ruler of Aleppo and Mosul, upset the delicate balance by appealing for a holy war against the Christians. He was, in the words of Ibn al-Athir "the gift of divine providence to the Muslims." A ruthless disciplinarian, he kept in being a permanent army rather than the annual levies of the old system of recruitment. His opportunity came with the death of Baldwin II after a failed attempt to take Damascus. Baldwin had his body dressed as a canon of the Church of the Holy Sepulchre, which he had sworn to defend. He wished to die in poverty as Christ had, in Jerusalem. His successor, Fulk, count of Anjou, had married his eldest daughter, Melisande, and was a man of great power and experience in Europe if not in the Near East. His misfortune was to be confronted by Zangi, the severe apostle of revenge on the infidel.

While Zangi made advances, capturing many of the Christian castles in Syria, the Byzantine emperor John Comnenus decided first to retake Antioch from the Latin Christians and then to ally himself with them on a Crusade against Zangi. King Fulk of Jerusalem persuaded Raymond, prince of Antioch, apparently to hand over the city to the Byzantines and join the imperial army in an attempt on Aleppo. This campaign petered out, and John Comnenus returned in disgust to Constantinople, gaining nothing. The truth was that the Latin Christian kings and princes opposed the Greek Christian armies as much as Zangi and the Muslim emirates did. A Christian holy war threatened the precarious position in the northeastern Levant as much as a *jihad.*

Zangi next tried to unite the Muslims against the Franks, but King Fulk of Jerusalem made an alliance with Damascus, which feared the rule of Zangi even more than amity with the infidel. So conciliation preserved the status quo. In point of fact, if Latin Christendom had been able to join with Greek Christendom, they would have presented an invincible force and possibly have extended the borders of their combined faith as far as Persia and into Egypt. As it was, their divisions were as ineluctable as those of their official Muslim enemies. Groups of small powers of whatever faith had to cohere temporarily in order not to be gobbled down by an empire.

The death of Fulk of Jerusalem in a hunting accident left the kingdom in the hands of a boy thirteen years old, his eldest son, Baldwin. Under the weak regency of his mother, Melisande, the far-flung county of Edessa was allowed in 1144 to fall into the hands of Zangi. The leaderless Kingdom of Jerusalem could not concentrate enough of its stretched forces to save its northern bastion. Zangi himself stopped the massacre of the Christians in Edessa, hoping to use his clemency as a means to attract the civilian populations of other Eastern cities under Frankish domination. As the Syrian bishop Abu al-Faraj Basil described the defeat:

> In fact, the Syrians and Armenians were brought out of the citadel, and they all returned to their homes safe and sound. Everything was taken from the Franj, however: gold, silver, holy vases, chalices, patens, ornamented crucifixes, and great quantities of jewels. The priests, nobles, and notables were taken aside, stripped of their robes, and led away in chains to Aleppo. Of the rest, the artisans were identified, and Zangi kept them as prisoners, setting each to work at his craft. All the other Franj, about a hundred men, were executed.

If the inability to concentrate their small forces at the right place and time was the curse of the Christian rulers, assassination was the death of the Muslim ones. Zangi received many titles, such as the Ornament of Islam and the Prince of the Faithful; but while he was pondering whether to march on Damascus rather than on Jerusalem to extend his own domain, he was murdered by one of his eunuchs, and his power disappeared with him in an orgy of plunder by his own troops. He left behind, however, a second son, Nur al-Din Mahmud, who put his father's signet ring on his own finger; he was to inherit Aleppo, while his elder brother had Mosul. Apparently, the threat to Edessa was over. It was recaptured briefly by a Christian force, then overwhelmed by the army of Nur al-Din. In attempting to escape in a war sortie, the remaining Christian population was exterminated, except for those sold into slavery. "Edessa was left deserted," Michael the Syrian wrote, "a hideous sight, infested with the bodies of its children, the home of jackals."

For Nur al-Din was a holy warrior as his father had not truly been. Even the Christian William of Tyre wrote of him that he was pious and wise and "feared God." His religion made him loathe the Franks. Diplomacy with them was a last resort. Edessa had fallen twice because of the religious schisms between the Latin church and the Greek Christian church, split forever in the age-old quarrel between Rome and Constantinople, which could not forgive the fact that the popes now appointed the patriachs of Jerusalem and Antioch, no longer the gifts of the imperial prelates. The long march to Jerusalem, indeed, had often seemed to the Byzantine emperors to be an assault on Constantinople on the way. And so it would prove to be. The suspicion was to turn into the fact.

For the time being, however, the massacre of the Franks at Edessa concentrated the mind wonderfully in Europe on a Second Crusade, as it was obvious that the Christian forces in the Levant could not concentrate themselves sufficiently to defend their major cities. This disaster in Outremer fuelled the fires of holy war in the West, just as Nur al-Din was doing in the Near East. The soldiers of the cross and the crescent would cease their manipulations for a trial of might and the main chance.

SIX

MANY THE TEMPLE

"There are people for whom money is more important than sand."

—Saladin

S t. Bernard of Clairvaux inspired the Second Crusade for the defence of Jerusalem. The French king Louis VII came to him for advice as if he were a "divine oracle." While the king wanted a little more than mailed pilgrims going to the defence of the Holy Land, the pope desired a full Crusade leading to more conquests in the Levant. Trying to reconcile the two attitudes, St. Bernard advised Pope Eugenius III to issue a bull *Quantum praedecessores,* the second of eight papal decrees that would call the Christian faith to arms. The bull vested control of any major Crusade in Rome, confirmed the absolution and privileges of Crusaders, and exempted them from paying interest on any money borrowed for making the sacred expedition. With salvation and finance assured, the Crusader was also exhorted to protect the Holy Land, which had been won by his forefathers. Edessa had only fallen because of the sins of a few predatory Christian knights. Their successors should restore the honour of chivalry as well as defend the Kingdom of Jerusalem.

At Vézelay at the end of March 1146, St. Bernard preached the Second Crusade to the kings of France and the assembled French nobles. His fervency and tongue of quicksilver, praising the remission of grievous crimes for all who took up the cross, provoked a gale of acceptance. His hearers cried out for the favours of Christ. Before too long, all the prepared red strips of cloth were finished. St. Bernard had to give up his red robe to be cut into pieces for those who would go east. His helpers became tailors and stitched the pledges of the holy pilgrimage onto the faithful. An orgy of commitment promised another holy war. After preaching later to the people of France, St. Bernard was able to write to the pope, "The Crusaders have multiplied to infinity. Villages and towns are now deserted. You will scarcely find one man for every seven women."

St. Bernard's sermons were almost impossible for a Christian to resist. The promise of absolution was paramount. In his letter to the English, he emphasised his message:

> Now is the accepted time, the day of abundant salvation. The earth has been shaken; it trembles because the Lord of heaven has begun to lose his land—the land in which, for more than thirty years, he lived as a man amongst men. . . . But now, on account of our sins, the sacrilegious enemies of the cross have begun to show their faces even there; their swords are wreaking havoc in the promised land. . . . What are you doing, you mighty men of valour? What are you doing, you servants of the cross? Will you throw to the dogs that which is most holy? Will you cast pearls before swine? O mighty soldier, O man of war, you now have a cause for which you can fight without endangering your soul; a cause in which to win is glorious and for which to die is but gain. . . .

> Or are you a shrewd businessman, a man quick to see the profits of this world? If you are, I can offer you a splendid bargain. Do not miss the opportunity. Take the sign of the cross. At once you will have indulgence for all the sins which you confess with a contrite heart. It does not cost you much to buy and if you wear it with humility you will find that it is the kingdom of heaven.

As before, the destination of the Crusaders was not always Jerusalem. The English contingent under Henry Glanville, constable of Suffolk, was joined by Flemish and Frisian forces; they reached the banks of the Tagus

River in Portugal on their way to the Mediterranean. There they were persuaded by Alfonso, the count and later king of Portugal, to join him in the attack on his future capital, Lisbon, then held by the Muslims. After four months of the siege, the Muslims surrendered, but were massacred, as they had been in Jerusalem. The principle of the bloody cleansing of the infidel had arrived at the western reaches of the Christian war against Islam. Few of the English Crusaders travelled on towards Jerusalem. Most remained as settlers of these newly conquered lands and began the long alliance between England and Portugal that would become a significant harbour in the history of the Atlantic Ocean.

The two major crusading armies, German and French, took the dangerous land route through the Balkans towards Constantinople. After pogroms and skirmishes with the imperial forces, both of the hosts reached the Hellespont. The French king, however, was accompanied by the protector of Jerusalem, Everard de Barre, the grand master of the Templars, with a whole regiment of new recruits for the military order. Efforts to proceed to the holy places through Anatolia by land ended as before in disaster. There was no help from the Byzantine armies, who were preoccupied by the attacks on the imperial possessions in Greece from Corfu by the Norman forces of King Roger of Sicily. The remnants of the French and German armies had to sail to the captured parts of Palestine. The sea was the only safe passport to the Israel of old. Although Raymond, prince of Antioch, tried to persuade the king of France to join him in a Crusade against the threatened *jihad* of Nur al-Din and assault Aleppo, the king was determined to honour his vow and proceed to Jerusalem. That was the true focus of the Crusade.

Followed to Palestine by King Conrad of Germany, the Crusaders decided to attack Damascus, a greedy decision against a friendly power that had combined with the Kingdom of Jerusalem to oppose the expansion of the influence of Nur al-Din. The combined Christian armies proceeded to the orchards outside Damascus; its ruler resisted their approach, summoned up reinforcements from Turkey, and threatened to deliver the city to Nur al-Din if his previous allies did not withdraw. In ignominy they did so. The Second Crusade was a fiasco. "The German Franj," in the words of Ibn al-Athir, "returned to their country, which lies far away beyond Constantinople, and God rid the faithful of this calamity."

The failure of this Crusade to the Near East, promoted by St. Bernard, was compounded by a change of emphasis in his Cistercian order. Jerusalem was not now held to be in Palestine, a geographical place set around the Temple Mount. It was also said to be Clairvaux, the head-quarters of the white monks. Pilgrims to the Holy Land needed to travel no farther than Champagne. As St. Bernard wrote to an English convert, his vow of worshipping at the Church of the Holy Sepulchre was fulfilled by remainining at the chief Cistercian abbey, where "his feet already tread the pavements of the Holy Jerusalem. This Jerusalem which is linked with the heavenly Jerusalem and which is entwined with her in all the deepest feelings of the human heart is Clairvaux."

The road to Jerusalem was still the way to God. Yet it was also a spiritual journey to heaven, not to a sacred site. By continual worship and praise of the Almighty at a monastery in Europe, the journey to Calvary became no longer necessary. When St. Bernard was given land outside the Holy City in order to find a Cistercian refuge there, he refused the gift. His monasteries were each a New Jerusalem. The monks did not have to visit the actual Via Dolorosa to follow Christ's footsteps towards Crucifixion. They could retrace his way around the Stations of the Cross in the abbey church. Jerusalem was widespread now. There were many roads to it.

Yet St. Bernard was also instrumental in founding the military order of the knights of the Temple of Jerusalem. These were the lances of the white monks, who dedicated their lives to guarding Christian pilgrims to the real holy places in Palestine. Although Clairvaux and the other Cistercian foundations might symbolise other Jerusalems, the Temple Mount was under the protection of knights in armour, who lived by the sword as well as by the principles of Christian charity. "These warriors are gentler than lambs and fiercer than lions," St. Bernard wrote of the Templars, "wedding the mildness of the monk with the valour of the knight so that it is difficult to know what to call them: men who adorn the Temple of Solomon with shields instead of crowns of gold." St. Bernard himself would never take ship to the Holy City and like many a pilgrim would confuse the Muslim Dome of the Rock with the destroyed Temple of the ancient king of Israel, over which the Christian warrior knights had raised the cross on high.

The construction of alternative Jerusalems was, indeed, another preoccupation of the Templars, who saw themselves as the builder-soldiers of Zerubbabel, who had set up the Second Temple with a weapon in one hand and a trowel in the other. The Templar knowledge of Byzantine and Near Eastern architecture was to contribute to the building of many of the great Gothic cathedrals, that extraordinary popular explosion of practical faith of the twelfth and thirteenth centuries after the birth of Christ. As late as Jacobean times, the son of Sir Christoper Wren would recognise the eastern influence on his father, which gave to him the sacred design for the cathedral of St. Paul's that crowns London. That same influence was also the origin of medieval ecclesiastical construction:

> What we now vulgarly call *Gothick* ought properly and truly to be named the *Saracenick Architecture refined by the Christians,* which first of all began in the East, after the Fall of the *Greek* Empire, by the prodigious Success of those People that adhered to Mahomet's Doctrine, who, out of Zeal to their Religion, built Mosques, Caravanserais, and Sepulchres wherever they came.

> These they contrived of a round Form, because they would not imitate the Christian Figure of a Cross, nor the old *Greek* Manner, which they thought to be idolatrous, and for that Reason all Sculpture became offensive to them.

> Then they fell into a new Mode of their own Intervention, tho' it might have been expected with better Sense, considering the *Arabians* wanted not Geometricians in that Age, nor the *Moors,* who translated many of the most useful old *Greek* Books. As they propagated their Religion with great Diligence, so they built Mosques in all their conquered Cities in Haste. . . .

> The Holy War gave the Christians, who had been there, an Idea of the Saracen Works, which were afterwards by them imitated in the West; and they refined upon it every Day as they proceeded in building Churches. The *Italians* (among which were yet some *Greek* Refugees), and with them *French, German* and *Flemings,* joined into a Fraternity of Architects, procuring Papal Bulls for their Encouragement and particular Privileges; they stiled themselves Freemasons, and ranged from one Nation to another as they found Churches to be built (for

very many in those Ages were everywhere in Building, through Piety or Emulation).

Sir Christopher Wren was himself a grand master Mason and had access to early documents of the craft. He had no doubt of the importance of the Knights of the Order of the Temple of Solomon and other Crusaders in bringing back Muslim ideas on architecture from the Near East, which then became broadcast throughout Europe. The *Old Charges* of the Masonic movement, which date back to the early fifteenth century, also stressed the influence of the Levant, particularly the medieval tradition of the building of the Temple of Solomon—so often confused by pilgrims with the Muslim shrine of the Dome of the Rock. The tradition was that King David had begun the building of a Temple of the Lord God in Jerusalem. He had made himself a patron of the Masons and had showed how highly he valued their craft. He had even given them a charge and control over their rules, and he had increased their wages.

When King Solomon had reached the throne of Israel, he pushed forward the completion of the Temple. He invited skilled workmen to Jerusalem from all the countries of the Near East. Among them were eighty thousand stonemasons. King Solomon selected three thousand six hundred of these to be Master Masons and direct the holy work. Hiram, King of Tyre, showed his friendship by providing the imperishable cedarwood for the Temple as well as his most skilled architect, also called Hiram. An expert in the sacred geometry of Euclid, the artificer Hiram was also a master of carving and engraving copper and brass. Both the Books of Chronicles and Kings took whole chapters of the Bible to detail the wealth and beauty of the Temple of Solomon with its golden palm trees and brass oxen and lions and cherubim and flowers and wheels and axletrees. But Hiram's special legacy to the Masonic movement was the making of the two great pillars of the Temple.

And he set up the pillars in the porch of the temple: and he set up the right pillar, and called the name thereof Jachin: and he set up the left pillar, and called the name thereof Boaz.

And upon the top of the pillars was lily work: so was the work of the pillars finished.

King Solomon himself declared that the Temple was the house of God and that he would look on it with favour and give it his holy name.

Then spake Solomon. The Lord said that he would dwell in the thick darkness.

"I have surely built thee an house to dwell in, a settled place for thee to abide in for ever. . . .

"That thine eyes may be opened towards this house night and day, even toward the place of which thou has said, My name shall be there. . . ."

King Solomon was also held to have instituted the customs and practises of the medieval Masons and other craft guilds, who had built his Temple. "Solomon confirmed the Charges that David his father had given to Masons," the earliest Masonic document, the *Cooke Manuscript* of 1410, declared. "And Solomon himself taught them their manners, but little differing from the manners now used." He was the grand master of the primal lodge at Jerusalem, while Hiram was the deputy grand master, the most accomplished designer and operator on earth. It would be the job of millions of later Masons to rebuild the Temple of Solomon in the New Jerusalems of tens of thousands of lodges across the Western world.

In nearly all of the earlier Masonic catechisms, the Question and the Answer confirmed the tradition of the founding of the first Masonic lodge at the west end of the Temple of Solomon, where two pillars of brass had been erected by Hiram. He was now given the further name of Abiff, which derived from the Hebrew word for father, as if Hiram were the father of all masons. He was said to have been martyred by three jealous fellow masons, because he would not tell them the secrets of the craft. In a catechism called after the two pillars of the Temple of Solomon, *Jachin and Boaz,* the examination ran:

QUESTION: *What support our lodge?*
ANSWER: *Three pillars.*

QUESTION: *Pray what are their names, brother?*
ANSWER: *Wisdom, strength and beauty.*

QUESTION: *What do they represent?*

ANSWER: *Three grand masters;* Solomon, *King of Israel;* Hiram, *King of Tyre; and* Hiram Abiff, *who was killed by the three fellow-crafts.*

QUESTION: *Were these three grand masters concerned in the building of Solomon's Temple?*

ANSWER: *They were.*

QUESTION: *What was their business?*

ANSWER: Solomon *found provisions and money to pay the workmen;* Hiram *King of Tyre provided materials for the building, and* Hiram Abiff *performed or superintended the work.*

Masonic historians chose several routes for the direct transmission of rites and practises from King Solomon's lodge at Jerusalem to the present day. The *Cooke Manuscript* stated that the foundation of masonry was geometry, the first of the seven liberal arts. Abraham taught Euclid geometry, and he taught the Israelites practical masonry in Egypt. These skills built the Temple of Solomon. The earliest four Masons, the Quatuor Coronati, were killed by the emperor Diocletian. Charles Martel, or Charles the Hammer, of France organised masonry there, while St. Alban and King Athelstan founded the craft in England. Later historians looked to Byzantine corporations as absorbing the teaching of the Jewish fraternities of Masons. The emperor Justinian himself was said to have exclaimed after the building of Sancta Sophia: "I have surpassed thee, O Solomon!" This influence was then passed on to the Teutonic guilds of Steinmetzen, which were certainly formed by the middle of the thirteenth century. The connection was demonstrated by the use of spiral columns in the architecture of the Byzantines and the Jews as well as in later Masonic lodges, building their own Temples of Jerusalem.

Another provenance for the Masons was through Roman building guilds learning from Jewish practises after the fall of Jerusalem and the final destruction of the third Temple there. Diocletian may have tried to destroy Christianity, whose founder was a carpenter, but he was lenient to the Collegia, or guilds, of Rome, many of whose members were already Christians. He did martyr four aristocratic patrons of architecture and also four Masons with an apprentice, Claudius and Nicostratus and Simphorianus and Castorius and Simplicius. They were to become the patron saints of Lombard and Tuscan builders and later of the medieval Masons of France and Germany and England. Their emblems are still to be seen at Rome and Florence, Nuremberg and Antwep and Toulouse—the saw, hammer, mallet, compasses, and square. These tools may also be found in Templar gravestones in the Holy Land and in Scotland. The confrontation of the early Masons with Diocletian was commemorated in an early poem:

> . . . *These holy martyres fowre,*
> *That yn thys craft were of gret honoure;*
> *They were as gode masonus as on erthe shul go,*
> *Gravers and ymage-makers they were also.*
> *For they were werkemen of the beste,*
> *The emperour hade to hem gret luste;*
> *He wylled of them a ymage to make,*
> *That mowt be worscheped for his sake . . .*

The emblems of these Roman martyrs were also those of the Collegia and have recently been excavated in Pompeii, carved on stone along with the cube and the plummet, the circle and the level. These symbols and the rules of the craft were bequeathed to the mysterious Magistri Comacini, a guild of architects who lived on a fortified island on Lake Como at the breakup of the Roman Empire. These were held to have taught the secrets of sacred geometry and construction methods to the Italian builders of Ravenna and Venice, and through them, to the art and trade guilds of the Middle Ages. Certainly, an edict of a Lombard king of 643 gave privileges to the Comacini and their colleagues. Their meeting places were called *loggia,* from which the word *lodge* was said to come. Their symbols included King Solomon's Knot and the endless, interwoven cord of Eternity.

Their heirs in France were given a pedigree. Their generic name was the Compagnonnage, and part of them were called Enfants de Salomon, the Children of Solomon. Along with later English Masons, they believed that King Solomon had given them a Charge and incorporated them fraternally within the precincts of his Temple. They also believed in the death of the martyr Hiram and the Quatuor Coronati. They were the craft guilds which constructed the greater Gothic cathedrals, sometimes under the guidance of Cistercian or Templar Master Masons, called the Fratres Solomonis. They first congregated in the twelfth century at the building of Chartres cathedral, which became a form of popular crusade, the construction of a New Jerusalem. There, the stained glass windows still commemorate the carpenters and the Masons who built it, and the tools and emblems of their trades.

The early building of abbeys in England under St. Alban and King Athelstan gave rise to a tradition of earlier Masonic guilds than in France, although their beliefs and practises were also said to derive from Jerusalem. The *Old Charges* considered that King Athelstan, the grandson of Alfred the Great, built castles and abbeys, "for he loved Masons well." He was meant to have called an assembly of Masons at York and to have issued them with a Charge. What was more likely was that, after the Norman Conquest, French Masons and their practises were imported to assist in the building of cathedrals and abbeys. In the five hundred years after the conquest of England more than a thousand abbeys, priories, hospitals, and colleges were founded, all built by Masons. By the fourteenth century, the word *lodge* was used of the meeting places of the craft. The *Halliwell Manuscript* advised a Mason to keep secrecy:

> The prevystye [privacy] of the chamber telle be no mon,
> Ny yn the logge whatsever they done.

And the very word *Ffre Maceons* or *Freemason* appeared at the end of that century, referring to a worker in freestone, a term already used for two centuries in the trade.

Other inquiries into Masonic origins predated the knowledge of the craft into Babylonian or Egyptian or Greek times, but all deriving from the Near East. In a reference to the Tower of Babel, one early Masonic catechism gave the Answer: "We differ from the Babylonians who did presume to Build to Heaven, but we pray the blessed Trinity to let us build True, High and Square, and they shall have the praise to whom it is due. . . ." Some historians believed that the Temple of Solomon was built by Masons who knew of the Dionysian and Eleusianian mysteries as well as divine geometry from the gods and the golden mean. To them, the Masonic mystery of the martyr Hiram was merely a reworking of the myth of the death of Orpheus, the great creator, in the Bacchic religion.

Still other diggers into the dust of the past looked to the Greek god Hermes, whom the Romans called Mercury, as the source of sacred geometry. The Christian Father Cyril of Alexandria had asserted the Christian Hermetic tradition: "Have you not heard that our native Hermes of Egypt divided the world into tracts and divisions, that he measured the country with a string, made ditches and canals, made laws, named provinces, set up contracts and agreements, re-discovered the calendar of the rising of the stars, and handed down certain crops, numbers and calculations, geometry, astrology, astronomy, and music, and, finally, the whole system of grammar which he himself invented?" Hermes was the creator of the seven liberal arts, of which the greatest was geometry.

At this point, the Greek god became confused with Euclid and Pythagoras in medieval Masonic thought, never very good on names or the periods of great men. Another tradition, recorded by the Jewish historian Josephus, that the arts of astronomy and music were carved on two pillars by Adam's son Seth, also became part of Masonic tradition—these pillars were to be recast by Hiram in the Temple of Solomon. Zoroaster, the ultimate magus, was also held to have inscribed all the seven liberal arts on fourteen pillars, half of brass and half of baked brick. It was these pillars and those of the Greek god Hermes, on which all true knowledge was inscribed, that were held to be rediscovered by Hermes Trismegistus, the founder of alchemy and the hermetic doctrine, which was so much to influence the Knights of the Order of the Temple of Solomon and, through them, the Masons.

For the Templars had seen themselves as followers of Zerubbabel, who persuaded King Darius to allow the rebuilding of the Temple of Jerusalem. They inherited the belief from the Gnostics and St. John that the Temple was the mystic centre of the world, and so they secretly resisted the power and authority of the popes and kings of Europe. Some black-and-white devices of their order, black octagonal cross against white habit, showed their Gnosticism and Manicheanism, the belief in the continuing struggle of the devil's world against God's intelligence. They bequeathed to the Masons the black-and-white lozenges and indented mosaic of their lodges. And before his death, the last of the official grand masters, Jacques de Molay, "organised and instituted what afterwards came to be called the Occult, Hermetic, or Scottish Masonry."

What all these theories of conspiracy and myth mixed with history had in common was that Masonic beliefs derived through the Templars from the mysticism of the Near East as well as from the Old and the New Testaments of the Holy Bible. A perfect catalyst between the legendary and the practical was the building of the House of the Lord by King Solomon in Jerusalem. Certainly, in the romances of the Middle Ages, Solomon and his Temple were second only to King Arthur and the Grail as a source of inspiration. "And it was precisely at that time," the leading researcher into the Temple of Solomon has written, "that the framers of the Masonic Legend were at work in developing the various aspects of the traditional history of their Craft."

It was also precisely at that time that the Knights of the Order of the Temple of Solomon guarded what was thought by pilgrims to be the king of Israel's Temple in Jerusalem, the octagonal shrine of the Dome of the Rock. Its builder, Caliph Umar, had cried on its completion: "Behold a greater than Solomon is here." The Templars passed on to the troubadours and craft guilds of Europe much of the rabbinic and cabbalistic lore about King Solomon, which had come from ancient times. Solomon was thought to be a magus, or wise man, a magician and a worker of wonders. He was meant to have foreseen the destruction of his Temple by the Babylonians and to have constructed a secret vault within the walls for the burial and the preservation of the Ark of the Covenant—a sacred treasure that has been the object of innumerable quests ever since its disappearance.

The Christian Fathers, Clement and Eusebius, had written of King Solomon's power over demons, and Gregory of Tours and the Venerable Bede wrote of the wonders of the Temple and its significance. "The House of God which King Solomon built in Jerusalem represents the Holy Universal Church, which, from the First of the Elect to the last man who shall be born at the end of the world, is built daily by the grace of her peaceful King, that is, her Redeemer." As Mount Moriah in Jerusalem was venerated as the stepping-stone of the Prophet Muhammad on his flight to heaven and paradise, the Temple of Solomon was also venerated by Muslims, who built the Dome of the Rock in its place. The mysticism of the

Sufis and the Manicheans and the Gnostics permeated the Christian crusading guardians of Mount Moriah with its converted mosques and
shrines, so that the military order of the Temple of Solomon believed that
it was the keeper of a house of God on earth, built by the Great Architect
of the world. They would pass on the mysteries of its construction to the
builders of other Temples and New Jerusalems across the world.

In another of their roles, the Templars were literally Master Masons.
They directed the building of their formidable castles such as Castle Pilgrim and ordained the shape of their octagonal chapels and circular towers. As the Fratres Solomonis, they introduced holy geometry from the
Near East into the creation of the Gothic masterpieces of France such as
Chartres cathedral. But there is no question that their secret ritual involved a belief in a sacred architecture, a single Creator of the world, and
the actual regulation of the teams of masons who built their thousands of
preceptories and churches across Europe and the Levant. As St. Bernard
had declared of Clairvaux, Jerusalem was no longer in Israel or Palestine;
but it might be rebuilt everywhere in Europe.

Certainly, the elevation of Chartres was a people's crusade through
stone and faith. A Compagnonnage was organised that included local citizens, who were rich and poor, to join the apprentices and the masons at
the quarry as well as at the building of the foundations. A form of remission of sins was given to those who pulled the huge stone waggons like
beasts of burden. It was a crusade to build at Chartres the Temple at
Jerusalem. By their works at the sacred edifice, these pilgrims could remain in their city and make it blessed. The Virgin Mary, the mother of
Christ, was the inspiration behind this spiritual task. She stood for the birth
and the growth of the divine against the sword of the warrior saints, Lon-
ginus and George and Michael. Out of herself came the House of God in
stone as well as in flesh, not the blood of the Lamb spilt in holy wars.

There was no question but that the Knights Templar took the architecture and wisdom of the Near East and transferred it to the West. Much
of this knowledge derived from the classical past, the Hellenic influence
that spread to Asia after the conquests of Alexander the Great, and the
legacy of the Roman and Byzantine Empires in the Levant. Now that the
Franks or the Franj had reached the Near East through the Crusades and
had established their first permanent military orders on the lines of the

Sufis and the Assassins, a certain understanding was being reached between Western feudal barbarism and Oriental urban sophistication. At the Sicilian courts of the Frankish kings, a century passed before the Viking berserkers were educated sufficiently by Arab scientists and philosophers into a form of civilisation. A similar process took place in the Kingdom of Jerusalem. After fifty years of coexistence with Islam, later generations of the Crusaders learned to learn and to transfer that learning back to their mother countries. History is a form of concertina. The classical world of the Mediterranean was squeezed into Asia, which then extended that heritage and its own discoveries back to Europe through the Western quest for Jerusalem, that catalyst of thought and feeling.

Yet a *jihad* still threatened the accommodation between Christian and Muslim. The folly of the leaders of the Second Crusade in attacking friendly Damascus suited the strategy of Nur al-Din. Advancing his army to the walls of that city, he began a programme of religious propaganda against the atabeg. He declared that he had not pitched camp outside Damascus to besiege it. He had come to defend it with his large army. "I well know," he wrote to the leaders of the Damascenes, "that you are unable to protect your provinces, and I am aware of your powerlessness, which led you to seek the aid of the Franj against me and extort from your poorest subjects the riches which you have lavished on the Franj. Such behaviour pleases neither God nor any Muslim." The governors of the city would have none of this argument, responding that the sword alone would decide who was to rule Damascus. "We have sufficient support among the Franj to chase you off, if you should attack." In spite of the mistakes of the Second Crusade, the king of Jerusalem did appear twice more with his army to deter Nur al-Din; but he was unable to mobilise his forces again on a third approach by the ruler of Aleppo. Moreover, he had lost the sympathy of most of the Damascenes by the previous crusading attack, while Nur al-Din had softened any resistance by his appeal for a holy war to be called by the united Islamic states of northern Syria. "I desire no more than the well-being of the Muslims," he declared, "*jihad* against the infidels, and the release of the prisoners they are holding. If you come over to my side with the army of Damascus, if we help each other to wage the *jihad,* my wish will be fulfilled."

This time in the spring of 1154, Nur al-Din did blockade the city and intercept its food supplies. Faced with such pressure, the citizens and most of the soldiers abandoned the cause of the atabeg. A Jewish woman threw down a rope from the deserted walls, which were scaled. So Nur al-Din took Damascus "to the great joy of the inhabitants and soldiers, all of whom were obsessed by their fear of famine and their terror at being besieged by the Franj infidels." Unfortunately, the considerable threat to the Kingdom of Jerusalem by this combined Islamic force to the north was devastated by an earthquake, which even threw down the towers of Aleppo. Yet the Christians could be trusted to provoke Islamic coherence and retaliation by their careless greed. King Baldwin III had allowed the Damascenes and the neighbouring Turkomans to pasture their flocks and herds near the fortress of Baniyas. In need of supplies and revenue, he seized the sheep and cattle and slaughtered their drovers. In a counterattack, Nur al-Din was able to surround and destroy nearly all the Christian troops, while the young king escaped only through luck back to Jerusalem. The majority of the couple of thousand knights who defended the Holy Land were killed or captured, and even William of Tyre thought that the defeat at Baniyas was justified. It was the vengeance of Our Lord upon the king of Jerusalem and his men for what "they had done to the Turkomans and to those of Arabia, when they treacherously killed and robbed those whom they had guaranteed upon oath." Nur al-Din was praised as a just and pious prince, even if he was a heretic.

Another despicable act of pillage was carried out by the ravenous and brutal Reynald de Châtillon, the new prince of Antioch. In combination with the Templars, he attacked the rebel Armenian king Thoros and installed the military order in Alexandretta, beginning a long alliance that would prove finally fatal for the Kingdom of Jerusalem. Reynald then switched sides and joined Thoros against the rich and ill-defended Byzantine island of Cyprus. It was raped and ravaged for three weeks, until an imperial fleet drove the Christian pirates away. This mayhem upset the equilibrium enough in the eastern Mediterranean for King Baldwin of Jerusalem to seek the friendship of the Byzantine emperor, Manuel Comnenus, who gave him his thirteen-year-old niece Theodora as a bride. Both of these allies by marriage and circumstance marched on Antioch, where Reynald played the penitent in order to survive, flinging himself barefoot in the dust at the feet of the emperor, who forgave him in spite of the sack of Cyprus. Now was the time to combine against Nur al-Din and seize Aleppo, but when the Islamic ruler offered to release all six thousand of his Christian prisoners, including the grand master of the Temple, Manuel Comnenus decided to retreat to Constantinople. He preferred to protect his own empire in the south by keeping the Frankish forces balanced in war against the Syrian Islamic groups, so that neither was powerful enough to strike at the imperial underbelly in Cilicia.

The death of King Baldwin III at the age of thirty-two did not lessen the ambition of the Franks. His successor was his younger brother Almaric, who was admired by his opponents as William of Tyre had admired Nur al-Din. "Never since the Franj first appeared in Syria," Ibn al-Athir wrote, "had there been a king to equal him in courage, cunning and cleverness." Almaric was no Crusader, however; he was an Oriental diplomat, and something of a scholar and a sceptic. William of Tyre even doubted that the new king thought Christian revelation to be superior to that of other religions. Almaric was not interested in a *jihad* as Nur al-Din was; but he wanted to expand his power and conquer Fatimid Egypt, then weak and riven by a series of palace revolutions. To forestall the Franks, Nur al-Din sent his best general, the Kurd Shirkuh, to restore the previous vizier of Egypt to power. This was easily achieved, and when King Almaric arrived with his army from Jerusalem he could make no progress until the vizier himself changed sides, needing a Christian alliance to offset the ambitions of Nur al-Din in taking over Egypt through Shirkuh and his army, which were now forced to retire. Another crusading victory in 1164 by Nur al-Din near Harenc, however, now made Almaric retreat to Jerusalem, the bulwark of his strength.

The lure of the Nile remained seductive. Almaric thought he needed powerful allies and asked King Louis VII of France to help him in return for the mastership of Cairo and even the keys of Jerusalem. Finding no support there, Almaric still decided to honour his alliance with the vizier and to oppose another incursion by Shirkuh, who inflicted a defeat on the Christian forces at Babain and then captured the great port of Alexandria. With the remnants of his knights and his Egyptian allies, Almaric returned to blockade Alexandria, compelling Shirkuh now to flee and the eventual surrender of the city, which had been left in the hands of Shirkuh's nephew,

Salah al-Din Yusuf, or Saladin, a young man of twenty-nine who was to become the scourge of the Chrisitan Levant.

Saladin had never wanted to accompany his uncle to the Nile. "In God's name," he had said, "even were I granted the entire Kingdom of Egypt, I would not go." Yet he went, and on his capture by Almaric he found himself treated with honour, a mercy that he would return in his own days of victory, even if he believed in the *jihad* as passionately as Nur al-Din. Almaric refused to press home his advantage and seize Cairo, respecting his allies as much as his enemies, although his bishops promised to take the sin of such treachery upon themselves "and have it absolved by the Pope." Instead, Almaric took the funds for his campaign from the vizier, an annual payment of one hundred thousand gold pieces. Egypt was effectively a protectorate of the Kingdom of Jerusalem. And yet it still had to be held by a Christian force with too few ships and men to keep even what they had taken before.

Another ally had to be found with sufficient resources to conquer the valley of the Nile and maintain an army of occupation. There was only one power sympathetic and near enough to be useful. At the last resort, Constantinople had always been trusted to stop Antioch and all of north Syria falling into the hands of Damascus, which might then become too dangerous to resist. In fact, Almaric revived the alliance with Constantinople with the express purpose of conquering Egypt before Nur al-Din and Shirkuh could, or the vizier again changed tack. The weakness of the Kingdom of Jerusalem was its lack of sea power, and the Byzantine fleet was more reliable and less avaricious than those of Genoa and Venice.

The ambition of the military orders, however, probably provoked Almaric into attacking his Egyptian ally before the arrival of the imperial navy. The subsequent slaughter by the Christian army of the population of the city of Bilbays almost matched the original crusading butchery at the capture of Jerusalem. In the view of the Islamic chronicler Abu Shama, if the Franks had behaved humanely towards the people of Bilbays, they would certainly have taken Cairo afterwards, "but it was God who, for His own ends, drove them so to act." Whatever the cause, atrocity as usual brought on resistance. The vizier bought off the ferocious invaders with tribute and sent for Shirkuh to save him. So the Christians withdrew and

Nur al-Din's troops entered Cairo in 1169 to become the masters of the city. The vizier was assassinated soon afterwards because of his unfaithfulness to the cause of Islam.

Shirkuh himself rapidly followed his adversary to the grave, leaving the young Saladin to be appointed as the master of Egypt in the name of Nur al-Din, with the Byzantine fleet and Almaric's army again preparing to attack the delta of the Nile. The port of Damietta was besieged, but it held out until a storm destroyed much of the imperial navy. The Christian forces had to retire with nothing gained. In fact, by their rashness, they had put into the hands of Saladin the key to Muslim unity. And although Almaric cemented the Byzantine alliance by marrying the emperor's great-niece Maria Comnena, he had shattered the seesaw of the strategy of defending Jerusalem, which involved always keeping the army ready in the Holy City to help defend the Christian principalities to the north rather than committing all of the small royal resources in the endeavour to seize a whole civilisation along the Nile.

So stretched had Almaric become in his southern campaigns that he was forced to concede to the two main military orders based in Jerusalem the defence of the Holy Land. This was, after all, their avowed purpose, but the problem was their independence and their rivalry. The orders of the Knights Hospitaller and Templar were the chief landowners in Outremer. They built and garrisoned the border castles. They were the permanent cavalry of the crusading kingdom. The Hospitallers had sent five hundred knights on the Egyptian campaign of 1158, in which the Templars had refused to participate. The first order was renowned for its charity and care of the sick, while the second order was more famous for its aggressive charges and its banking practises, for it lent money to Christian and Muslim traders alike. From the point of view of Almaric, however, neither order owed him allegiance; their sovereign was the pope in Rome, not the king in Jerusalem. And the interests of Rome did not always prove to be those of Jerusalem.

The failure of the Christian campaigners against Egypt allowed Saladin to consolidate his power there. The death of the last young Fatimid Shi'ite caliph allowed him to follow the instructions of Nur al-Din and impose the Sunni faith on Egypt, thus ending a long schism in Islam. The Shi'ite Isma'ilis, however, were appalled by the news, and there was an

Assassin attempt to kill Saladin. But his piety and frugality, his preference for a simple relationship with his troops rather than for the pomp of power, gave him a growing reputation. Even before the death of Nur al-Din in 1174, Saladin's reputation was beginning to eclipse that of his overlord. Indeed, the ageing ruler of Damascus was becoming so incensed by the independence of the new ruler of Cairo that he was preparing to invade Egypt himself to restore his authority. He had noted that Saladin, in the opinion of Ibn al-Athir, "was holding off from fighting the Franj in fear of having to unite with him under his command." The death of Nur al-Din, however, gave Saladin the opportunity to proceed north against Damascus in advance of pronouncing a *jihad* against Jerusalem. He had to unite the Islamic powers of the Near East before he could overwhelm the Christian kingdom. Only thus could he present himself as the heir of Nur al-Din, not his hesitant underling in the counterattack against the infidel.

For the kingdom of Jerusalem only existed on Muslim sufferance. So King Thoros of Armenia warned Almaric I, giving him pity along with advice, according to the *Chronicle of Ernoul:*

> "Sir, I am very sorry for you and for the country; for you are not king, except only as long as the Muslims wish; you will only keep the country for as long as the Muslims wish. And I will tell you how this is. There are Muslims living in all the towns of your country. . . . If it so happened that a Muslim army entered your country it would have help and information from the peasants of the land, both food and services. If it turned out that the Muslims were defeated, your own people would help them to safety; and if you were defeated, it would be your own peasants who would do you the worst harm."

SEVEN

THE FALL OF
THE HOLY CITY

"My saddle is my council chamber."

—Saladin

As Machiavelli was to declare in *The Prince,* half of a man's life lay in his skill or character and half in his opportunity or luck; but when necessity came, it would strike him down. Saladin's character had made him the effective sultan of Egypt. His opportunity was the necessity that laid low his two leading rivals. Soon after Nur al-Din died, Almaric also met his fate through an incurable attack of dysentery. The Kingdom of Jerusalem passed to Baldwin IV, a youth of thirteen who was a leper. Only the Byzantine emperor Manuel Comnenus was left, who might threaten Saladin's future hegemony over the Levant. And two years later, in 1176, he was totally defeated by the Seljuk Turkish army under Kilij Arslan II at Myriokephalon. After the annihilation of his army, the emperor died, leaving a successor who was another child and Anatolia to the new Muslim power.

Although Saladin had appeared to be the rival of Nur al-Din in his last years, the older ruler of Damascus had been the teacher of the young Kurdish officer, particularly in the arts of preaching the *jihad* and forcing unwilling Muslim allies into the holy war. Ibn al-Athir reported on the techniques used to compel the emir of Diarbekir to join the anti-Crusade. The emir complained that Nur al-Din deluged the Sufis and *mullahs* with lists of the crimes of the Christians against the Muslims of Syria. He asked their help with their prayers and their calling on the faithful in the mosques to join in a sacred struggle. Such pressure was then exerted on the emir that he thought his own subjects would rebel against him if he did not give support to Nur al-Din in his efforts to recapture Jerusalem. When his people read and heard of Nur al-Din's religious propaganda, they would weep and curse the emir, "calling God's venegeance on me. That is why I cannot help but march against the Franj."

This use of public opinion against potentates who dragged their feet was the legacy of Nur al-Din to the young Saladin, whose name, Salah al-Din, meant "Protector of the Faith." His youth had been spent in the study of the Koran, his young manhood in the service of Nur al-Din's *jihad.* "The fight for God's cause," his biographer, Baha al-Din, wrote of him, "was a true passion with him. . . . He talked of nothing else, and all his thoughts and cares were with weapons and soldiers. He gave all his attention to those who spoke of the holy war and urged the people to take part in it."

Nur al-Din had also left as his heir a child of eleven years old. This testament gave Saladin the opportunity to demand the guardianship of his old teacher's boy. "I shall come to the court of my master's son," he declared, "and repay to the child the benefits which I received from the father." Such apparent benevolence was the last thing that the acting regents in Damascus and Aleppo wanted. In fact, they sought to revive the old alliance with Christian Jerusalem to resist the surging power of Cairo. But as so often before, Damascus fell out with Aleppo in a power struggle for the possession of the young heir to the whole of Nur al-Din's domain, which now included Mosul and Mesopotamia. So the Damascenes sent for Saladin to represent their claims against Aleppo, and he was able to proclaim himself as the rightful guardian of the heir to the crown. He advanced on Aleppo with his army, but he was forced to retreat after the Christian army came to its defence from the Kingdom of Jerusalem. This alliance of Aleppo with the infidels gave Saladin the chance to proclaim himself the ruler of Damascus on the grounds of the apostasy of Nur al-Din's heir. He was the true holy warrior of Islam, seeking to disentangle its diplomacy from any alliance with the Frankish states of Outremer.

The first regent of the leper King Baldwin IV was soon killed in a conspiracy. His replacement was Raymond III, count of Tripoli, the first cousin of the deceased Almaric. Two years before, he had come out of prison in Aleppo after eight years of captivity. Yet he immediately advocated a combination with his captors against Saladin, who wrote of him that he had "placed the people of Aleppo under the protection of the Cross and infected them with his hatred of Islam." Knowing that he would have to bide his time, Saladin agreed to a truce with the Kingdom of Jerusalem in 1175, well aware that he would have to unite the Muslim world by other means before he could continue the *jihad* and occupy the Holy City. But incredibly, the leper King Baldwin IV emerged as a formidable warrior at the age of fourteen, even defeating Saladin's brother in raids upon the territories around Aleppo and Damascus.

Saladin continued the policy of Nur al-Din through his chief of propaganda, al-Fadel. His message to the discontented Syrian emirs was that of their old master. "In the interests of Islam and its people we put first all of that which will combine their forces and unite them in one purpose. . . . Loyalty can only be the consequence of loyalty. We are in one valley and those who think ill of us are in another." By his usual magnanimity in victory and justice in government, Saladin wooed the Muslim people and the Copts and the Jews in the Near East, even if their leaders opposed him. Alexandria had a Jewish community of three thousand at this time, as did Damascus, while the two thousand Jews of Cairo had two synagogues and a rabbi recognised as their leader. The Spanish rabbi Moses Maimonides found the condition of the Jews in Christian Palestine so deplorable that he moved on to Egypt, where he wrote his *Guide for the Perplexed* and became the doctor to Saladin's son. His brother traded in jewels through the commercial routes guarded by Saladin, particularly after he had taken the Crusader fortress at Aqaba by the Red Sea. There the trade in spice and gems and porcelain was carried in *dhows* to the Far East, and Saladin taxed the exchange of goods to pay for his fortification and irrigation projects in Egypt.

Having a truce with the Franks, Saladin was able to return to his rich base and develop his army and his revenue. A minor Crusade by Philip of Flanders with new large forces from Europe led Saladin to make a cavalry attack on the Holy Land, which ended in a rare reverse. Although only sixteen years old, King Baldwin IV made a sally with his supporters from Ascalon joined by the Knights Templar from Gaza. They surprised Saladin in a wadi southeast of Ramleh and nearly killed him. He was lucky to escape and lost his army. This strange setback, however, merely made him more determined to retake Jerusalem. That was his assurance to the caliph of Baghdad, who was still the official overlord of the Muslim world in the Near East.

The Templars insisted that King Baldwin should again control the fertile plains near Baniyas and build a fortress at Jacob's Ford on the Jordan River, a base for any future attack on Damascus. The castle was built, but it could not be defended. A rash assault by the Templars resulted in a defeat by Saladin; the grand master, Odo of Saint-Amand, became his captive and died in prison. Saladin stormed the new fortress and killed all the Muslim renegades and the Christian crossbowmen, who had been particularly lethal to his troops. But he could not advance on Jerusalem. He had to consolidate his empire towards the East, Mosul and Mesopotamia, from where Western civilisation had originated.

Again, he made a truce with the Kingdom of Jerusalem in order to unite his fragmentary empire before he could pursue the *jihad* to recapture the Holy City. Once Mosul was set in place in the chain of alliances, al-Fadel reassured the caliph of Baghdad, "the whole armed might of Islam will be co-ordinated to engage the forces of unbelief." Not only would Jerusalem fall, but Constantinople and Christian Georgia. The new Abbasid caliphate of Saladin could cleanse the world, turning all the churches into mosques. Before that final *jihad,* however, the way to Jerusalem and the Christian East lay through the Muslim West. Alliance preceded triumph.

"When God gave me the land of Egypt," Saladin said, "I was sure that he also meant Palestine for me." But to unite Islam in a final *jihad,* he needed Christian provocation. He had not long to wait. At the time when he finally took Aleppo, Reynald de Châtillon plundered a caravan of pilgrims on their *Hajj* to Mecca. He followed up this violation by joining some Red Sea pirates to raid the ports which served Medina and Mecca itself, now under the protection of Saladin. A boat full of Muslims on their way to the sacred shrine of the Ka'aba was sunk. "All were taken by surprise," Ibn al-Athir wrote, "for the people of these regions had never before seen the Franj, either merchant or warrior." Saladin's brother in Egypt sent out a fleet which destroyed the pirates. The captives were beheaded in Mecca for trying to violate the holy places. And Saladin was given his reason to declare another *jihad*, particularly when Reynald repeated the outrage in 1186, plundering another caravan bound for Mecca and taking its survivors, including a sister of Saladin's, into his castle at Kerak for ransom. He expressed his defiance by saying, "Let your Muhammad come and rescue you." This action, according to the *Estoire d'Éracles,* "was the cause of the fall of the Kingdom of Jerusalem."

Meanwhile, that kingdom had begun to split and crack just as the Muslim states had done before the advent of Saladin. With the death of the leper king, there had been a struggle over the regency of the new heir, Baldwin V, a boy of seven years old, who died a year later. He was succeeded in a palace coup by Guy of Lusignan, who had married the princess Sibylla, the mother of the king. A weak ruler, who was unable to control the aggressive hawks such as Reynald and the Templars, King Guy decided to attack his rival Raymond, count of Tripoli, who immediately turned to Saladin for support. The roles in the religious wars were reversed. Some of the Christians were seeking an alliance with the Muslims to defend themselves in their own civil strife.

Calling for support in the *jihad* against Jerusalem, Saladin found reinforcements from the Turks and the Kurds as well as the Arabs. He asked the count of Tripoli to allow a reconnaissance by seven thousand of his cavalry under safe-conduct through the count's territories. The Knights Hospitaller and Templar decided to ambush the Muslim horsemen near Nazareth with only a hundred and thirty knights and three hundred soldiers. Their charge ended in a massacre. Only three of the knights survived, including Gerard de Ridfort, the grand master of the Templars. It seemed a prelude to total disaster.

When news reached Jerusalem that Saladin had massed an army of twelve thousand horsemen, including a bodyguard of a thousand *mamluks* from Egypt, and even more foot soldiers, stiffened in the holy war by volunteer Sufis and *fida'is,* the Christians knew that they had to concentrate their forces or die. Count Raymond of Tripoli must rejoin the fold. The patriarch of Jerusalem and leading knights were sent to him. They reproached him, according to Ibn al-Athir, about his alliance with Saladin, saying: "You must surely have converted to Islam, otherwise you could never tolerate [the massacre of the Templars and Hospitallers] which has just happened." The count agreed to a reconciliation and to place his troops under the command of King Guy in Jerusalem. And so the Christian army managed to field its largest army: twelve hundred knights, two thousand Turcopole mercenaries, and ten thousand infantrymen. The Relic of the True Cross led the vanguard.

If strategy was the strength of Saladin, aggression was the weakness of the Christian leaders. Saladin decided to incite an attack from his infidel enemy. He took the city of Tiberias and besieged the wife of the count of Tripoli in the citadel. He then arranged his army behind the twin peaks of the Horns of Hittin in a fertile plain backed by the waters of Lake Tiberias. To fight him, the Christian army would have to advance across a waterless valley, which would sap their strength, if they were harassed by light cavalry on their march. The question was, would the bait be taken?

Count Raymond of Tripoli counselled caution. "Tiberias belongs to me," he said in the report of Ibn al-Athir, "and it is my own wife who is besieged." Yet he would rather avoid a confrontation and ransom his wife later. Reynald accused him of exaggerating the strength of Saladin's army and preferring to cooperate with the infidel. "The fire is not daunted," he said, "by the quantity of wood to burn." Later that night, Gerard de Ridfort went to the tent of King Guy of Jerusalem, counselling attack as always. He said that the Templars would sell their white mantles if their recent humiliations were not avenged. "Go and have it announced throughout the army that all should arm and every man go to his company and follow the standard of the Holy Cross."

So the grand master of the order dedicated to defend the Temple at Jerusalem advised the strategy of assault outside its walls that would lead to the loss of the Holy City. King Guy advanced at dawn into the snare set by Saladin. Harassed and parched and baked by the sun in their scalding armour, the knights and soldiers dragged their way to the Horns of Hittin, to find that Saladin's forces had cut off access to fodder and water. There Jesus was supposed to have preached the Sermon on the Mount against war. That night, the *fida'is* set fire to the dry grass and scrub. Smoke and flame choked the Christian army, now maddened with thirst. The men would have to break through to the lake in the morning, or die of thirst.

Certainly, Frankish chivalry was at its best under pressure. If it could not achieve grace, it could achieve a sort of martyrdom. The infantry were doomed to exhaustion and slavery. Yet the knights repulsed an assault by Saladin's cavalry, and then struck back at his tent. If he were killed, his army would collapse. Count Raymond of Tripoli's charge ended in futility. The Muslim ranks opened in front of him, and he and his men thundered forward to nothing. The other charges nearly succeeded. In the reported words of Saladin's son of fifteen:

"I was at my father's side during the battle, the first I saw with my own eyes. The king of the Franj had retreated to the hill with his own band and from there he led a furious charge against the Muslims facing him, forcing them back upon my father. I saw that he was ashen pale and distraught, and he tugged at his beard as he went forward, crying: 'Satan must not win.' The Muslims turned to counter-attack and drove the Franj back up the hill.

"When I saw the Franj retreating before the Muslims I cried out for joy: 'We have beaten them!' But they returned to the charge with redoubled ardour and drove our army back towards my father. His response was the same as before, and the Franj retired back up the hill. Again I cried, 'We have beaten them!' but my father turned to me and said: 'Be silent; we shall not have beaten them until that tent falls!' As he spoke the royal tent fell and the sultan dismounted and prostrated himself in thanks to God, weeping for joy."

In victory, Saladin did not show his unusual magnanimity. The sacred places of Islam had been assaulted, pilgrims had been killed, truces broken. This was a holy war for Jerusalem, the third sacred city in Muslim eyes. The chief violator of God's law, Reynald de Châtillon, was denied water and refused to become a Muslim. Saladin struck at his head with his own sword. A bodyguard finished off the traitor to the divine. All of the captured two hundred knights of the Temple of Jerusalem and of the Hospital of St. John were ransomed from their captors by Saladin and given to the Muslim mystical orders, the Sufis and the *fida'is,* to behead. Some of these, Imad al-Din reported, "slashed and cut cleanly and were thanked for it; some refused and failed to strike and were excused; some made fools of themselves and others took their places." Others laughed as they killed the Templars and the Hospitallers. Saladin detested these infidel warriors in a *jihad*. They never held that an oath with an infidel was worth a damn. They followed a higher law, as he did. He would try to extirpate his chief enemies.

In taking over the major cities of Palestine, however, in his encirclement of Jerusalem, Saladin knew that clemency prevented the need for a long siege. Acre capitulated without resistance as its population was promised mercy. Saladin tried to persuade the Italian merchants to stay and continue trading, but most of them left for Tyre. The small cities and towns of the Holy Land also surrendered, the Christian inhabitants trusting to the justice of Saladin. Jaffa resisted the advance of Saladin's brother with an army from Egypt; he broke through the walls and sold the citizens into slavery. Saladin continued to take all the major ports, Beirut and Ascalon, which was yielded in return for the release of King Guy and the master of the Temple; Gaza also fell, although it was held by the remnants of the Templars. But Saladin bypassed Tyre and did not seize Tripoli nor the citadel of Tortosa. It was his greatest mistake. He left landing places for a Third Crusade from the West.

Yet he would now have Jerusalem. Only two knights had been left to defend its city after the catastrophe at the Horns of Hittin; but their ranks were swelled by refugees from the countryside, terrified at Saladin's advance. Some sixty thousand people were now packed into the walls of the medieval city. Saladin allowed Balian of Ibelin, lord of Nablus, to enter the Holy City merely to remove his wife and children to Tyre; but Balian was persuaded to become the leader of the defence. He threatened Saladin with a scorched city, if he did not spare the inhabitants of Jerusalem from another massacre, the savagery which the Christians had previously visited on the place. As he declared:

> "O Sultan, be aware that this city holds a mass of people so great that God alone knows their number. They now hesitate to continue the fight, because they hope that you will spare their lives as you have spared so many others, because they love life and hate death. But if we see that death is inevitable, then, by God, we will kill our own women and children and burn all that we possess. We will not leave

you a single dinar of booty, not a single dirham, not a single man or woman to lead into captivity. Then we shall destroy the sacred rock, al-Aqsa mosque, and many other sites; we will kill the five thousand Muslim prisoners we now hold, and will exterminate the mounts and all the beasts. In the end, we will come outside the city, and we will fight against you as one fights for one's life. Not one of us will die without having killed several of you."

Deterred or impressed by this threat, Saladin agreed that the people of Jerusalem would be treated as prisoners of war, if they surrendered. They could ransom themselves and most of them did, for two hundred and twenty thousand dinars. It was a remarkable act of grace by Saladin. For he had sworn to his army in an address delivered before Jerusalem that he would take the *jihad* to its bitter end. The Dome of the Rock had been profaned by raising the cross above it and pretending that it was the Temple of Solomon. He had reminded his troops that the Prophet, Muhammad, had ascended to the seventh heaven from that carved rock, which was also the resting place of the prophet Abraham. There, too, the Muslims would receive justice on their Judgement Day. Saladin had vowed to restore Jerusalem to Islam, in the testimony of Imad al-Din, and "not to leave until he had honoured his word and had set his feet in the place where the Prophet had set foot." With the unconditional surrender of the city, however, Saladin kept his Koranic faith. He allowed the patriarch Heraclius to escape to Tyre with loaded chests of treasure on payment of the common ransom of ten dinars a head. His charity was such that Dante recognised him among the worthy pagans such as Achilles and Homer just outside the gates of hell, while he entered the *chansons de geste* as a hero almost the equal of Roland and Lancelot.

The first mission of Saladin in Jerusalem was to renew it as a Muslim holy city, which it would remain effectively for the next eight centuries. He entered its walls on Friday, 2 October 1187, the same day in tradition that Muhammad had mounted from the sacred rock on Mount Moriah to heaven. The golden cross was cast down from over the Dome of the Rock and the Templar headquarters in the al-Aqsa mosque, and all the Christian symbols and dressings were removed, and the walls sprinkled with rose water. A great service of thanksgiving was held, in which the Qadi of

Aleppo prayed that Saladin's empire might spread over all the earth. Such praise angered the caliph of Baghdad, who claimed that his armies had conquered Jerusalem, provoking Saladin to ask where they were at the time. "By God!" he declared, "I conquered Jerusalem with my own troops and under my own banners." But as he held all the three Muslim sacred cities under his protection, he already appeared too powerful to the rulers of Baghdad.

When they had captured Jerusalem, the Crusaders had added exclusion to genocide, forbidding for a period the presence of Muslims and Jews within the walls. Now Saladin returned the compliment. Frankish and Latin Christians owing allegiance to Rome were forbidden the Holy City; but Greek Orthodox Christians looking to the patriarch in Constantinople and Copts and other Christian believers were allowed to remain within and visit Jerusalem. In the struggle between the sacred centres, Saladin preferred the Second Rome of Byzantium to the first one, where St. Peter had founded the rock of the Latin church. Saladin also resisted advice from his zealots to raze the Church of the Holy Sepulchre and plough other Christian churches into soil. "What is the use of wrecking and destroying the seat of their admiration," Ibn al-Athir made Saladin ask, "the site of the Cross and the Sepulchre and not all the edifice?" If all churches were razed to the ground, Christians would still come to Jerusalem. He chose conciliation rather than blood feud. He invited the Jews back to their sacred city to live in peace with the Muslims there. He was greeted across the Mediterranean ghettos as the new Cyrus, allowing the dispersed Jews back to the site of the Temple of Solomon, although it was now covered by the Dome of the Rock. There was a fresh wave of immigrants to the Holy Land, including Sephardic scholars, enthused by a belief that Saladin's victory promised the advent of another Messiah, who would pass through the Golden Gate to the Temple Mount to repossess the centre of Israel.

The fall of Jerusalem still could provoke a crisis of faith and conscience in Western Europe. Yet the call of Pope Gregory VIII for a Third Crusade was not as urgent or fervent as his predecessor's trumpets and clarion calls. Although the kings of France and England were forced by threat of excommunication to give up their wars and vow at Gisors to take the cross, Henry II of England was too old and sick to stagger towards Jerusalem, while Philip Augustus of France was struggling to preserve his lands from the Plantagenet threat in western France. But Henry's death released his son, King Richard, to fulfill his vow to proceed to the East; his resolve was followed by a popular pogrom against the Jews in London and Norwich and York; to go to Jerusalem usually meant to persecute those seen as the enemies of Christ. In addition, much of French chivalry, led by the counts of Champagne and Bar and Brienne, set off for the reconquest of Jerusalem, aided by fleets from Pisa and Genoa. A counterattack from Tyre by the released King Guy of Jerusalem had invested Acre with its Muslim garrison, and there the crusading reinforcements could land, although their vast encampment was again threatened by Saladin, now conscious of his mistake in leaving the new Crusaders with easy access from the sea to Palestine.

A third and more dangerous foe, the German emperor, Frederick Barbarossa, also took the cross, inspired by the legendary Charlemagne's Crusades against the Moors. He set off with more than fifty thousand men to defend the Holy Sepulchre. He chose the fatal land route through the Balkans and on to Constantinople, where he bickered with the Greek emperor; but he moved onwards through Anatolia, where the Seljuk Turks preferred to give him safe passage. For they were as uneasy about the power of Saladin as the Byzantines were. Perhaps this crusading host from Germany could remove a threat to all of them, whatever their religion. Frederick Barbarossa reached Cilicia and the eve of a victory against Saladin. He was seventy years old, however, and had a heart attack bathing in a cold river after a hot day's ride. His death dissolved his army and made him the material of legend. Along with King Arthur, he was thought for centuries to be asleep in a mountain, ready to burst forth with his knights to recapture the Holy City. Ibn al-Athir took his sudden death as the gift of God. If the German emperor had not died on the borders of Syria, "men would write today that Syria and Egypt had once belonged to Islam." The emperor's son Frederick of Swabia reached Acre eventually with only two thousand men.

Philip Augustus of France and the count of Flanders reached the camp outside Acre before Richard of England, who stopped on the voyage to ravage Sicily on behalf of his sister Joanna, the widow of the late king, before proceeding to conquer Cyprus as a supply base for the Third

Crusade. Energetic and brutal with a certain royal code and dignity, he was a serious challenge to Saladin. Eventually, Acre was to yield to the Christian reinforcements that surrounded its walls, after a siege of two years—as long as that of Antioch, where the First Crusade had almost foundered. Epidemics of dysentery and cholera decimated the besiegers; but now recruits and supplies continued to arrive from Europe. Sea power was the secret of the Christian success, and Saladin coud not resist this tide against him. His only success was again to capture Gerard de Ridfort and have the grand master of the Temple beheaded as his brothers in the military order had been after the victory at the Horns of Hittin.

Although the Crusader camp was divided over who should be the next king of Jerusalem when it was retaken—the English backed the present king, Guy of Lusignan, while the French supported his rival Conrad of Montferrat, who had married the dead King Almaric's second daughter, Isabella—they were united in their determination to take Acre before they marched on the Holy City. And when they did force the surrender of its three thousand heroic defenders, they spared their prisoners for the promise of a large ransom, the release of the same number of Frankish captives, and the return of the True Cross, the necessary symbol of their faith and long struggle. But when Philip Augustus returned to France, leaving his forces behind him, King Richard ordered all the Muslim prisoners beheaded in public, because Saladin had delayed in sending the ransom and the True Cross. And so, through barbarity, King Richard rekindled the fires of the holy war.

He saw that the future of the Kingdom of Jerusalem lay in its command of the sea. Therefore he decided on a coastal Crusade to reoccupy the ports of the Holy Land, where any future expedition from Europe would find a secure berth. He fought a classic campaign along the beaches of the Mediterranean that outfoxed even Saladin. He knew that Jerusalem could not be retaken without capturing its nearest outlet to the sea, Jaffa. He marched along the coast with his western flank protected by his fleet and his eastern flank protected by his dogged infantry and lethal archers, with the knights held in reserve in the centre to charge down any incursion. At Arsuf, north of Jaffa, Saladin tried a battle, but he was beaten off by these inexorable tactics. Jaffa fell, and King Richard began negotiating with Saladin's brother, al-Adil, to find the least costly route to the Holy

City. For news of his brother John's misrule of England in his absence had begun to trouble his prolonged quest for salvation in the East.

The negotiations were singular and showed King Richard almost as much of a diplomat as a warrior. "As far as we are concerned," he told Saladin's brother, "there are only three subjects of discord: Jerusalem, the True Cross, and territory. As for Jerusalem, it is our place of worship, and we will never agree to renounce it, even if we have to fight to the last man. As for territory, all we want is the cessation of the land west of Jordan. As for the Cross, for you it is only a piece of wood, for us its value is beyond price." Saladin replied that Jerusalem was as holy to the Muslims as to the Christians: He would not abandon the city. Ignoring its Jewish and Roman heritage, Saladin said that the territory of Palestine had always been Muslim, while the Christians had occupied it briefly. "As for the Cross, it was a great thing to hold, and we will surrender it only in return for some important concession on behalf of Islam."

Negotiations continued, including the possible marriage of King Richard's sister from Sicily to Saladin's brother, the negotiator. But such a convenient arrangement between the cross and the crescent was doomed to failure. King Richard's sister angrily refused to give herself to a Muslim. Especially in marriage, the two religions could not meet. And they were irreconcilable over the possession of Jerusalem. King Richard mobilised his forces at Jaffa and began the first of two advances on the Holy City. Saladin had been deserted by most of his army, and he did not know how to stop the Christian advance. The biographer of the sultan of Cairo and Damascus, Baha al-Din, illustrated the conflict between strategy and religion when the goal was the irreducible Holy City. Just as the Christians had marched around its walls many times in prayer before the assault which took it, Saladin now relied on his faith for its defence. In the words of his witness:

> The Franj—God damn them—had come up and camped at Bait Nuba, a few days' march from Jerusalem. The Sultan was there, having posted advance guards in close contact with the enemy and sent out spies and reconnaissance troops. Thus he obtained the news of a firm decision taken by the enemy to besiege Jerusalem and give battle. This frightened the Muslims. The Sultan summoned the emirs and

informed them of the critical situation in which the Muslims found themselves, and consulted them on the advisability of staying in Jerusalem. The emirs began by blustering, but their real intentions were quite different, each of them asserting that he would not in the least mind staying in the city, that the whole of Islam would be exposed to danger: they, they said, would remain, and he was to take a detachment of the army and go out to encircle the enemy as had happened at Acre. His job would be to cut off the enemy's supplies and to harry them. Theirs would be to defend the city. On this decision the council broke up, but Saladin remained firm in his resolve to stay in the city in person, well aware that if he did not stay no one would. When the emirs had gone home, one of them returned to say that they would not stay unless Saladin's brother al-Adil, or one of his [own] sons, stayed behind to command and support them. Saladin realised that what they really meant was that they would not hold out, and this troubled and perplexed him.

That night, the Thursday night, I was on duty beside him from sunset until it was almost dawn. It was winter, and we were alone but for God. We discussed this project and that, examining the implications of each in turn, until I began to feel concerned for him and to fear for his health, for he seemed to be overwhelmed by despair. I begged him to lie down on his bed, in the hope that he might sleep a while. He replied: "Perhaps *you* are tired," and rose. Scarcely had I returned to my rooms and settled to a task than dawn broke and the muezzin's call to prayer resounded. I almost always made my morning prayer with Saladin, so I went back to his room, where he was washing himself. "I have not shut an eye," he said. "I knew that," I replied. "How did you know?" "I did not sleep either, there was no time for it." We prayed together, and again took up the usual problem. "I have had an idea," I said, "that may be of use, God willing." "What is it?" "Turn to Almighty God, call on him and have trust in him to resolve this terrible dilemma." "How should we do it?" "Today," I said, "is Friday. Your Majesty should wash before going to the Friday prayer and should perform the public prayer as usual in the Mosque al-Aqsa, on the spot from which the Prophet ascended on his journey to Heaven. Offer certain alms secretly by the hand of someone you trust and then pray two *raka'at* between the muezzin's first and second call, prostrating yourself and invoking God Almighty—on this subject there is an authentic *hadith* of the Prophet saying: My God, all my earthly power to bring victory to your Faith has come to nothing; my only resource is to turn to You and to rely on Your help and trust in Your goodness. You are my sufficiency, You are the best preserver! God is too generous to let your prayers go to waste."

Saladin did exactly as I advised. As usual I was at his side during the prayers: he performed two *raka'at* between the first and second call, and I saw him prostrate, with tears running down his white beard and onto his prayer-mat, but I could not hear what he said. . . . The very same day a message came from 'Izz al-Din Ibn Jurdik, captain of the advance guard, to say that the Franj were on the move. Their whole army was mounted and moving that day toward the plain. There they halted until the afternoon and then retired to their tents. On the Saturday morning a second messenger brought word that they had repeated this manoeuvre, and during the day a spy reported that a quarrel had broken out among the Franj. The French held that it was absolutely essential to besiege Jerusalem, while the King of England and his supporters did not want to put all Christendom in jeopardy and his own men in danger in that mountainous, waterless land—for Saladin had ordered that all the springs around Jerusalem were to be blocked up. So they went out to take council, for their custom is always to hold councils of war in the saddle, mounted on their horses. They decided to put the whole matter into the hands of ten men and to abide by their decision. On Monday morning came the joyful news that they had withdrawn and were returning to the region of Ramleh. I saw with my own eyes this evidence of Saladin's faith in God.

So the Muslim commitment to holding Jerusalem broke the Christian vow to retake it to the last man. King Richard had to return to England. He could only negotiate the best possible terms for Christian pilgrims to have access to the holy places. As always, delaying tactics had won the longest day. The potentates of Europe had to return to rule their own domains before they could force the arid way to Jerusalem. The only problem before this necessary accommodation lay in the person of Conrad of Montferrat. King Richard of England was overruled by the assembled Frankish barons, who preferred the claims of Conrad to King Guy of Jerusalem. Indeed, Conrad was the most formidable warrior with a reputation for cunning and ruthlessness. Yet within a few days of his election to the crown, he was stabbed to death by Assassin killers. King Richard was accused of instigating the murder; but he had no dealings with the Assassins. The relationship between the Templars and the Isma'ili sect had broken down before the disaster at the Horns of Hittin, when the Templars had murdered Assassin envoys to the king of Jerusalem, seeking an alliance against the rising power of the Sunni Saladin. It was Saladin who had come to terms with the Assassins after they had attempted to murder him, and Ibn al-Athir pointed the finger at Saladin as the man responsible for the murder of Conrad. Certainly, in the Near East at that time, assassination was diplomacy by other means. With Conrad gone, King Richard and Saladin could reach an agreement over Jerusalem.

First, a new Frankish king had to be chosen, less aggressive and more palatable to the divided Christian brokers of power. The count of Champagne was crowned as King Henry II; he was King Richard's nephew as well as the nephew of the king of France. He acquiesced in Richard's solution to the problem of Jerusalem. It would remain a Muslim protectorate, while Christian pilgrims should have access to all the holy places, including the Church of the Holy Sepulchre. The king of Jerusalem would retain all the coastal strip won back by the Third Crusade, except for refortified Ascalon, the gateway to Egypt, which would be restored. "I want your friendship and affection," King Richard wrote to Saladin. "You are no longer allowed to send all your Muslims to their deaths any more than I am all our Franks."

The Muslim emirs had also lost their appetite for a *jihad*. In a final attack on Jaffa, they had been routed by King Richard and some Pisan infantrymen, although they had outnumbered the infidels by ten to one. "Unlike other princes," Saladin said sourly to his supporters, "I do not prefer a life of ease to the Holy War." His adviser al-Fadel had warned him that nobody would follow him now except for money. He might summon them in the name of God, but they thought he was calling on them for his own ambitions. The war between him and King Richard was a stalemate. Both of them had to reach a truce to return to their bases to renew their resources.

Therefore Saladin allowed the Crusaders to pray in Jerusalem, led by Hubert Walter, the bishop of Salisbury, who was shown the Holy Cross. He asked Saladin to allow the Latin mass to be celebrated in the Church of the Holy Sepulchre as well as the Greek rite. Saladin agreed, and so in a sense, the Crusade was a success and Rome did reach Jerusalem again. King Richard himself turned away from the Holy City, hiding the sight of its walls under his shield, because he could not capture it and fulfill his crusading vow. But he did ensure that European pilgrims could now worship in the places where Christ had lived and died.

The realities of warfare in Palestine had led to a mutual acceptance and a form of coexistence. Neither the Crusaders nor Saladin could defeat each other totally. In the end, the religious hatred that had led to the beheading of Christian and Muslim holy warriors ended with the toleration of the worship of Latin and Greek Christians along with Jews in the Muslim city of Jerusalem, dominated by the Dome of the Rock, once again under the crescent rather than the cross. The strike for Jerusalem by the Crusaders was already blunted by the building of other Temples of Jerusalem in the Cistercian abbeys and Gothic cathedrals and fledgling Masonic lodges of Europe. And Rome was increasingly promoting itself as the primary Holy City with its living church founded by St. Peter, somewhat more relevant than the site of the death of Christ. Its rival was rather Constantinople, the Second Rome and home of the Greek rite, than Jerusalem. The Fourth Crusade, indeed, would prove whether the objective of these expeditions was the supremacy of Rome or the conquest of the Holy Land.

EIGHT

GOD'S OWN

"Kill them all: God will look after His own."

—Arnald-Almaric, the abbot of Cîteaux

Saladin did not long survive his initial triumph at Jerusalem. Six years later, his death at Damascus led to the slow crumbling of the Ayyubid Empire that stretched from Cairo to Mosul, from Aleppo to Mecca. The inescapable quarrels among his sons and heirs would end with *mamluk* control of the richest prize, the land of Egypt, and the preservation of the Christian coastal strip which still was known as the Kingdom of Jerusalem, now imperilled by the accidental death of Henry of Champagne, who fell out of a window. The backing, however, of the new and forceful Pope Innocent III for the king of Cyprus, Almaric of Lusignan, united the two Crusader kingdoms left in the Levant. Their survival depended in their combination and dissension within Saladin's empire.

Another death, however, prevented the Christian recapture of the Holy City. The young German emperor, Henry VI, harboured the same ambitions as had Frederick Barbarossa, perhaps on Constantinople, certainly on Jerusalem. He sent the advance guard of a mighty Crusade under the command of Conrad, the archbishop of Mainz, to Palestine. The German knights advanced into Galilee to find that Jerusalem had largely

117

been stripped of its defences. Enthusiasm for a *jihad* seemed to have expired at the bier of Saladin; but a relieving army appeared from Egypt to chase the fresh Crusaders away. The legacy of Archbishop Conrad, however, was the foundation of a new military order of Teutonic Knights, based on a hospice at Acre and modelled on the Knights Hospitaller of St. John. Initially, the members of the German order were also the defendants of the holy places, although later their role would be to create a Christian empire in the pagan lands of the eastern Baltic with their headquarters at a New Jerusalem at Marienburg to the rear of an incessant battleground against the Slavic peoples.

While the Emperor Henry VI was preparing a massive armada at Messina in Sicily, he died at the age of thirty-two years. The destination of his huge expedition was unclear. He had forced the Byzantine emperor, Alexius III, to pay him a huge indemnity in order not to invade his empire. Sacred regalia in Constantinople had to be melted down to pay the "Alamanian" tax. The Byzantine historian of the period, Niketas Choniates, affirmed the German monarch's designs on the Greek Second Rome as the Eastern capital of a new world empire. Even if his strategy was debatable, there is no question that Henry VI saw Constantinople as the key to Jerusalem. Only with its resources would Latin Christendom hope to hold on to a retaken Palestine.

The Byzantine Empire, indeed, under the Comneni and Angeli dynasties had preserved the Latin principalities of the West to offset the threat of the Seljuk Turks and the Muslim lords of Aleppo and Damascus. The emperor Manuel Comnenus had been feared by Saladin more than any Western ruler. "The master of Constantinople is a proud despot," he had informed the caliph of Baghdad, "a Goliath of infidelity, the sovereign of an empire which has lasted for many years, the head of Christianity which everywhere acknowledges its supremacy and gives it homage." The chief threat from the West had been the Normans based in Sicily, the second city in the realm. The papacy was also a menace, because it insisted on the submission of the Greek patriarch of Constantinople to the See of Rome. The emperor Alexius III had written to Pope Innocent on his election: "We are the only two world powers: the single Roman Church and the Single Empire of the successors of Justinian; therefore we must unite. . . ." Yet the papacy insisted on ecclesiastical supremacy with the Latin rite set over the Greek. Such pride meant an assault on the pretender.

The fleets of the maritime Italian cities, Genoa and Pisa and particularly Venice, also represented dangers to Constantinople; so a Golden Bull was granted to various doges, which gave Venice extraordinary trading privileges in the Bosphorus and elsewhere. In 1171, Manuel Comnenus had seized a thousand Venetian ships in imperial ports; but eleven years later, alternative traders from Genoa and Pisa had been massacred and the Venetians recalled as hostile friends. The glory of the Byzantine navy was only a memory. The policy of exchanging blows and bribes between the rival Italian fleets was playing with Greek fire, that naval missile that burned even the sea.

When Pope Innocent III decided to preach a Fourth Crusade, he did not look to the Italian naval powers for his recruits. They carried pilgrims and warriors to the Holy Land, they did not provide them. He sent his emissary, Fulk of Neuilly, to proclaim a new holy war in the fertile grounds of northern France and the Low Countries, where the counts of Champagne and Flanders along with Simon de Montfort and Geoffrey of Villehardouin took up the cross. In a general letter, Innocent III complained about the Muslim triumph in the sacred sites. "Our enemies insult us and say, where is your God who can free from our grasp neither Himself nor you? We have polluted your sanctuaries, seized the objects of your adoration, and violently attacked the Holy Land. In spite of you we keep in our hands your father's cradle of superstition. . . . Where is your God? Let Him rise and help you! Let Him show how He protects you and Himself!"

Initially, the plan of the Fourth Crusade was to assault Egypt before attempting to seize Palestine with an army of thirty thousand men. An agreement was signed with the aged Doge Dandolo of Venice on the terms of transport—eighty-five thousand silver marks for the largest fleet ever assembled by the lagoon city. Unable to pay the fee in full, and with a change of leader because of the death of the count of Champagne, the Crusaders under the north Italian Boniface, the marquis of Montferrat, gave their support to a Venetian sortie against the port of Zara on the Dalmatian Coast, which had seceded to the king of Hungary. And when the fleet set out, in the words of Robert of Clari, "it was the best thing to behold that had ever been seen since the beginning of the world . . . it seemed that the whole sea was aswarm and ablaze." Zara was soon captured, incurring the wrath of Pope Innocent, who excommunicated the Crusaders, writing to Boniface, "Instead of reaching the Promised Land, you thirsted for the blood of your brethren. Satan, the universal tempter, has deceived you. . . . The citizens of Zara hung crucifixes upon their walls. In spite of the Crucified you have stormed the city and forced it to surrender." After showing his temper, the pope listened to the appeals of the Crusaders and pardoned them so that they could proceed to Palestine, but he would not lift his anathema on the Venetians, who had no intention of sailing towards Jerusalem.

Another destination had suggested itself. The present Byzantine emperor had dethroned and blinded and imprisoned his predecessor, Isaac II, whose son Alexius Angelus had escaped on a Pisan ship to the west. Appearing at Zara, Prince Alexius promised to put the Greek church under the sway of the Latin rite at Rome, if his father were restored to the imperial crown. He would also pay a large indemnity and commit Byzantine forces to the Crusade, as well as giving Venice trade and territorial concessions.

The deviation on the route proved too tempting to resist. "The Franks and all their chiefs have loved the gold and silver which the son of Isaac has promised them," the contemporary *Chronicle* of Novgorod stated, "and have forgotten the precepts of the Emperor and the Pope." Certainly, the greed of the Crusaders for the booty of the richest city in Christendom was a motive for the detour to the Bosphorus; but Venetian ambition was also a guiding factor. Even Pope Innocent III unofficially approved of establishing the supremacy of Rome over Constantinople, while the successor of the German crown, Philip of Swabia, also had the ambitions of his predecessor to found an Eastern empire. The pretender Prince Alexius was able to compound these mixed motives into a philosopher's stone that would transmute the leaden journey towards Jerusalem into a voyage to the Golden Horn.

To the Crusaders, the sight of Constantinople was almost that of a paradise fallen to earth. "They never thought there could be in all the world so wealthy a city," Villehardouin marvelled, "when they saw the high walls and magnificent towers that encircled it, the rich palaces and mighty churches, so many that no one would have believed it who had not seen it with his own eyes." Its capture seemed to Villehardouin the greatest enterprise anyone had undertaken since God had created the world. In point of fact, the Byzantine capital's walls were in disrepair, its fleet was reduced to a few hulks, and its only good soldiers were the Anglo-Saxon mercenaries of the Varangian Guard. Although these imperial troops beat off an assault by land, the Venetians rammed and broke the chain that barred their ships from the Golden Horn, then they scaled the seawalls and took twenty-five of the towers. Emperor Alexius III fled with his jewels, so the citizens of Constantinople cleverly took the blind Isaac II from prison and restored him to the throne. The object of the diverted Crusade had been achieved. Prince Alexius was made regent and then crowned as the coemperor. His problem was now to redeem the reckless promises he had made to the Franks encamped across the Bosphorus. For the imperial treasury was nearly empty, and none of his Greek subjects would accept submission to Rome.

Some of the Crusaders were persuaded that they had reached a city almost as holy as Jerusalem because of the quality and quantity of its sacred objects. Villehardouin wrote that it possessed as many relics as all the rest of Christendom. The Muslims might have captured a piece of the True Cross at the fall of the first Kingdom of Jerusalem; but Constantinople possessed the Holy Shroud or Veil, contained in a version of the Grail, which had come into the hands of the Byzantines in 943 at the siege of Edessa. The treasurer of the Pharos chapel warned the Crusaders not to molest the blessed cloth. "In this chapel," Mesarites wrote, "Christ rises again, and the Shroud with the burial linens is the clear proof. . . . They still smell of myrrh and are indestructible since they once enshrouded the dead body, anointed and naked, of the Almighty after his Passion." Robert de Clari saw the sacred linen in the Church of St. Mary Blachernae, where "was kept the Shroud in which Our Lord has been wrapped, which stood up straight every Good Friday, so that the features of Our Lord could be plainly seen there." The imprinted cloth was kept in a golden vessel which hung on silver chains, a Grail that contained the blood of Christ.

The Muslims had never understood the Christian passion for worshipping what they saw as idols. The Franks seemed the servants of a piece of wood, which was called the cross. "They are bidden to adore it," Imad al-Din wrote after the True Cross had been captured at the Horns of Hittin. "It is their God; before it they bow their heads in the dust and bless it with their lips . . . they would lay down their lives for its sake, and they look to it for their salvation. They make other crosses in its image and address their homage and vows to it in the temples of their cult." Even more puzzling seemed the veneration of statues and mosaics of the Virgin Mary and Child, an abomination to the Muslims. Al-Usama recorded a Templar showing him such an image. "There," the Templar said, "is the infant God." To which al-Usama added, "May God rise above what these impious men say."

To the wandering Crusaders, however, on their expedition to Constantinople, the incitement of the holy relics was almost greater than of the royal treasures. The pope and the archbishops of Western Europe wanted these objects of adoration in the churches of the Latin rite, while the Greeks could hardly tolerate the Franks ogling and coveting the most venerated symbols of their faith. A mob attacked the Italian quarter of Constantinople, burning down the shops of the Genoese, the Pisans, and the Venetians, who retaliated by pillaging the Muslim quarter in a parody of a holy war. With the two emperors unable to pay them off, the Venetians and the Crusaders threatened that they would take by force what was not given them under agreement. Another riot against the invaders in the city led to a son-in-law of the deposed Emperor Alexius III being proclaimed emperor under the title of Alexius V; he then disposed of the fourth Alexius and his blind father to verify his claim to the throne. This coup ended any chance of settlement with the Venetians and the Crusaders, who could now claim that they were avenging the murder of the true emperors, whom they had restored. It was truly a mission against impiety and injustice.

Before assaulting the city, Doge Dandolo (for Venice) and Boniface, the marquis of Montferrat (for the Crusaders), agreed on a just division of the future spoils, with the lion's share going to the Italian maritime power. To satisfy the pope, a Latin patriarch would be elected to rule from the great basilica of Sancta Sophia, while the sacred relics of Christianity would be divided among the Western conquerors. There was no thought that the Byzantine Empire had protected Christian Europe from the assaults of nomadic hordes and Islamic invaders for eight hundred years. The

Greeks now were considered perfidious and effete, and their faith appeared almost heretical in its resistance to the authority of Rome. It was a good time to establish a Latin empire on the rubble of a Hellenic one.

"Calling upon the name of Christ,"—these were the opening words of the treaty between the conspirators against Constantinople—"we must conquer the city with the armed hand!" This treacherous crusade to elect a Latin emperor to govern "to the glory of God and the Holy Roman Church and Empire" began with another assault from the sea, which was repulsed. But the usurper Alexius V could not prevail against the besiegers and fled to preserve the remnants of the Byzantine Empire outside its capital. For three days, the Franks and the Venetians pillaged the greatest city in Europe. Libraries were plundered, the Church of the Holy Apostles and the imperial tomb of Jerusalem and Sancta Sophia were robbed, nuns were violated, and the sacred relics were stolen. "Since the world was created," Villehardouin noted with his usual hyperbole, "never had so much booty been taken in any city!" Niketas Choniates contrasted the good behaviour of the Muslims under Saladin at the recapture of Jerusalem in 1187 with the savagery of these "forerunners of the Anti-Christ" at the sack of Constantinople seventeen years later. Even Pope Innocent III was horrified at the barbarism shown by the Crusaders in their rape of the Second Rome, the rival imperial city of God. But he was won round to a qualified approval of the enterprise, lifting his sentence of excommunication from Doge Dandolo and the Venetians, although they insisted on another Venetian, Thomas Morosini, becoming the new patriarch of Constantinople instead of allowing Rome to make the appointment.

The victor of the aborted Fourth Crusade was Venice, which secured the best ports in the eastern Mediterranean and most of the Aegean Islands and Crete and large areas of Constantinople, where Dandolo took on the title of despot at the age of ninety. He was to die soon, but he had created in 1204 a Venetian Empire by manipulating a Crusade that never reached Jerusalem. The Latin Empire of the Crusaders would only hold Constantinople for fifty-seven years; but when it was recovered by the Greeks under Michael Palaeologos, it was too late to restore the glory and the strength that had been Byzantium.

The Christians had imitated the Muslims in fighting among themselves and enfeebling their own power, when only an alliance between Rome and

Constantinople could ever sustain a Kingdom of Jerusalem. By focusing on the supremacy of the See of St. Peter rather than the conquest of the Holy Land, Innocent III acquiesced in the diversion of the Fourth Crusade from retaking the City of God to reducing the Second City of Christendom. This precedent for sending a crusade to fight the heretics or the pagans or the infidels outside Palestine was to prove fatal to the concept of the Christian holy war. The enemies of Rome could now be massacred in the south of France as well as the Levant, in North Africa as well as Galilee. A crusade was a crusade was a crusade, even with the loss of its eventual direction towards Calvary.

In the cradle of courtly romance where the troubadours sang of the quest towards the East, apostates appeared and had to be rooted out. The new crusade was a form of Christian self-destruction. The victims, the *cathari,* or pure ones, were called heretics, as the Knights Templar would be in their turn a century later when the Holy Land would be lost. Since their foundation by Hugh de Payens, the Templars had been closely connected with the Court of Champagne and Provence and the Langue d'Oc. The writers of the medieval romances had made them the Knights of the Grail. The patrons of the culture of the south of France, certainly the richest and most civilised in Europe in the twelfth century, supported the Crusades and died while serving upon them. But the kings of France coveted the independent principalities of the south, and the popes distrusted the increasing power of the Cathar priests called *perfecti,* who wanted to reform the faith.

Both the Cathars and the Templars were influenced by Manichean and Sufi and Islamic doctrines as well as by early Christianity and the Cabbala. They believed the flesh was corrupt and life was an ascension to the spirit rather like the quest for the Grail. Lucifer, or the Devil, had brought about the Creation of man. Plato was right in the *Gorgias* when he quoted Euripides, "Who knows, if life be death, and if death be life?" Also right was the Grail King in *Diû Krône.* "We only seem to be alive, in reality we are dead." Through the mystical feast known as the *manisola* and the chaste kiss of reception into the faith called *consolamentum,* the *perfecti* took their initiates into the path of the spirit. This religion was certainly more pure and personal than Catholicism at the time, for an individual was made responsible for his or her own soul by an ascetic way of life. Cathar influences were evident in the quest for the Grail and in the early crusading quest for the holy city of Jerusalem. It was a tragedy for European expansion that the Albigensian Crusade was turned against a source of the previous Crusades to the East.

The heresy of the Langue d'Oc had caused concern in Rome for many years; but the provocation of open war lay in the assassination in 1208 of the papal legate by a servant of Raymond VI, the count of Toulouse. Innocent III declared the murdered man to be a holy martyr, killed by apparent fellow Christians. A crusade was declared against people the pope called heretics, "worse than even the Saracens." Just as the split between the Sunnis and the Shi'ites had bedevilled Muslim unity, so now the division between the Church of Rome and its reformers, inspired by puritan beliefs from the Near East, threatened the cohesion of Christendom. What made Innocent III's anathema even more ironical was that Raymond IV, then count of Toulouse, had been one of the leaders of the First Crusade, which had actually captured Jerusalem. Now that ferocity of a holy war was returned on the south of France itself.

As in the previous assaults on the Holy Land and on Constantinople, there were territorial as well as spiritual motives behind the crusade. The count of Toulouse was one of the greater princes of Europe, almost the equal of the king of France, who later would also destroy the Knights Templar for threatening his power. Paris was almost excluded from the Atlantic by the French possessions of the Plantagenets on the English throne. It desired access to the Mediterranean through the lands ruled by the counts of Toulouse. And though King Philip II himself refused to take the cross and attack his cousin's domain, he accepted that his vassals could well do so. Arnald-Almaric, the abbot of Cîteaux, toured the north of France with the bloodstained habit of the murdered legate and, as William de Puylaurens testified, "reached an agreement with the King and the barons, while various popular preachers began, in the name of the Apostolic authorities, to call for a war against the heretics, promising indulgences like those usually given to Crusaders who crossed the seas in order to save the Holy Land."

One of the lords who joined the crusade against the deviant Christians of the Midi was Simon de Montfort, who had refused to attack Constantinople on his way to Palestine in the Fourth Crusade. Yet now he did turn his sword on his own countrymen, probably looking for a fiefdom in the sun for himself. The previous Crusades had encouraged a class of noble mercenaries, who confused their ambitions over earth with the search for a place in heaven. Crusaders not only gained the remission of their sins, but also a moratorium on their debts, as well as a share of the plunder from their conquests and a stake in a captured country. Although the road now wound towards Béziers and Carcassone rather than Galilee and Jerusalem, it was a shorter route that promised more rewards.

By his fatal decision to use the weapon of the crusade against the heretics at home, Innocent III would lose the moral authority of the church, when it called for a holy war. And as in the destruction of Constantinople, he would demonstrate that the authority of Rome was more important to the papacy than the struggle against the infidel and the pagan. Although the Cathars did not believe in damnation or hell, because the power of Satan was only exercised in the material world, they were doubly damned in the view of the Holy See because they rejected the necessity for the Catholic priesthood. Each Cathar might approach God directly and become one of the *perfecti* after many years of abstinence and prayer. A saint could be self-made during life without the need for beatification after death.

The counts of Toulouse had not been able to check the spread of heresy in their domains. Raymond VI had *perfecti* at his court, while many of his nobles were related to Cathar families. At first Raymond decided to resist the Frankish crusade gathering at Lyons; but then he decided that submission was the better part of valour. He humiliated himself at Saint-Gilles, where the papal legate had been murdered; he was flogged by the birch, a halter was put round his neck, and he swore to take the cross himself against his own subjects and vassals, to remove all Jews from office, and to deliver up all heretics. Essentially, he accepted the control of Rome over his lands. And by joining the ranks of its invaders, he hoped to spare the people from the worst excesses of medieval warfare.

That was not to be. The first city to be invested, Béziers, fell immediately and the butchery was as savage as the capture of Jerusalem. Hardly a citizen escaped; the buildings were sacked and burned. In a notorious remark, Abbot Arnald-Almaric answered the question of distinguishing for punishment good Catholics from heretics by the words, "Kill them all: God will look after His own." He boasted after the massacre that twenty thousand people had been slain by the sword, regardless of age or sex. This outrage was both an excessive reaction to church propaganda that damned the people of the Langue d'Oc as children of Satan and a deliberate policy of terror. As William de Tudela wrote, the leaders of the crusade agreed that any place which refused to surrender should have all its defenders killed, "thinking that afterwards no man would dare to stand out against them because of widespread fear when it was seen what they had already done."

The young Raymond-Roger, viscount of Trencavel, had already decided to retreat with the best of his forces to the impregnable fortress of Carcassonne, where he could withstand an assault. But after a fortnight's siege, he surrendered himself as a hostage in order to preserve the lives of those within the citadel; these were allowed to depart as long as they left their possessions behind them. And so the crusaders captured more spoil and a fortress that would serve as the base for the completion of the expedition. In recognition of his ruthlessness as well as his martial qualities, Simon de Montfort was elected as the new viscount of Béziers and Carcassonne. He was charged by Rome with extirpating all heresy in the south of France, and he followed his charge with grim persistence. To some Catholics, he seemed like the flail of the Almighty, a second Judas Maccabaeus; to the Cathars and the church reformers, he appeared proof that the Devil did rule the earth. He continued a policy of terror, blinding and cutting off the noses of the defenders of Bram and sending them under the guidance of a one-eyed man to deter the occupiers of a neighbouring castle. And he was in charge of three mass burnings of the *perfecti,* who gladly suffered the stake and the flame in their martyrdom. They would rather char then recant.

Yet the ferocity shown towards the Cathars merely hardened their resistance. Raymond VI was now excommunicated, and Simon de Montfort moved against his capital at Toulouse, where the Catholics and the Cathars were roughly equal in their numbers and fought street battles against each other. For the first time, he was repulsed and forced to withdraw to face a threat from the rear. King Peter of Aragon had won a great victory in 1212 against the Moors at Las Navas de Tolosa and now protested to the pope about the diversion of a Christian crusade to the Langue d'Oc, when he needed the knights under Simon de Montfort to complete his victory against Islam in Spain. Innocent III was reminded of his priorities in the use of holy wars and reprimanded de Montfort, rather late in the day. "Not content with taking up arms against heretics, you have also fought, under the banner of the Crusade, against Catholic peoples." The indulgences given to the Crusaders for fighting against heretics were abrogated and transferred to campaigns against Islam in Spain or in the Holy Land. Rome seemed to have recovered a spiritual compass to steer its policies of aggression in the right direction.

Although the pope forbade King Peter to attack de Montfort, the ruler of Aragon had his own designs on the Langue d'Oc and invaded it with two thousand knights and a large army. Opposed by de Montfort with a force of half that size, King Peter and his royal guard were killed in an astonishing assault at Muret, where the two lines of battle met with such a shock that "it sounded like a whole forest falling under the axe." The Aragonese army retired over the Pyrenees, leaving de Montfort to resume the siege of Toulouse, which still resisted him. Joined by Prince Louis, the son of the king of France, and further Frankish Crusaders, he received the submission of the heretic city; its count fled, its walls were razed, it submitted to the orthodox Catholic faith.

At the Fourth Lateran Council of 1215, the count of Toulouse and his vassals were formally dispossessed for supporting heresy in their former domains. The suzerainty of the Langue d'Oc was given to Simon de Montfort. And yet in the *Chanson de la Croisade,* the pope was made to express doubts about his whole policy, saying: "Let Simon hold this country and rule it! My lords, since I may not deprive him of it, let him guard it well if he can, and take care that his claws are not clipped. For never while I live shall a crusade be preached to go to his aid."

The victory over Crusaders against Islam had guaranteed the dominion of Simon de Montfort; it was not the fruit of his own triumphs over the infidel. Even Innocent III had questioned his own strategy of losing one Catholic potentate to fight another with the goal of suppressing heresy. This was hardly the conquest of Christianity over the forces of darkness. It had led to the slaughter of hundreds of thousands of believers in the Church of Rome at the bloody hands of fellows of the same faith. The calling of such an original holy war within Christendom would lead to the crusade being used as a device of Italian diplomacy. The currency of faith was already debased and would end in dross.

The deposed count of Toulouse and his son Raymond were welcomed elsewhere in the south of France, at Marseilles and Avignon, where the people wished to retain their independence. For Simon de Montfort had already done homage to the king of France for his new fiefdom in the Midi, conferred at the Lateran Council. The question now appeared to be the maintenance of the independence of Provence rather than the suppression of the faith of an Anti-Christ. With a new army raised under the leadership of his energetic son, the old count of Toulouse could now resist Simon de Montfort. With the death of Pope Innocent in 1216 and help from Aragon, the count occupied Toulouse again and slaughtered the garrison of Franks. And finally after a long siege, de Montfort himself was killed by a stone fired from a gun by the women of Toulouse; it shattered his head to pieces. The crusade was also broken apart by the death of its leader, and this effort to destroy heresy by preaching divine vengeance was turned into the mere conquest of Provence by France. As the *Chanson de la Croisade* declared of Montfort: "If one may seek Christ Jesus in this world by killing men and shedding blood . . . by winning lands through violence and working for the success of empty pride; by supporting evil and eliminating good; by slaughtering women and slitting the throats of children—why, then he should wear a crown and shine with brilliance in Heaven."

This resistance and show of independence brought about the retribution of the past. Prince Louis arrived with a further army of crusaders and mercenaries and put Marmende to the sack and massacre, killing all its population of five thousand souls. But another siege of Toulouse failed, and Prince Louis and his crusaders had to retire to Paris without taking the southern city. Perhaps nothing was more significant in the mental conflict within the Capetian dynasty as to the right path to take in seeking grace by feats of arms, than the purchase of the Crown of Thorns by King Philip Augustus II from the ransackers of Constantinople. He housed this sacred object in the Sainte-Chapelle, built on a fortified island in the Seine in the heart of his capital. He had bought the symbol of Christ's martyrdom to live in his own city. To visit it was to pray in Paris. There was no need to take a pilgrimage to the old Jerusalem, when a new one was being built in the north of France. If there were still to be crusades, these should be in French interests against heretics on the borders, where the acquisition of territory would increase the security and revenues of the nation.

The old count of Toulouse died and begged to be buried in the Hospital of St. John at Jerusalem; but as he was still excommunicated, his wish was denied, although his skull was later kept safe by the Knights Hospitaller. The young count, Raymond VII, took back the rest of Provence, while the son of Raymond-Roger, viscount of Trencavel, also regained Carcassonne. A certain restoration of legitimacy appeared to be the legacy of the Albigensian crusade. But Rome and Paris still coveted the mastery of the territory. On the death of his father, King Philip Augustus, the new king, Louis VIII, demanded of Pope Honorius III that he could become sovereign of the south of France, if his naked grab for land was legitimised by the soiled name of crusade with indulgences for him and his barons and with excommunication for anyone who attacked him while he was away on his conquests. The Fifth Lateran Council pronounced the king of France the legitimate overlord of the Langue d'Oc, giving him the divine and legal excuse to conquer his way to the Mediterranean Sea.

Avignon held out against the French army for three months before it was forced to capitulate, but Toulouse did not, and the king himself died at the age of thirty-seven years. But the regent was his determined religious wife, Blanche of Castille, and she wanted the Midi for her eldest son. She had reserves sent to the crusaders who were applying a scorched-earth policy outside Toulouse. A fresh harshness of treatment towards the Provencal city was tempered by the evangelical work of St. Dominic with his new order of Black Friars, dedicated to the struggle against heresy in the Langue d'Oc. Their fanaticism increased the habitual ferocity of the crusaders against apostasy and infidelity. The saint himself was given inquisitorial powers to convince and convert heretics to the orthodox faith. The order of friars was born of this crusade against deviant Christians, while the bitter inheritance of inquisitions against those who protested against the corruption of the Catholic Church as well as those who selected a different way to God would write in blood the history of Europe for many centuries to come.

In the end, the settlement of this internecine holy war was through an arranged marriage. Raymond VII of Toulouse had only one daughter, Jeanne, and she was betrothed at the age of nine to another child, Alphonse of Poitiers, the second son of Blanche of Castille. The Langue d'Oc was her dowry, which her father only continued to rule as a dependant of France. The count of Toulouse would now be obliged to hunt down all heretics, to refuse to employ them or the Jews, and to resist all opponents to the marriage and the French alliance. He admitted waging war against the Holy Roman Church and the king of France, but he was relieved from excommunication because of his repentance. Like his father, he had to submit to being scourged for his sins with a rope round his neck in an act of public penance in the forecourt of Nôtre Dame. His degradation was the price of the preservation of the lives of the survivors from the long crusade against Provence.

Although the See of Rome seemed to dominate the Midi through the control of France, the Cathars were not defeated. They had allied their heresy with the independence movement. And the arrival of the full inquisition to the Langue d'Oc, spearheaded by the Dominicans, provided the martyrs a resistance cause. Even the bones of previous Cathars were condemned and exhumed and burned. The submissive count of Toulouse himself rebuked the Inquisition for leading men into error rather than towards the truth, but he could not dissipate the terror caused by their denunciations in their hunt for victims.

Although this systematic persecution drove the Cathars underground, they maintained their organisation in the forests and the mountains. And at the castle of Montségur, they had their headquarters in an inaccessible rock outcrop with colonies of adherents living in the caves and village below. The Dominicans referred to the citadel as the Synagogue of Satan, the very term used by the Cathars to describe the Church of Rome. On the eve of a rebellion against French authority by Count Raymond VII of Toulouse, a band of knights from Montségur assassinated seven monks who were serving as Inquisitors. This was a declaration of open war on Rome, and the failure of Count Raymond's revolt left Montségur in 1243 at the mercy of French reprisals. After a long siege of nine months, Montségur capitulated and its obdurate Cathar defenders were burned alive and became the stuff of legend.

Yet Montségur was a fortress, not another Temple of Solomon or Castle of the Grail, although that holy object was meant to have been removed with the Cathar treasure before the fall of the strongpoint. It was the practical headquarters of an Eastern belief that had infiltrated Christianity and that was prevalent elsewhere, particularly in Lombardy and the Balkans, rather as Alamut had served in the Isma'ili sect of the Assassins. It was a *protest* against the Catholic church, which would lead to the great later schism of Protestantism, also an independence movement that would undermine the authority of the Catholic church now also under pressure to defend its territorial claims in Italy.

That divided country was already split in a civil war between the Guelfs, who supported the papacy, and the Ghibellines, who supported the Holy Roman Emperor. The papacy preached another series of crusades throughout the thirteenth century, particularly against heretics on home soil and the foreign German emperors, whose base was now in Sicily—Frederick II and his sons Conrad and Manfred. The mistake of using the device of crusades to wage wars on behalf of the papal states, caught between the jaws of the kingdom of Sicily and the Holy Roman Empire of northern Italy and Germany, was a blind folly more dangerous than any heresy to the church. To demean the mission of Rome into the defence of the power and possessions of an earthly city was to destroy its symbolism and strength as a heavenly city, the New Jerusalem, the rock of faith built beside the Tiber as a reflection of heaven.

Most of the Cathar knights who escaped the slaughter at Montségur were received into the military order of the Temple of Solomon, which was already permeated with puritan and Oriental influences. Although Catharism would officially be persecuted from existence in the Langue d'Oc, its spirit would remain to burst out again in the religious civil wars of the sixteenth century. The apparent victory of Rome did not extinguish the embers of the revolt against it. The memory of a misdirected holy war is a bitter heritage. The wrongs perpetrated in the name of a particular church set the children's teeth on edge for generation after generation. As the massacre at Jerusalem still lodges in Muslim minds, so that of Béziers still irritates the Langue d'Oc. The sword of the unjustified faith is rarely forgiven, the wound never heals.

NINE

SAVIOUR OR ANTI-CHRIST

Thus the Church became a new polis, and the paradoxical link between the soul lost in irredeemable sin and its impossible yet certain redemption became an almost platonic ray of heavenly light in the midst of earthly reality: the leap became a ladder of earthly and heavenly hierarchies.

—Georg Lukács, *The Theory of the Novel*

The wandering peoples of Europe were still marching towards Jerusalem. From Normandy to Flanders to Lorraine and Germany, popular piety erupted in crusades of the poor and the landless, who were often called *pueri,* or "boys" or children. Two young men named Stephen and Nicholas had visions of Jesus in 1212 in northern France and the Rhineland, and they formed mobs of the dispossessed, who wandered south towards Rome and the Mediterranean. These travellers were not children, but they had a childlike faith that by procession and peaceful example, they could liberate the Holy City and recover the True Cross, which had only fallen into the hands of Islam because of the pride and folly of the Frankish knights. Between Easter and winter, these hordes of believing beggars travelled towards the sea, then dispersed or were sold into slavery by the merchants of Genoa and Marseilles. Some joined the church reformers called the pacific Waldensians, who had survived the Cathar crusade in Provence. For the "Children's Crusade" was as much a peasants' revolt against the corrupt authority of the Church of Rome as a dream of reaching Jerusalem itself. Had not St. Bernard denounced the riches of the great Abbey of Cluny in these terms: "The walls of the church are indeed wealthy, but her poor are needy. She clothes her stones with gold and leaves her children to go naked. The eyes of the rich are delighted at the expense of the poor. The delicate find good things to gratify their palate, but the miserable find nothing to satisfy their hunger."

To the church, indeed, such resistance to its authority was a pestilence. It was an infection, according to Isidore of Seville, which was caught by one man and spread to many. Raymond V, the count of Toulouse, had said that the heresy of the Cathars had infected the bowels of his city, while the orthodox Rainer Sacchoni wrote of "the poison which they drink from the mouth of the ancient serpent"—the devil of the Manicheanism of the Balkans and the Near East. When Catharism spread to England in the movement called the *Publicani* and was denounced by King Henry II at Oxford, he called the disease a form of leprosy. He had the stripped heretics expelled to die of cold and neglect, and so "the kingdom of England was cleansed of the infection" in the account of William de Newburgh. This "pious rigour" eliminated the plague by contradicting the Christian doctrine which the heretics had themselves denied: "I was hungry, and you gave me meat: I was a stranger, and you took me in."

The crusade against the Cathars had already debased the concept of using weapons to enforce a mission, said to be sacred. "Where one of her sons has done wrong," Hugh de Saint Quentin wrote of French intervention in the Langue d'Oc, "Rome should not send her eldest son to destroy him. It would be better to rebuke him gently." Two other knights, Palazi and Tomier, also criticised the change of direction of the attack towards heretic Toulouse. "He who abandons the Holy Sepulchre does not have a sincere faith in God. The priests and the French do little about the shame inflicted on the Lord, but God will be avenged on those whose greed has cut the voyages to Acre and Syria." A crusade of poor travellers would hardly restore the new resources that the Kingdom of Jerusalem needed to survive.

During the next hundred years, there were three other abortive crusades by shepherds and poor peasants with the aim of reaching Jerusalem. They came from the same area of northern France and the Low Countries and the Rhineland, which would always be vulnerable to millennial preaching and would remain a compost heap of dissent against the power of Rome. This smouldering triangle had contained the first sparks of the revival of trade and industry in the eleventh century. Here the manufacturing towns had swelled to burst out from the armour of feudal society with their demands for guilds and civic rights. The *genii* of the period had worked at Aachen in Lorraine at the Court of Charlemagne and his successors—John Scotus Erigena and Alcuin—while later original thinkers had taught between Cologne and Paris—particularly Abelard. They had fertilised and incited certain social conflicts—the townsfolk against the merchants, the peasants against the seigneurs, the women against male domination, the laypeople against the clergy, the rising middle classes against the feudal lords and the church. Yet without a passionate Christian faith, none of these forces of dissent could have ignited. Efforts to achieve freedom from the local bishop or the knight rarely meant that the citizen or the farmer rejected the spiritual authority of Rome.

There was a general recognition of the divisions of society. In a famous phrase, there were those who worked, those who fought, and those who prayed. Few except the Cathars had denied that the representatives of St. Peter still held the keys of heaven and of absolution. The popular crusades, however, could not accept the earthly hierarchies that led through the Catholic church and the pope to the heavenly angels sitting below the throne in the City of God. They wanted to reach a real Jerusalem through their faith without the benefit of misdirection by the church. Unworldly though the belief was and doomed to failure, it did presage a revolt against the power of Rome that would result in the great schisms of Renaissance Europe, the Protestant splits from the Catholic faith, which would lead to more holy wars than were ever fought between Sunnis and Shi'ites in the Near East.

Tragically, the pogrom against the Jews was a part of the popular crusades as it had been in the knightly ones. The mendicant and the missionary friars, the Franciscans as well as the Dominicans, more and more saw the Jews as the Anti-Christ. St. Augustine's tolerance towards them and their religion as witnesses of the City of God was changed to Pope Gregory's condemnation of the Talmud in 1236, while the persecution of Jewish communities, particularly in France, became a regular method of extortion throughout the thirteenth century. The king of France himself, Louis IX, was a crusader, who once said that the best way to argue with a Jew was to stick a sword into him. The missionary element in the new crusades with their Inquisitions against heretics was encouraging a fanaticism which would destroy any tolerance between the three founding faiths of the Levant.

As mysticism and millennialism began to permeate western Europe leading to outbreaks of rebellion among the Christian poor, so messianism and visions of the Apocalypse revived among the threatened Jewish communities. The excommunication of backsliders became more virulent, the hope of the return of the Messiah in Jerusalem more prevalent. Despairing after the Spanish, authorities also condemned the Talmud as blasphemous, the great scholar Nahmanides, or the Ramban, returned to Palestine to await the end. He found few Jews left in Jerusalem, but he encouraged them to reconstruct their synagogue and a centre for study of the Talmud. Their Torah scrolls had been taken away for safety, but these were now returned. And there the increasing number of Jewish pilgrims and some settlers might pray in the synagogue, still known as the Ramban. "Many come to Jerusalem, men and women from Damascus [and other parts]," Nahmanides wrote in a letter, "to see the place of the Temple and to mourn over its destruction. And he who has been privileged to see Jerusalem in its ruin will be privileged to see it restored to its glory."

Visions of Jerusalem both as a heavenly city and as the goal of a pilgrimage continued to stimulate the medieval imagination. Before maps of the actual site were brought back by returning Crusaders, the city was seen as that place described in the Book of Revelation and in the words of mystical preachers. In the *Beatus* of St. Sever, the plan of the Holy City demonstrated twelve gates and angels, one with a measuring rod: In the *Scivias* of the missionary Hildegard of Bingen, the City of God was a parallelogram set in a circle on a mountain. In Dante's *Divine Comedy* Jerusalem was described at the centre of the known globe, while Islamic influences on the Italian poet situated the entrances to hell and heaven there. But with actual descriptions coming back from the Kingdom of Jerusalem, the *Passionale* at Stuttgart showed the inner city surrounded by circular walls, while the plan at Cambrai Library put the holy *polis* in the more factual shape of an irregular rectangle with curving streets showing

The Seal of King Baldwin I of Jerusalem, showing the Church of the Holy Sepulchre, the Tower of David, and the Dome of the Rock.

A Seal of the Knights Templar, showing the Dome of the Rock crowned by the cross.

The Seal of Louis VII of France.

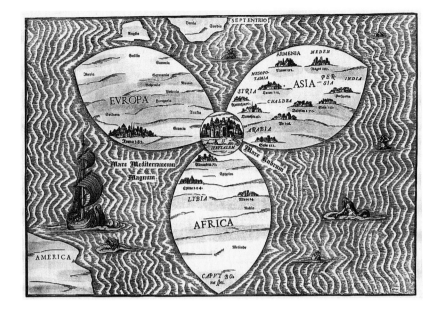

A map of the world designed in the form of a trefoil with the city of Jerusalem as the central piece. Woodcut, originally published in a book by Henry Buenting in 1581.

A probable portrait of Saladin, c.1180.

Muslim cavalry. From an etching by Erhard Renwick, 1486.

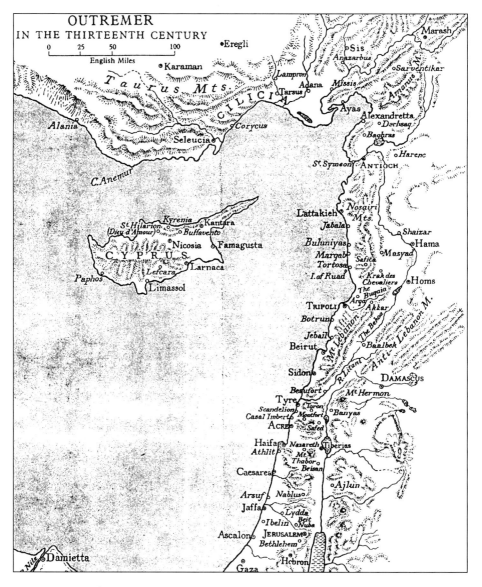

Outremer in the thirteenth century. From Steven Runciman's *A History of the Crusades, Volume III: The Kingdom of Acre* (Cambridge University Press, 1966).

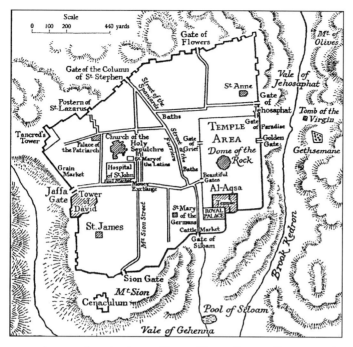

Jerusalem under the Latin Kings. From Steven Runciman's
*A History of the Crusades, Volume II: The
Kingdom of Jerusalem* (Cambridge
University Press, 1968).

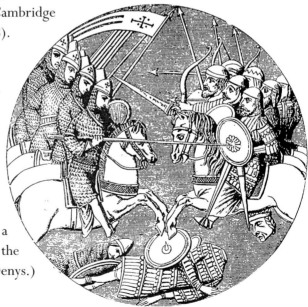

The earliest represen-
tation of the Knights
of the Military
Orders in battle
against the Muslims.
Godfrey de Bouillon
leads the Christians.
(An engraving of a
window in the
Church of St. Denys.)

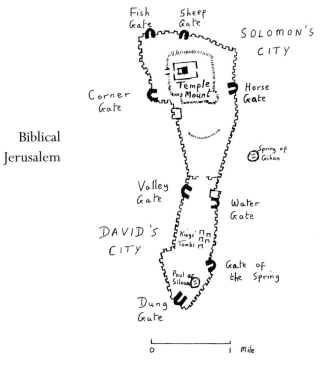

Biblical
Jerusalem

Fish
Gate
Sheep
Gate
SOLOMON'S
CITY
Temple
Mount
Horse
Gate
Corner
Gate
Spring of
Gihon
Valley
Gate
Water
Gate
DAVID'S
CITY
Kings'
Tombs
Gate of
the Spring
Pool of
Siloam
Dung
Gate

0   1 mile

The Destruction of
Jerusalem from the
Book of Maccabees.

vic oziam non bumane virtutis sed diuine gratie fatereetur. In ea vastatione fuit ea hominū strages ea fames miseroz funesta necessitas: Que si et ozdine nosere cupis Josephum lege. Non audita sed visa et cōmunia sibi cū ceteris referentur. Aeneas denicp Lit° romā cū patre suo Vespasiano triumpho celeberrimis egit. Simone qui vrbis exidij causa fuit in triūpho pducū postea laqueo p totā ciuitate traxerunt multis confossus vulnerib° interfecerūt. Vespasian° templi pacis edificauit vbi iudeoz preciosioza instrumēta si delicet tabulas legis penetraliū vela. τ alia multa reposuit. Ea aūt vrbis visq ad adriani principatus tpa latronū sicarioruq facta est receptaculi. Et p quiquagita annos: deinde ciuitatis misere reliquie. Quā postea Adrianus impatoz menib° τ edificijs instaurās τe suo noie belyam appellaut: et diu° Hieronym° ab

Quinta seculi etas Hic incipit et ortum babuit a captiuitate iudeoz in Babiloniam duratqz vic̃ ad christi iesu domini nostri natiuitatem per annos. 5 90. quis in hac supputatione aliqui aliter sentiunt. Unde qui recte captiuitatis annos numerare voluerint ab vndeamo Sedechie regni an no vt Eusebius ponit. nunc septuaginta captiuitatis annos in secūdū Darij annus terminabunt. Joseph° et diuus Hieronimus a.is. Josie regis vsq ad teraum Lyri regis annus. Honnulli ab vltimo regis Joacchim anno computant vsq ad vltimum Lyri annum. Et sane sentiendo septuaginta illi anni qui in tercio vel vltimo Lyri anno terminantur. proprie captiuitatis iudaice anni dicuntur. Illi vero qui in secdo Darij terminantur proprie complete transmigratiōis sunt. Et hec principalioz et precipua sacre scripture era bal

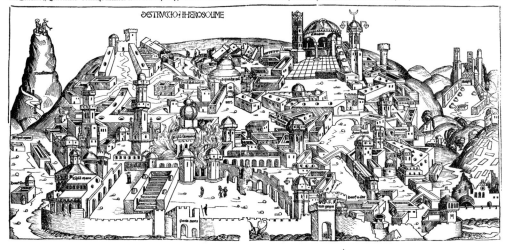

ÐESTRVCIO IHEROSOLIME

The destruction of Jerusalem. From the book by H. Schedel, 1492.

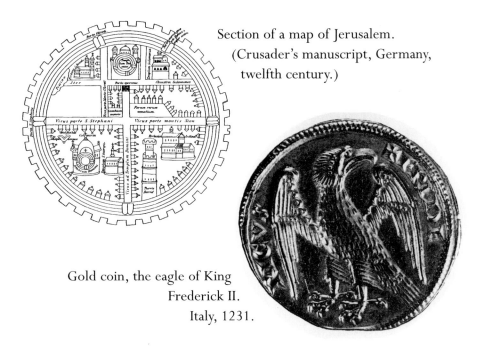

Section of a map of Jerusalem.
(Crusader's manuscript, Germany,
twelfth century.)

Gold coin, the eagle of King
Frederick II.
Italy, 1231.

Section from
a map of
Jerusalem.
(Crusader's
manuscript,
twelfth century.)

The Seal of King Baldwin I of Jerusalem, depicting the Tower of David,
twelfth century.

The Seal of the Archbishop of Caesarea, depicting the walls and the
tower of the city, twelfth century.

the ways from the Church of the Sepulchre to the Dome of the Rock. It was not that imagination was giving way to naturalism so much as that the unearthly and actual Jerusalem existed simultaneously in the minds of most Crusaders, high or low.

In a sense, the elevation of the Jerusalem of the other and this world within the dissenting regions of Europe was a deliberate counterattack on the pretensions of Rome, trying to supersede the original bedrock of the Christian faith with its own claim to be the foundation stone of the Christian church, through the mission and martyrdom of St. Peter. In the utopian vision, Jerusalem could never be replaced as the image of the City of God upon earth. There the Temple had been built, there the Son of God had been the sacrifice for the sins of man. However much Rome might try to become an alternative for the Holy City with its ordered hierarchies rising towards a disciplined hereafter, its obvious policies against heretics and against threats to the papal states of central Italy muddied its divine claims. And with the succession of a strange young man of destiny to the throne of the Holy Roman Empire, the conflict between northern European aspirations and papal supremacy would lead to the most unlikely Crusade of all, a designed accommodation with Islam after a show trial of strength, which would yield Jerusalem back to Christianity without a fight.

Frederick Hohenstaufen, who was to be known as Stupor Mundi, "the Wonder of the World," had the backing of Pope Innocent III, when he was elected at the age of eighteen years old to the throne of Charlemagne. He immediately took the cross to join a Fifth Crusade, although his relationship with Islamic thought from his childhood at the court of the kings of Sicily had already made him an admirer of the Koran rather than a scourge of the infidel. In the Kingdom of Jerusalem, a new intervention from Europe was not welcome. As the bishop of Acre, James of Vitry, informed Pope Honorius III, the start of another round of holy war would ruin the trade and endanger the security of the Christians already in Palestine. There were three thousand merchants from Genoa and Pisa and Venice trading in Cairo at the time, while the Egyptian sultan al-Kamil had no wish to disturb his good commercial relations with the West. But in 1218, three fleets from England and France and Frisia arrived to reinforce Duke Leopold of Austria, and these forces succeeded in capturing the port of

Damietta in Egypt the following year. Although the Egyptian sultan did not want a *jihad,* the arrival of the severe Spanish cardinal Pelagius turned the enterprise into a conflict of the faiths. He intended to take Cairo and destroy the Ayyubid Empire, which protected the three great holy cities of the Near East. When the young Emperor Frederick II would respect his vow and arrive with his army, the Nile would become a Christian delta.

Yet Frederick did not come, and the fearful Sultan al-Kamil made an astonishing peace proposition. He would deliver Jerusalem with its walls dismantled, along with the True Cross and all of Palestine west of the Jordan River to the Crusaders in return for their withdrawal from Egypt. The knights and lords of Outremer wanted to accept this generous and extraordinary offer, which was the whole point of any religious Crusade—the possession of the Holy Land. But Cardinal Pelagius refused. He wanted more, even the conversion of the "perfidious and worthless" infidels to Catholicism. The Christian army marched on Cairo and became bogged down in silt. The Muslim forces cut the dykes and marooned the Frankish armies, compelling them to save their skins by a complete evacuation of Egypt. The refusal to accept the gift of Jerusalem was the prelude to total humiliation. The intransigence of Pelagius had cost Rome the mastery over the Holy City.

There was a new missionary fervour in the ranks of the Crusaders. James of Vitry, who understood the compromises necessary to survive with Muslim neighbours in the Near East, came near to condemning the tactics of the zealous Franciscans and Dominicans, who were now arriving to preach and to convert unbelievers. As he wrote, "the Saracens listen willingly to the Minor Friars when they speak of the faith of Christ (*also a Muslim prophet*) and the teaching of the Gospels. Yet when their words openly contradict Muhammad, who appears in their sermons as a perfidious liar, they strike the friars without respect, and if God did not protect them marvellously, they would almost be murdered and driven from the cities."

Before Frederick II left on his Crusade to the Holy Land, he had married Yolanda, the daughter of John of Beirut, and so had acquired a claim to the title of the king of Jerusalem. An Arab diplomat, Fakhr al-Din, was sent to report on Frederick's behaviour in his court at Palermo. To his surprise, the Ayyubid ambassador found that the German emperor spoke fluent Arabic and admired Islamic thought, while he had nothing but contempt for the pope and most of Western civilisation. Frederick now began a long philosophic correspondence with the sultan of Cairo on the nature of the universe and the soul, which was a prelude to assessing the outcome of an expedition to take up his claim to the title of king of Jerusalem. He even allowed his Muslim guards and advisers to pray in the direction of Mecca, and he did not respect the papal decree of the new pope, Gregory IX, in 1227, forbidding the call of the *muezzin* to prayer by the followers of Muhammad. He concentrated his Muslim subjects in the city of Lucera in Apulia and recruited some of them to protect him from Catholic fanaticism.

Indeed, Gregory IX would not tolerate Frederick's consorting with Islam. He excommunicated the German emperor because he had not fulfilled his oath to go on a crusade. This obvious use of spiritual power against temporal dominion provoked condemnations of the papacy from imperial supporters. "The cross was given so that one might be redeemed from sin," Frederick noted. "Now that one is denied this by the ban, how can one save one's soul?" It was a fair question, which was also ironical. After all, the Crusade to the East was a method of redeeming sins and saving one's soul. Yet excommunication had not been used before to condemn those who had not yet gone. Peire Cardenal was correct in the motive for the anathema. "Kings, emperors and nobles used to rule the world," he wrote. "Today I see sovereignty held by the clergy through robbery, treachery, hypocrisy, violence and preaching." The Roman church was anxious to make Europe its own and expel Emperor Frederick from his own inheritance.

In point of fact, Frederick was quite happy to be prodded on to his mission to the East. His friend the sultan of Egypt had fallen out with his brother in Damascus, who was now acting as the sovereign over Jerusalem. The sultan said that he would help deliver the Holy City to Frederick without much of a fight. Yet as Frederick set out, the brother of the sultan died, leaving him to take possession of Palestine and besiege Damascus. The coming of a new Crusade to Palestine was no longer welcome. And on his arrival at Acre, the emperor found that the guardian warriors of the Holy Land, the Templars and the Hospitallers, would not serve him because he had been excommunicated. Only the Teutonic Knights would fight with a fellow German, even if he had fallen out with the pope, who was actually gathering an army to invade the imperial lands in southern Italy and calling it another Crusade.

With trouble at home, Frederick was not prepared to protract negotiations with the sultan of Egypt about the surrender of Palestine. He put on a show of strength, marching his small forces, including his own imperial guard, recruited mainly from Arabs in Sicily, towards Jaffa and building its ruined walls again. He also appealed to al-Kamil to help him save face in the West, writing to him: "I am your friend. It was you who urged me to make this trip. The Pope and all the Kings of the West know of my mission. If I return with empty hands, I will lose a lot of prestige. Pity me and give me Jerusalem, so that I may hold my head high!" The sultan was not unsympathetic, but he knew of the consequences of an easy surrender of the Holy City. So he replied, "I must also take account of public opinion. If I deliver Jerusalem to you, not only would it lead to the Caliph [of Baghdad] condemning my action, but also to a religious revolt that would threaten my throne."

The solution was to pretend that there would be a long and bloody war if there was not a compromise. And for the first time in history, two of the militant religions of the Near East agreed to share the Holy City. The Temple area on Mount Moriah along with the Dome of the Rock and the al-Aqsa mosque would stay in Muslim hands with the right of Islamic worshippers to enter the city and pray there. Emperor Frederick was given control of the rest of Jerusalem along with Bethlehem; a corridor of land running to the sea at Jaffa; western Galilee with Nazareth, and the lands around Sidon. Frederick was even permitted to rebuild the walls of the Holy City. Peace was declared between Christian and Muslim for ten years, except for the principality of Antioch, and all prisoners were to be released on both sides.

At first, this treaty seemed a triumph of reason and accommodation. The Qadi of Nablus gave Emperor Frederick the keys of Jerusalem and took him there to be crowned. Because he was excommunicated, no Catholic priest would carry out the ceremony, so he went to the Church of the Holy Sepulchre and put the crown of the Kingdom of Jerusalem on his own head. It showed that he was the sovereign there without any need of intercession from the Church of Rome. His diplomacy had won

Jerusalem for the Christian faith, his understanding with Islam triumphed without the benefit of a Crusade declared by the pope.

The Qadi of Nablus was amazed at Emperor Frederick's behaviour when they visited the Dome of the Rock and the al-Aqsa mosque. Finding a priest with a Bible trying to enter the mosque, Frederick dressed him down, asking, "What brings you to this place? By God, if one of you dares step in here again without permission, I will pluck out his eyes!" And that night, the Qadi asked that prayers should not be called by the *muezzin* so that the emperor should not be disturbed. But Frederick objected the following morning, telling the Qadi that he had done wrong, "for if I spent this night in Jerusalem, it was above all to hear the *muezzin*'s call in the night." But for all that, the Muslims were hardly impressed by Frederick's presence. He was covered with red hair except where he was bald, Ibn al-Jawzi noted, and he was shortsighted. As a slave, he would have been worth two hundred dirhams.

Frederick's feat in negotiating the transfer of Jerusalem did not earn the forgiveness of his Christian foes. His gains seemed as indefensible as his cowardly conduct. The Holy City could not be held if it was connected by a sleeve of land to the sea. And the Templars were outraged. They were sworn to the defence of the Temple, which was held to be on the site of the Dome of the Rock, while their headquarters had been in the al-Aqsa mosque—and these very places had been left to Islam. The barons of Palestine were also furious at Frederick's self-coronation, for he was not the king of Jerusalem, but only the regent for his small son by Queen Yolanda. The Templars even informed al-Kamil that they would aid in the German emperor's assassination. Informed by his friends of this plot, Frederick decided to leave for Sicily to defend his lands there against papal attack. As he left, he was pelted with dung and offal by the butchers of Acre. Reeking and filthy, the saviour of Jerusalem sailed away from his brief kingdom.

Islamic fury against Sultan al-Kamil was even more extreme. "As soon as the news that the Holy City had been ceded to the Franj became known," Ibn al-Jawzi recorded, "the lands of Islam were swept by a mighty storm. Because of the gravity of the event, public processions of mourning were organised." He himself was ordered to speak of the matter in the great mosque of Damascus. "The new disaster that has befallen us," he declared, "has broken our hearts." Worse was to happen, because al-Kamil took

Damascus, forcing his nephew to flee to the fortress of Kerak, from where he staged a lightning raid against Jerusalem to destroy its new fortifications. Yet he also was forced to recognise the suzerainty of the Franks over the Holy City when his uncle died and he needed the support of the infidels in a family war against his cousins for control of the Ayyubid Empire. And so Jerusalem remained precariously in Christian hands, like a nut caught in the crack that divided its enemies.

To make matters worse for the Kingdom of Jerusalem, a series of Christian civil wars began. On his voyage towards the Holy Land, Emperor Frederick had accepted his sovereignty over Cyprus, expelling the Ibelin family and leaving it under the control of five *baillis* of his choice. In a counterattack, John of Beirut defeated the army of the *baillis* and became regent of the island until the majority of its boy king, Henry. But the resources of the island were not used for the defence of the Holy Land. In fact, the Ibelins had to defend Cyprus and Palestine from reinforcements sent out by Emperor Frederick, who had his excommunication lifted after a truce with the pope. Internecine strife was destroying the unity of Christendom in the Near East as much as in Europe.

The kingdom of Armenia had long coveted the principality of Antioch. Their ruling families were related by marriage, and there were rival claimants for the small Crusader outpost against Aleppo and the Ayyubid Empire. After a series of invasions, the Armenians captured Antioch and installed their candidate as its prince for a period of three years, after which he was ousted. Excluded from the terms of the peace between the European Frederick and Sultan al-Kamil, Antioch continued to harass and annoy the Muslims. The Templars in particular did so from their border fortress at Baghras until they were decimated in a raid on the nearby castle of Darbsaq. As always, the military orders had an unholy capacity for upsetting the equilibrium of the Levant.

At the end of the ten years' truce between Emperor Frederick and Sultan al-Kamil, the Muslim cause was weakened by the death of their leader, opening the way to a renewed civil war between his Ayyubid heirs. Pope Gregory IX sought to exploit the opportunity by preaching another Crusade, which was headed by the king of Navarre and other Frankish nobles. A thousand knights reached Acre, where a decision was made to attack both Egypt and Damascus. Part of the army was defeated at Gaza, but the quarrels between the Ayyubid cousins allowed the Kingdom of Jerusalem to make contradictory alliances with both Damascus and Egypt, securing its fortresses and frontiers for a while. Yet the Templars and the Hospitallers were now almost at open warfare with each other, and anarchy was the form of government of Outremer. The Templars even burned the great mosque at Nablus and massacred its citizens, as though holy war were not a thing of the past.

A fatal alliance by the Templars with Ismail of Damascus, one of the claimants to the Ayyubid Empire, provoked the final loss of Jerusalem, the desecration of its Christian sites, and another massacre of its people. Ismail had offered the Templars and the crusading kingdom a part of the plunder in another expedition against his rival Ayyub in Egypt, but he was suddenly attacked in Syria by the remnants of a ferocious war band of ten thousand Khwarismian Turks, urged by Ayyub to act as guerrillas behind his rival's lines and to pillage their way to join the Egyptian forces in the south. Moving from Damascus to Galilee, the Khwarismians reached Jerusalem in the summer of 1244. The Holy City was hardly defended. The monks and nuns of the Armenian convent of St. James were slaughtered, as were the Latin and other priests of the Church of the Holy Sepulchre, which was set on fire after the bones of the kings of Jerusalem had been ravaged from their tombs. Much of the rest of the city was put to the torch, while of the six thousand citizens allowed to leave under safe-conduct, only three hundred reached Jaffa and the sea. After this further massacre, Jerusalem was destined to slip from prominence to relative insignificance, except in the visions of the faithful. As the thirteenth-century German monk and pilgrim Burchard of Mount Zion noted, "At this day there are very few inhabitants for so great a city, because the people within dwell in continual terror."

With their Muslim allies from Damascus, the response of the Christians in Acre was to march against Egypt. Raising the largest army put in the field since the disaster at the Horns of Hittin, the Crusaders and the Damascenes attacked a large Egyptian force under the young *mamluk* emir Baybars at La Forbie near Gaza. The Khwarismian horde routed the Muslim troops on the Christian side and took the Frankish knights in the flank. The grand master of the Temple was killed, the grand master of the Hospital taken prisoner. Less than a hundred knights survived death or capture to hold out in the fortress of Ascalon. The coastal Kingdom of Jerusalem seemed doomed, but was again given a lease of life because of the Muslim war of succession. In a counterattack, Ayyub seized Damascus and later the Khwarismians were annihilated, after taking up the cause of Ismail. This victory was followed by the reduction of Ascalon, and Ayyub seemed set again to unite Saladin's old domains. Yet two threats, one from within and one from outside, would destroy the dynasty. The *mamluks* and the Mongols, slave warriors and steppe horsemen, would inherit most of the Near East.

Under Jenghiz-Khan, the upstart and nomadic Mongols had raided as far as Bulgaria as well as capturing Baghdad. Other expeditions devastated Russia and Hungary and were poised to invade western Europe, before their recall because of the death of the Great Khan Ogodai. Later, the Seljuk Turks and then the Armenians were routed and made their submission. The Christian kingdoms seemed under threat in both Europe and Outremer, and yet nothing was planned except another crusade by King Louis IX of France against Egypt. The chosen enemy was the old one and the wrong one, the crusade was misplaced, the present danger was misunderstood.

For the Muslims had been more destroyed by the Mongols than the frontiers of Christendom. To the long-suffering Ibn al-Athir, the incursion of the Mongols seemed to be the beginning of the end of the world. He lamented that what was happening was so horrible that he did not dare mention it:

"It is not easy to announce that death has fallen upon Islam and the Muslims. Alas! I would have preferred my mother never to have given birth to me, or to have died without witnessing all these evils. If one day you are told that the earth has never known such calamity since God created Adam, do not hesitate to believe it, for such is the strict truth. Nebuchadnezzar's massacre of the children of Israel and the destruction of Jerusalem are generally cited as among the most infamous tragedies of history. But these were nothing compared to what has happened now. No, probably not until the end of time will a catastrophe of such magnitude be seen again."

For the papacy, the advent on the world scene of the emperor Frederick II also seemed to herald the coming of the end of the world. In 1239, Pope Gregory wrote to the archbishop of Canterbury about the Hohenstaufen sovereign and quoted the Book of Revelation: "A beast arose out of the sea . . . it opened its mouth to utter blasphemies against God." Frederick was seen as one of the signs and forerunners of Armageddon, perhaps the Anti-Christ himself who would briefly reign on earth before the rule of the resurrected Jesus Christ. But as an apocalyptic figure, he also appeared to imperial supporters and even dissenters and the followers of the popular crusades as another Messiah, who would overthrow the corrupt papacy and lead all true Christians to Jerusalem and the Promised Land. Even after his death in 1250 at the age of fifty-seven, he was to attain the legendary position of his forebear Frederick Barbarossa, a mystical figure who might rise again to usher in an era of peace with the Muslims and an urban Eden to pilgrims to the holy places. His accommodation with Islam had, after all, regained Jerusalem, and his followers would become rebels against Catholic orthodoxy. Their vision of an earthly paradise of peace in the Near East would incite their protests against the wars and Inquisitions in the name of the faith still preached by Rome.

TEN

FINAL LOSS

"It profiteth a man nothing that he should delight himself with God."

—The Book of Job

 King Louis IX of France had a merciless piety. Nothing stood between him and doing right. Nothing he did would he accept as wrong. He was a man of his cruel word: He never broke it except in dealing with heretics and infidels. With the pope driven from Italy itself in 1245 by the "Anti-Christ" emperor Frederick II, and the barons of Outremer decimated after their defeat near Gaza the year before, the king of France could see well the necessity for another champion of Christendom to take the field in Europe and the Near East. For three years, Louis IX prepared his Crusade, a time which enabled Emperor Frederick to inform his friend the sultan of Egypt of the impending attack. Then an armada sailed from Marseilles and Genoa to concentrate all forces in Cyprus before an assault on the Nile delta, now considered the acceptable detour on the road to Jerusalem.

Damietta was again the objective. After all, it was considered so valuable that the Holy City had been offered in exchange for its possession. After a fierce battle on the beaches, the Muslim forces evacuated the port city, which fell without a siege. The great mosque was turned into a cathedral, and the three military orders along with the three Italian maritime trading cities were assigned headquarters and concessions. Again Sultan Ayyub offered Jerusalem in exchange for Damietta, but the king of France would not trust or treat with the infidel. On his deathbed, the sultan ordered his advance guard forward to Mansourah, which stood between the Crusaders and Cairo. And then he died, leaving the defence of Egypt to his widow and an aged general.

Finding a ford across the river that separated the Christian and Muslim camps, the Templars and the Frankish knights surprised the Islamic forces and routed them, killing their general and pushing them back into the alleys of Mansourah. The astute emir Baybars, the victor of La Forbie, kept the gates of the city open and allowed the rashness of the European cavalry to cause its self-destruction. Assailed in the narrow streets by *mamluks* and crossbowmen, the charge was turned into a carnage. Only five of three hundred Templars survived. The king of France had followed the sortie by crossing the river, and he repulsed the counterattack of the *mamluk* cavalry, which was driven back into Mansourah. Now the Christians could claim a sort of victory from their defeat. Although their new camp was besieged, they had enough men to hold it; but they were stranded in the dust, unable to proceed and hardly to withdraw. A slow retreat along the Nile ended in a total surrender, with King Louis himself put into chains. On every night for a week, three hundred of the prisoners were beheaded, but then King Louis was allowed to redeem the rest by the payment of a million bezants and the surrender of Damietta.

While the king of France survived, the last Ayyubid sultan of Egypt did not. A *mamluks* revolt of these Turkish Circassian slaves led by Baybars murdered him and installed the senior *mamluk* general in power in Egypt. He respected the terms of the Frankish evacuation, although the amount of the ransom was reduced and the wounded prisoners were killed. Louis IX remained in Outremer, trying to profit from a new divide between *mamluk* Cairo and Ayyubid Damascus in which he might regain Jerusalem as Emperor Frederick had; but his diplomacy came to nothing. Although he treated both with the Isma'ili sect of the Assassins and with the advancing Mongols as possible allies against the Ayyubid heirs and the *mamluk* pretenders, he failed to reach more than an understanding with them not to attack each other. And after four years at Acre, he sailed back to France, achieving nothing except a further weakening of the power of the Kingdom of Jerusalem.

As in ancient Rome, so in Egypt. Long ago the mercenary imperial guard had taken over the role of emperor, and now the *mamluk* slave warriors were the masters of the Nile. They had two primary enemies to conquer before they would turn their attentions towards the Christian remnants along the shores of Palestine. The first were the true heirs of Saladin, who had extended the Ayyubid Empire as far as Mosul. The second were the Mongols, who had set up a Persian Ilkhanate after Hulegu, whose wife was a Nestorian Christian, had destroyed the Assassins at Alamut in 1256 and captured Baghdad two years later. His progress appeared irresistible. To the Christians of Asia, he seemed a new Emperor Constantine with his Christian queen, come to save Jerusalem. The following year, the Mongol cavalry took Mosul and Aleppo and Damascus itself, eliminating the last of the Ayyubids. In these cities, the Muslims were massacred and the Christians were spared. Then the Mongols swept on a year later towards Jerusalem, as once the Huns had launched themselves on imperial Rome.

It appeared that the rule of Islam in the Near East was finished. For the king of Armenia and the prince of Antioch had joined Hulegu and his Christian queen, although she preferred the Greek Orthodox rite to the Latin one. At this time, the Christian kingdoms of the eastern Mediterranean were surrounded by the Mongols and had to accommodate or die. Only the *mamluks* in Egypt resisted the advance of the mounted tribesmen from central Asia. It was fortunate for them that Hulegu himself and most of his army had to move east to solve a question of the Mongol succession, while his Christian deputy Kitbuqa was left to hold the recent conquests with inferior forces. Although the *mamluks* themselves were quarrelling over the succession to the sultanate of Egypt, they found a formidable way to advance with the emir Baybars towards Galilee. The Christians at Acre gave them a safe-conduct and supplies to confront the Mongols: for they could not. And in 1260 at Ayn Jalud, also called the Pools of Goliath, the *mamluks* surrounded the charging Mongols and destroyed them and beheaded their general Kitbuqa in a decisive victory that preserved the power of Islam in the Middle East.

For the Mongols had believed in Shamanism until this period, and it was touch and go whether they would be converted to the doctrines of Jesus Christ or the Prophet, Muhammad. If the Christian Kitbuqa had reached Egypt and had overthrown the last major Islamic power this side of North Africa, the Christian elements in the Mongol camp would have been strengthened. But as it was, the *mamluks* were to grow in power and reforge the Ayyubid Empire and destroy the Kingdom of Jerusalem and Antioch and the vestiges of Christian control of the Levant. Soon after Ayn Jalud, the *mamluks* retook Damascus and Aleppo. These successes were followed by a conspiracy led by the emir Baybars, in which he killed the current sultan and was elected in his place. A formidable Turk and an able strategist, he would make Egypt into the supreme power of Islam by the end of the thirteenth century.

For the Christian European kingdoms were dissipating their religious zeal in unholy wars. After the death of Emperor Frederick II, his son Conrad was displaced by his bastard brother Manfred, who became theoretically king of Sicily and Jerusalem. The papacy disapproved of the usurpation, and Urban VI found a new candidate to replace the Hohenstaufen dynasty, the ambitious and ruthless Charles of Anjou, the youngest brother of King Louis IX. Taxes were raised to equip an army on another "Crusade": On the death of Urban a new French pope, Clement VI, called on Charles of Anjou to invade Italy. He defeated and killed Manfred in 1265 at the battle of Benevento and three years later captured and beheaded Conrad after a fight at Tagliacozzo. The Hohenstaufens were nearly extirpated, and Charles of Anjou began to dream of an Italian empire to link with his French possessions and to dominate Constantinople and the Near East. When Pope Clement died, he blocked the appointment of a new pope, who might challenge his authority, and he diverted his elder brother's martial piety into a futile Crusade against North Africa, which threatened Sicily with a Muslim invasion. King Louis was persuaded that the emir of Tunis was ready to become a convert to the Christian faith and would do so under threat. Louis led a French fleet to Tunis in the heat of summer, where plague did the work of defence. The army was rotted by disease and the sun. The king of France died, and many of his nobles and men. Charles of Anjou saved the expedition and received a bribe from the emir of Tunis to sail away. The last words of the pious Louis were said to be, "Jerusalem, Jerusalem."

He had been misdirected. And for the next six hundred and fifty years there would be no Christian Crusade against the Islamic occupiers of Jerusalem. The Christian and Jewish presence there would be dependent on *mamluk* and later Seljuk tolerance. In a strange forecast of a holocaust to come, the Jews were made to wear yellow turbans in the Holy City, while the Christians had to wear blue ones. Yet more Jews returned after the example of Nahmanides, who had declared it was a religious duty to settle in Palestine "incumbent upon each generation; binding upon every one of us, even in time of exile." By the fourteenth century, the pilgrim Isaac ben Joseph ibn-Chelo found quite a numerous Jewish community in the sacred site:

> Among the different members of the holy congregation at Jerusalem are many who are engaged in handicrafts such as dyers, tailors, shoe-makers, and other trades. Others carry on a rich commerce in all sorts of things and have fine shops. Some are devoted to science, as medicine, astronomy and mathematics. But the greater number of their learned men are working day and night at the study of the Holy Law [the Torah and Talmud] and of the true wisdom, which is the Cabbala. These are maintained out of the coffers of the community, because the study of the law is their only calling. There are also at Jerusalem excellent calligraphists, and the copies are sought for by strangers, who carry them away to their own countries. I have seen a Pentateuch written with so much art that several persons at once wanted to ac-quire it, and it was only for an excessively high price that the Chief of the Synagogue of Babylon carried it off with him to Baghdad.

Yet ibn-Chelo found himself excluded from the Temple Mount by the Muslim authorities. They would not allow him to set foot in the al-Aqsa mosque nor in the Dome of the Rock. "Alas, by reason of our sins," he lamented, "where the sacred building [the Temple of Solomon] once stood, its place is taken today by a profane temple, built by the King of the Ish-maelites [the Muslims] when he conquered Palestine and Jerusalem from the uncircumcised [the Christians]." Yet the Jews were allowed still to say their prayers at the Western Wall, which was built on the approaches to the ancient Temple and remained "one of the seven wonders of the Holy City."

Meanwhile, the new sultan of Egypt, Baybars, planned the end of the Kingdom of Jerusalem as well as the Christian powers of Armenia and Antioch, which had aided the Mongols. Hulegu died in 1265 and his passing removed the greatest threat to Cairo. Baybars attacked the Christian strongholds in southern Palestine. He captured Caesarea and Haifa and then the Hospitaller castle of Athlit followed by the Templar fortress at Safed, which dominated Galilee. When the Templars surrendered on the promise of a safe-conduct to Acre, Baybars showed no mercy and had them all beheaded. He was bringing the *jihad* again to the Holy Land.

The next objective of the sultan of Egypt was the destruction of the northern Christian states. Attacking from Aleppo, he routed the Armenian army and occupied and plundered the capital of Sis, preventing the kingdom from anything but a defensive policy. In 1682, he stormed Antioch and killed or enslaved its whole population in an orgy of brutality and humiliation. The principality, which had been the northern bastion of the Christian world in the Levant for nearly two centuries, was now devastated and its importance gone. The Templars abandoned their fortress at Baghras and retired to Palestine for the last struggle, which was surely to come.

Sultan Baybars gloated about his cruel triumph. In a letter to the surviving prince of Antioch, Bohemond VI, he declared:

> Oh, if only you had seen your knights trampled by our horses, your houses looted and at the mercy of everyone who passed by, your treasure weighed in the scales, your women sold in the market-place four for a gold coin. If only you had seen your churches utterly destroyed, the crucifixes torn apart, the pages of the Gospels scattered, the tombs of the patriarchs trodden underfoot. If only you had seen your Muslim enemy trampling down your altars and holy of holies, cutting the throats of deacons, priests and bishops, the patriarchate irremediably abolished, the powerful reduced to powerlessness! If only you had seen your palaces given over to the flames, the dead devoured by the flames of this world before being devoured by the flames of the next

world, your castles and all their attendant buildings wiped off the face of the earth, the Church of St. Paul totally destroyed so that nothing is left of it, and seeing all this you would have said: "Would to God that I were dust."

An English Crusade reached Acre in a forlorn attempt to save the Holy Land. For Baybars was picking off the inland castles one by one, even capturing the impregnable Krak des Chevaliers in Syria. King Henry III of England had taken the cross, but he was too old to fulfil his vow. So he sent his son and heir Prince Edward with a thousand knights towards Jerusalem. Edward was sickened at the connivance between the Christians and the Muslims in Acre. The Venetians and the Genoese competed in supplying Sultan Baybars with all of his war materials, while the knights of the kingdom of Cyprus would not join him in a mainland Crusade.

Embassies to the Mongols provided Prince Edward with temporary assistance, but their priorities had nothing to do with the recapture of the Holy City. And when Baybars employed one of the last communities of Assassins in Syria to strike down this intruder at Acre, Prince Edward was badly wounded and barely escaped with his life. Disillusioned as so many of the Crusaders were by the difference between the dream of Jerusalem and the reality of Levantine politics, he returned home to be crowned on the death of his father. All he had achieved was a ten-year truce with Baybars, that the coastal strip of the Kingdom of Jerusalem might still survive on *mamluk* sufferance.

The new pope, Gregory X, had sailed with Prince Edward to Palestine, and he commissioned a report on why the crusading movement had gone wrong. Gilbert de Tournai reported that the people of Europe were frequently taxed for the recapture of Jerusalem; but many of these Crusades never took place. It was rather like Christ throwing the money changers out of the Temple, which could only be purified by their absence. The German bishop Bruno of Olmütz claimed that Crusades to the Near East were out of date and should be directed against the pagan Slavs in northern Europe. William de Tripoli was more of a missionary. He thought that the Mongols would destroy Islam, and a peaceful conversion of them would ensure that the Holy City would remain in Christian hands without a fight. But Humbert de Romans took a harder line, preaching another armed Crusade to the Near East; there, the true faith could only follow the sword. He wrote against the debasement of the militant ideal, the loss of zeal for the recapture of Jerusalem through sloth and sin.

Although the advice was excellent, Gregory X had frittered away the flame of holy war in the embers of papal self-interest in Europe. The struggle for supremacy between the kings of the rising nation-states and their feudal barons was superseding the push towards the East and spiritual salvation. Oddly enough, as Giotto and Dante, Wolfram von Eschenbach and Pisano, St. Thomas Aquinas and St. Francis of Assisi were preaching the unity of the Latin world, so its potentates were practising the division of the Christian nations and fomenting the schisms in the faith that would lead to the religious civil wars between Protestants against the Catholics and Rome. Mortal and military ambitions would destroy Europe as much as they did the Levant.

After another campaign in Anatolia, Baybars, the sultan of Egypt, died. Since the time of Saladin, he had been the ultimate menace to the remnants of the Kingdom of Jerusalem, now reduced to a few coastal cities stretching from Acre through Tripoli and Tortosa to isolated Lattakieh. The reason that the Christian preserve had remained viable was the provision of commercial opportunities. The fleets of Italy dominated the Mediterranean, and they carried the trade of Asia to Europe. The Templars, however, had taken the role of the armed guards of state money, and thus they became the bankers of the Near East and other European countries, although Genoa and Venice were trying to replace their role in Europe. This strange translation from the defenders of Jerusalem to the merchants of Muslim and Christian commerce was to condemn the Templars to the self-destruction that was the ruin of the Crusaders. As a Templar predicted from Acre in despair: "Anyone who wishes to fight the Turks is mad, for Jesus Christ does not fight them any more. They have conquered, they will conquer. For every day they drive us down, knowing that God, who was awake, sleeps now and Muhammad becomes powerful."

The death of Sultan Baybars only prolonged the agony of the Kingdom of Jerusalem. It could expect little more help from the West, and indeed, in a fresh truce with the new *mamluk* sultan Qalawun, it was obliged to betray another Crusade before this could leave Italy. "If a Frankish king sets out from the west," the accord stated, "to attack the lands of the sultan or his son, the regent of the Kingdom [of Jerusalem] and the Grand Masters of Acre shall be obliged to inform the sultan of their action two months before their arrival." The agreement was the same against any Mongol incursion: The two enemies must alert each other, but then they were free to make terms to ensure their own survival. In spite of these precautions, however, a last fatal alliance presented itself to the Christian coastal strip in Palestine. The grandson of Hulegu, the Ilkhan Arghun, suggested to them the deliverance of Jerusalem in combination with an assault on Egypt. This lethal proposal was a toxic hope.

A Christian and Mongol alliance remained the dread of Islam. To forestall such a threat, the sultan Qalawun decided to sever the Frankish worm crawling along the coast of the Near East by slicing through its second city, Tripoli. Using catapults and a blockade, Qalawun captured the city after a month of conflict. He continued the policy of brutal deterrence practised by the Mongols and his predecessor, Baybars. "The population fell back to the port," the young emir Abu al-Fida of Hama noted. "There, some of them escaped onto ships, but most of the men were massacred, the women and the children were seized; the Muslims took a huge quantity of booty." The city was then demolished, its walls razed to the ground. If there were other expeditions from the West, another stepping-stone into the Holy Land would be gone.

With the sack of Tripoli the citizens of Acre trembled. This remained as the last major *entrepot* of the Christian Near East. King Henry II of Cyprus pled with Pope Nicholas IV to preach yet another Crusade, but he was still bound up in Italian affairs as were the other rulers of Europe in matters close to home. A rabble from Lombardy and Tuscany, however, answered the call and was transported by Venetian galleys to Acre. There they provoked a drunken riot, which ended in the killing of the Muslim merchants in the city. Although William de Beaujeu, the grand master of the Templars, advised that the perpetrators should be delivered to the sultan of Egypt for his vengeance, this cautious advice was not taken. An army was assembled in Cairo to eradicate the infidel nuisance, and a belated attempt by William de Beaujeau to buy off retribution was again refused in Acre.

Although Qalawun died on the march north, his son al-Ashraf Khalil took an oath to complete the campaign. A year later in 1291, a large force with more than a hundred catapults and mangonels arrived outside Acre, defended now chiefly by the knights of the military orders, which had recalled their members from Europe to defend this last major bastion of Christendom in the Holy Land. The Pisans and the Venetians also had their own quarters and fought fiercely in defence of their trading privileges. King Henry II brought in from Cyprus another hundred knights and two thousand soldiers; but these reinforcements were not enough to defend the extensive walls and towers of the city. Breaches were being made by the flung stones, and deep mines were dug by the Muslim engineers. Too few were resisting too much and too many.

The outer wall and towers were eventually abandoned, and in a general assault on the inner wall, the Accursed Tower was lost and William de Beaujeu was wounded unto death in an attempt to retrieve it. Pisan and Venetian Cypriot ships took off the fugitives. For the Muslims were repeating their tactics of Tripoli, killing or enslaving all the Christian survivors. In a heroic resistance, the Templars held out in their citadel on the shore for a week, sending away their treasure to safety in Sidon. And when the Muslim attackers finally broke inside the stronghold, they had so battered the structure that it crashed about their heads, killing two thousand of the assault troops along with the last defenders, who like another blinded Samson, appeared to pull down the pillars of the Temple to crush themselves along with their enemies.

As Abu al-Fida noted, Acre fell on the hour and the day of the month when the Franks had taken it from Saladin nearly a hundred years before and had also massacred and enslaved its population. The ferocity of the recapture was a delayed tit for tat. "Thus Almighty God," Abu al-Mahasin observed, "was revenged on their descendants." The memory of mercilessness breeds retribution. God struck fear into the hearts of the Franks still remaining on the Syrian coast, Abu al-Fida recorded without surprise. They quickly evacuated Tyre and Sidon, where the Templars again fought a determined last-ditch action from their Castle of the Sea, before falling back on Tortosa.

Beirut and Haifa soon surrendered, to be followed by the two Templar castles at Athlit and Tortosa itself. The survivors of the military order retreated to the fortified island of Ruad, two miles offshore from Tortosa, and they maintained there for twelve more years the final strongpoint of Outremer, created by the Crusades and doomed by the Western loss of faith in that bloody mission to the East. Such a clearance was not dreamt of, even by Abu al-Fida. "Thus were the Franj, who had once nearly conquered Damascus, Egypt and many other lands, expelled from Syria and the coast. God grant that they never set foot there again!"

To a pupil of Nahmanides in Jerusalem, the fall of Acre seemed a prelude to the coming of the Messiah, which could not happen while the Christians remained in Palestine. "Let no man think that the King Messiah will appear in an impure land; and let him not be deluded into imagining that he will appear in the Land of Israel among the Gentiles." Nahmanides himself had not disapproved of the concept of the religious cleansing of the Holy Land, even if it were first done by Muslims against Christians. He evoked the memory of Joshua, ordered by Jehovah to slaughter the Canaanites. "We were enjoined to destroy the nations if they make war upon us," he wrote. "But if they wish to make peace, we shall make peace with them and let them stay on certain terms. But we shall not leave the land in their hands or those of any other nation whatsoever."

There were hardly enough Jews yet in Palestine even to populate Jerusalem. They had been scattered by persecution in the Diaspora throughout the Near East and Europe. The reconquest by Islam of the Levant left only the Mongols preventing the Muslims from counterattacking the West and taking the *jihad* into Europe. There were still, however, the Hellenic islands and mainland taken from the Byzantine emperors by the Latin Crusaders, although Constantinople had been regained by the Greek dynasty and faith. Moreover, the sea power of the kingdom of Cyprus, and the Templar and Hospitaller fleets, were a formidable barrier against Arab expansion to the west, particularly when these were aided by the navies of the Italian maritime cities. The election of Jacques de Molay as the last grand master of the Temple created a strange final opportunity for a Mongol and Christian alliance that might force the *mamluks* back to the Nile delta.

The Ilkhan Ghazzan of Baghdad had been converted to Islam; but he was sympathetic to Christianity through his mother, and he hated the *mamluk* slaves, who had become sultans in Egypt. In 1300, he retook Damascus, which surrendered to his authority. The extraordinary Catholic Arabist and visionary Ramon Lull travelled to Syria on the news of the invasion, hoping to kindle an alliance between the Christians and the Mongols, which would lead to the recapture of Jerusalem; for Ghazzan had already announced his intentions to advance on Egypt. In alliance with Jacques de Molay and the Templars now based in Cyprus, he had defeated the *mamluks* before Damascus. He restored authority over Armenia to the Christian king Hethrom II, and installed de Molay and the Templars for a summer in the Holy City. But they could not hold it. A counterattack by the *mamluk* forces resulted in the defeat of the Mongol and Armenian army at Marj-al-Saffar and the loss of Damascus again. A valiant conflict at Ayati near Tarsus resulted in an Armenian victory four years on and the preservation of that Christian kingdom; but Palestine was irrevocably gone. Although Ghazzan struck again in 1308 and reached Jerusalem itself, no power in Europe would enter into a Mongol alliance in exchange for the Holy City. Felix Fabri later gave an account of the good Emperor "Casanus," who offered Jerusalem back to the Christians. Eight years afterwards, unfortunately, he died. His successors were Muslims; the Persian Ilkhanate began to crumble. The power of Islam over the sacred sites of the Levant was complete.

The loss of the Holy Land essentially ended the true purpose of the three military orders, which were its defenders. The Teutonic Knights transferred their crusading purpose to Prussia in a quest for a new dominion in the East Baltic lands at the expense of the pagan Slavs. The Hospitallers regrouped on Rhodes, which became their island fortress for more than a century against the rising power of the Seljuk Turks. Yet the Templars were now doomed by the loss of their reason for existence, as well as condemned for their wealth and possessions in western Europe. Their own fidelity and the envy of great princes ensured their downfall. In his extraordinary efforts to reconcile the faiths of the Prophet, Muhammad, and Jesus Christ, Ramon Lull in his book *Liber de Fine* had preached the peaceful conversion of the Near East by missionary friars, but the conquest of southern Spain and North Africa by a Rex Bellator, or Warrior King, who would unite all the military orders under his command. King Philip IV of France had already announced his intention to mount a new crusade, and the new pope, Clement V, was a Frenchman, who had established himself at Avignon rather than Rome, as if to commemorate the French crusade against the Cathars in defence of Catholic Orthodoxy and

European self-mutilation. He connived with the French king to destroy the Templars for their wealth and independence, for acting as a financier and military force within the sovereign state.

By the end of the thirteenth century, the Templars had rivalled and surpassed the Genoese and the Lombards and the Jews as the leading bankers of the time. They owned some nine thousand manors across Europe, all of which were free of taxes, and they provided security for the storage and transport of bullion. The treasury of the king of France was normally kept in the vaults of the Temple in Paris; the king himself took refuge there when threatened by mobs. The only cash drafts which were readily redeemable were issued by the Templars. They had become the financiers of the Levant, and later of most of the courts of Europe. When King Louis VII had accepted a large loan from the order, he noted that the money must be repaid quickly, "lest their House be defamed and destroyed." Even the Muslims had banked with the Templars, in case the fortunes of war should force them to ally themselves with the Christians. Though usury was forbidden to Catholics in the Middle Ages, the Templars added to the money they banked or transported by paying back an agreed sum less than the original amount, while a debtor returned more than his debt. The Paris Temple became the centre of the world's money market.

The European kings who founded their nation-states were always short of money. They regularly turned on their bankers, Italians and Jews; they defaulted on their loans and expelled their creditors. The Templars were particularly vulnerable to such treatment. They had lost the Holy Land, their arrogance was almost royal, while their secrecy provoked slander. Something of their notorious pride could be seen in an exchange between King Henry III of England and the Master of the Temple in London. When the king threatened to confiscate some of the order's lands for his treasury, because the knights were raving with pride and haughtiness, the master replied, "What sayest thou, O King? Far be it that thy mouth should utter so disagreeable and silly a word. So long as thou dost exercise justice, thou wilt reign but if thou infringe it, thou wilt cease to be King." The implication was that he might be deposed by the Templars.

Pride, or *superbia,* was considered the worst of the sins in the Middle Ages. To this, the Templars added secret rituals and diplomacy, which added to the envy and hatred of them by the princes and the people. They were seen both as the poor knights of Christendom and as rich conspirators against the state and public welfare. When King Philip of France imprisoned more than six hundred of the three thousand Templars in the country in 1307, according to Inquisition records, their interrogation and torture produced confessions which corroborated medieval superstitions, but that were the result of applying force and pain. They were not the evidence of truth.

Guiot de Provins, the contemporary monk who belonged to many holy orders and condemned his own time as "vile and filthy," testified to the Templars' integrity, praising them above all other religious orders. He found them dedicated unto death, ascetic knights whom his shrinking flesh could admire and refuse to join.

> Better far be cowardly and alive,
> Than dead, the most famous of them all.
> The Order of the Templars, I know well,
> Is beautiful and excellent and sure—
> But keeping healthy keeps me from war.

Yet those brought up from birth to be knights, who had no hope of marrying or inheriting lands of their own, had often preferred to rise to the command of a Templar castle in the Levant or Spain rather than to subsist on a feudal lord's charity in Europe. Merit in battle and organisation meant promotion in the order. Rarely was feudal rank important in the election of the grand master of the Temple, although the increasing wealth and power of the order tended to attract more ambitious and greedy men to try and gain its leadership.

The last apparent grand master, Jacques de Molay, was not one of these. Experienced in war, illiterate in diplomacy, he fell victim to his own limitations. Among many other French Templars, he confessed under torture to heresies and abominations. Yes, the Templars were homosexuals, forced to kiss the mouth, navel, and anus of their initiator. Yes, novices were made to spit on the cross. Yes, the Templars had worshipped the devil Baphomet, which was a jewelled skull or a wooden phallus. They also worshipped the devil in the form of a cat, in the presence of young virgins and female devils. Thirty-six of the Paris Templars died under torture within a few days of their arrest, and the remainder were confessing to a hotch-potch of the diabolical and sexual fantasies of their age. Above all, the Templars were made the scapegoat for the loss of the Holy Land; they were accused of selling to the Muslims what they had fought to hold.

This was the only charge against the Templars that had some basis in truth. Over the years, they had become politicians of the Christian faith, more ready to accommodate themselves to Muslim rulers and customs for the sake of their own interests than to attack with the sword every evidence of Islam. This policy, combined with the facts that they spoke Arabic and, unlike other Christian orders, wore long beards in the Muslim fashion, played into the hands of their detractors. Opponents of the Templars did not forget that their first home had been a mosque, built on the site of the Temple of Solomon in Jerusalem. A visiting Muslim envoy had been allowed to say his prayers to Allah there, facing Mecca, though the mosque had been converted into a Christian church. The Templars themselves often pointed out that the Virgin Mary, to whom they were dedicated, had her place in the Koran. They knew of the esoteric doctrines of the East; their discipline of prayer, fasting, and scourging for sins was severe enough to satisfy the most rigorous Muslim; and they knew that their position in the Levant was tenable only as long as they had Arab allies and the Arab world would remained divided. When the Templars were accused of worshipping the phallic idol called Baphomet, they were really being accused of dealing with the worshippers of Muhammad.

Obscene and ridiculous as most of the charges against the Templars were, the order was open to attack by the secular state for its pride, its independence, and its secrecy. Homosexuality, and the coarse gesture of spitting on the cross, may possibly have existed in some Temples. Yet, on the whole, the Templars suffered because the kings of Europe wanted to centralise their states. The Kingdom of Jerusalem and the Templars were the victims of the revolutionary kings who turned their attention to their own countries rather than to uniting Christendom. The Templars had estates all over Europe, while their income in many fiefs was greater than that of the feudal lord. Though the goods of the Templars were finally made over to the Hospitallers, precious little slipped out of the hands of the kings; and the Hospitallers were careful to refuse such possessions as might lead them into conflict with the secular power.

Jacques de Molay, who had ruined his sect by ordering it to surrender and confess, ended by retracting his confessions and denying all the evil he had spoken of his order. In 1314, when he was brought out onto a scaffold in front of Nôtre Dame to receive his sentence, he declared: "I confess that I am indeed guilty of the greatest infamy. But the infamy is that I have lied. I have lied in admitting the disgusting charges laid against my Order. I declare, and I must declare, that the Order is innocent. Its purity and saintliness have never been defiled. In truth, I had testified otherwise, but I did so from fear of horrible tortures." He was burned alive the following day.

So ended the Templars as a known power, the victims of the greed of kings and of their own pride and wealth. As a contemporary poet asked:

The brethren, the Masters of the Temple,
Who were well-stocked and ample
With gold and silver and riches,
Where are they? How have they done?
They had such power once that none
Dared take from them, none was so bold;
Forever they bought and never sold . . .

Until they were sold to satisfy the greed of the royal person, in whom the state was sovereign and indivisible.

Many of the Templars escaped, some from France with their galleys and their treasure. They joined in the crusades of expansionary Europe under other names. The German Templars merged into the Teutonic Knights in their campaign towards the pagan northeast. As good sailors, they helped to transfer those northern crusades from land to sea. The province of Magdeburg was called "our Jerusalem," while the crusaders of western Germany and Flanders were asked to follow the Franks who had won victories "in the distant East."

The Templars who escaped from France to Portugal buttressed the order there, which was centred at its main stronghold at Tomar. They were well-received because of their experience in navigation. In the Levant, their sailing ships had led in using the compass and the lateen sail rig, which they had adopted from Arab *dhows* and steersmen. The very word they used for a boat, *barca*, or bark, was a shortened version of the Arab word *baraka*.

And the innovative Portolan maps of the Atlantic coast of Europe and the Mediterranean and North Africa, so different from the Ptolemaic maps previously in European use, seemed to have derived from their trading experience and knowledge of Arab cartography, since these first appeared soon after the suppression of the Order of the Temple of Jerusalem with its skills that it withheld from its commercial rivals. Whatever the Templar refugees brought with them, they were incorporated into a similar order, the Knights of Christ. The ships of the renamed order sailed under the eight-pointed red cross of the Templars. The explorer of Africa, Vasco da Gama, was a Knight of Christ, and Prince Henry the Navigator was to become a grand master. Their mission was another crusade—to convert to Christianity the pagans of Africa and afterwards Asia. Religion followed the sword.

In Scotland, where some of the Templar French knights with their resources reached their headquarters at Balantrodach, or Temple, they would join with the powerful St. Clair earls of Rosslyn to support the army of King Robert the Bruce, which defeated the army of King Edward II of England in a final charge at Bannockburn. As a consequence, the suppressed military order did not lose its privileges in Scotland. Templar courts and properties continued to exist there for two centuries. Although the Hospitallers were given authority over their proscribed rivals, they never ingested them wholly. To this day, the Oath of Fealty of the Scottish Templars reaffirms their continuance by Robert the Bruce:

> "Inasmuch as the ancient realm of Scotland did succour and receive the brethren of the most ancient and noble Order of the Temple of Jerusalem, when many distraints were being perpetrated upon their properties, and many heinous evils upon their persons, the Chevaliers of the Order do here bear witness.

> "Chevaliers of the Order do undertake to preserve and defend the rights, freedoms and privileges of the ancient sovereign realm of Scotland. Further they affirm that they will maintain, at peril of their bodies, the Royal House of the realm of Scotland, by God appointed."

The Templars had sworn to maintain the Temple of Jerusalem in Palestine. Now they were sworn to maintain the Temples of the New Jerusalems in Scotland. Through the king's appointments to the Royal Order of Scotland and the St. Clair appointments as grand Master Masons of Scotland for five centuries, the Templars and their esoteric doctrines were translated into the democratic Scottish Rite of Masonry. The knights of the sword and the trowel, who had built another Temple in ancient Jerusalem, would become the Scottish Masons, who were to build hundreds of Temples of Jerusalem in their many lodges. The shrine would be translated to the north.

The actual Crusades to the East had not achieved their purpose, the Christian conquest of the Holy Land. What they did was to transfer back to Europe much of the civilisation of the Hellenic and Arabic Near East. Without question, the Islamic urban ethos that stretched from Córdoba to Baghdad was superior in the arts to the feudal warrior states of the early European Middle Ages. The science and the architecture and sometimes the agriculture of the Near East was brought back in sweaty chain mail to enrich the West. This was the victory of the failed Crusades towards Jerusalem that came home. They would now provoke counter-crusades by the *mamluks* and the Seljuk Turks, some of whom had already led the *jihads* against Christianity—Zengi and Nur al-Din, Baybars and Qalawun. Unfortunately, the Mongols had destroyed the flower of Arab medieval civilisation in Baghdad, and the *mamluks,* who had been slaves, and the Seljuks, who had been shepherds, had neither the discrimination nor the taste to uphold this original summer of Islamic culture in the first three centuries of this millennium. A crusade may destroy progress in the blessed places, where it returns.

ELEVEN

FALSE DIRECTIONS

"The Holy Land has been so utterly lost that nobody so much as thinks about recovering it."

—The pilgrim Felix Fabri in 1483

The suppression of the Knights Templar was meant to provide funds for a new Crusade to take Jerusalem. William de Nogaret, the chief counsellor of King Philip IV of France, had advised his master that the funds seized from the suppressed military order would transport an army to the Near East. In 1313, the king did take the cross at a huge feast and ceremony; but as he died in the following year along with Pope Clement V, there was no holy expedition. It was the beginning of a long series of persecutions and exactions with the aim of raising finance to reconquer Palestine that was to end in the scandal of the sale of indulgences, which would help to foment the Reformation. So many Crusades announced, so many tithes and taxes collected, so few sailings to Outremer. The crusades, indeed, of the fourteenth and fifteenth century appeared to be more Christian civil wars than assaults on the infidel. The coinage of Christ was clipped, the currency of retaking Golden Jerusalem was debased.

National rivalries in Europe replaced any preoccupation about a sacred mission overseas. The Hundred Years War between the English and the French began in 1337, while France and Aragon and Norman Sicily and the German Empire contended for power in Italy and over the papacy. Natural and financial calamities also hobbled European expansion. The Black Death—the Parthian shot of the retreating Mongols—killed off a third to a half of the Latin West, as well as depopulating Egypt and Syria. And the collapse of the banking houses of Florence and Genoa halted the spread of Mediterranean commerce. And so the Crusades floundered until an unlikely revival under the leadership of the king of Cyprus, Peter of Lusignan. In 1362, King Peter travelled through western Europe, soliciting support for his new venture against Islam; he reached Poland and Hungary, Denmark and England. Pope Urban V granted him a title and other financial assistance, while indulgences for the remission of sins were distributed to the Crusaders. With reinforcements from the Hospitaller fleet, King Peter assembled a navy of more than one hundred and fifty ships to transport his fourteen hundred knights and ten thousand infantrymen to Egypt. For his secret destination was Alexandria. It was the old strategy. If Alexandria were taken, it could be exchanged for Palestine as well as paying back the costs of the undertaking.

Taken by surprise, the port fell within a day, after the Crusaders had fired the gate to the customhouse. Precedent was followed in a savage sack and massacre—even the property of the Venetian and Genoese merchants was grabbed. Seventy shiploads of plunder were taken aboard, and in the conflagration, two of the three landward gates were destroyed. This made the city indefensible against a *mamluk* counterattack from Cairo. Although King Peter wished to remain and barter the Nile port against Jerusalem, the Hospitallers and other nobles insisted on withdrawal, outweighing the impassioned appeal of the papal legate Peter Thomas that the possession of the Holy City lay in the retention of Alexandria. After the evacuation of Egypt, King Peter did propose a peace with the *mamluks* in exchange for Palestine; but with no troops on the ground, his terms for a truce were scornfully rejected.

The *mamluks* were themselves in decline and their sea power was negligible. More threatening to Western Christendom would be the rising power of the Turks, who would take over most of the Arabic world in the name of the Ottoman Empire and pierce the heart of Europe, so that future crusades would have to defend Western capitals rather than reach out towards Jerusalem. Yet the dreams of a return to the Holy Land were to continue for the next two centuries, even after Constantinople would be lost to the Turks. Three French kings, Charles VI, Charles VIII, and Francis I, would never give up their inherited ambitions to retake Outremer. In 1518, when there would again be peace between France and England, Francis I would offer himself "for the recovery of the Holy Land and for the increase of the faith and Christian religion." And the pope of the time, Leo X, could declare in hope of a fresh Crusade: "Be glad and rejoice, O Jerusalem, since now your deliverance can be hoped for."

Yet there was no hope of deliverance, while the Catholic church itself split Europe during the Great Schism, which began in 1378 and lasted for forty years. Rival popes based in Rome and Avignon declared crusades against each other. While England and Portugal and Hungary and Poland and Scandinavia and Flanders backed St. Peter's, France and Aragon and Castille and Sicily and Scotland adhered to the other camp in Provence. English crusaders went to Flanders and northern Spain to earn their indulgences, while two French-led crusades against Islam ended in futility at Mahdia in Tunisia and in disaster at Nicopolis on the Danube, where the Hungarians left the Frankish knights to be slaughtered by the Ottoman Turks, who had expanded onto mainland Europe to control much of Greece and Bulgaria and Serbia, surrounding the enclave of Christian Constantinople. Although an assault by the Tartar warlord Timur killed the Ottoman sultan Bayezid and destroyed the Turkish state, it quickly revived to resume its threat against the Christian Balkans. The capital that the Ottoman rulers desired was not the Holy City of Palestine, but that of the Bosphorus, which was the bridge between Europe and Asia Minor.

Rent by dissension, the papacy had perverted the aim of the first Crusades. Now it preached that there could be no return to Jerusalem before opposition was suppressed at home. Islam without was less dangerous than heresy within. As Boniface VIII had declared in 1300 of the expedition of Charles of Valois: "When Sicily has been stabilised, and other rebels in Italy subjugated and restored to obedience to ourselves and the Holy See, it will be possible to be more useful and efficient in producing appropriate aid for the Holy Land." The path to Palestine lay through an Italy that served Rome. So knights who had taken the cross to fight the Muslims, were now diverted to fight fellow-Christians. During the Sicilian wars, money collected for a Crusade to deliver Jerusalem was spent in the struggle against Palermo. Papal territorial ambitions overcast the commitment to control the city where Jesus Christ was crucified.

So Rome aroused antagonism from those who still believed in the primacy of the assault on the infidel, and from the kings and nobles and clergy who had to collect the misapplied taxes for internecine crusades, which appeared to be unjust wars. As the *Lollard Conclusions* declared: "Indeed, it is robbery of poor folk when lords get indulgences from punishment and guilt for those who aid their army to kill a Christian people in distant lands for temporal gain." The five crusades declared against the dissident Hussites of Bohemia were savage in their failure: All prisoners were put to death. And yet, it was less a war with Christian division than of Czech nationalism against German control, a fatal combination of patriotism with protest against church corruption that would destroy Catholic unity and tear Europe apart in religious civil wars, used by kings to increase the power of their states under the banner of the cross.

The commercialisation of the crusading faith was bringing the church into disrepute. The sale of indulgences to excuse the buyer from taking part in holy wars was as much a scandal as granting them to looting crusaders against other Christian people, held to be unbelievers because of papal policy. The humanist reformer Erasmus would denounce the idiocy of those who thought that buying a piece of paper would ensure entry past St. Peter at the gates of heaven, while the pardoners who sold these divine chits were wicked beyond credence. The persecuted sects, however, the Cathars and the Waldensians, the Hussites and the Lollards, were becoming sceptical about the concept of a holy war. Christian pacifism was born among some of the Cathars, who believed that the shedding of human blood prevented the achievement of salvation. The Waldensians took up passive resistance, and after the Hussite wars, the Czech Brethren also rejected war and violence, an attitude that passed on to the Anabaptist Swiss Brethren. The perversion of the concept of the Crusade from the possession of the Holy City into the persecution of anti-Roman groups provoked a disgust of war itself and the hypocrisy of its preaching as a just cause. Christ as the God of love appeared to be more true than the militant Jesus.

As Martin Luther was to declare, "If I were a soldier and should see as the flag of my army the colours of a cleric or a cross, even if it were a crucifix, I would run away as if the devil himself were after me." He also declared that the Church of the Holy Sepulchre was not significant, "the actual tomb, which the Saracens held." Worse were the murder and burial of the Holy Writ by the friars and the Inquisitors. To read the Bible was more important than to trudge to Jerusalem.

Yet the zeal for reaching God's city on earth remained a part of general and royal imagination. The mystics such as the Catalan doctor Arnold of Villanova declared that Jerusalem would be recovered when the "Lost Emperor" defeated the Anti-Christ, when a second Charlemagne came to the rescue of the Holy Land. Before he was to invade Italy in 1494, King Charles VIII of France believed that he would cross the seas to Palestine from Rome, while the marquis of Cadiz would declare to King Ferdinand of Aragon that he would expel the Moors from Granada, and then subdue all Africa, "take the Holy House of Jerusalem . . . and put the banner of Aragon on Mount Calvary." With the coming of printing to England, William Caxton followed his version of the Bible with an English translation of the medieval romance, *Godfrey de Bouillon or the Siege and Conquest of Jerusalem,* still a popular subject. And during one of the last Catholic mass protests in English history, the Pilgrimage of Grace of 1536, Lord Darcy handed out lead badges of Christ's five wounds left over from a previous crusade to North Africa. A residual belief in a just and sacred war survived the waning of the Middle Ages and the coming of the Reformation, in spite of the blistering attack on the preaching of any crusade in reforming texts such as the *Consultatio* of Erasmus:

> Every time that this farce has been acted out by the popes, the result has been ridiculous. Either nothing came of it, or the cause actually deteriorated. The money, people say, stays stuck to the hands of the popes, cardinals, monks, dukes, and princes. Instead of wages, the ordinary soldier is given licence to pillage. So many times we have heard the announcement of a crusade, of the recovery of the Holy Land; so many times we have seen the red cross surmounted on the papal tiara, and the red chest; so many times we have attended solemn gatherings

and heard of lavish promises, splendid deeds, the most sweeping expectations. And yet the only winner has been money. We are informed by the proverb that it is shameful to hit yourself on the same stone twice; so how can we trust such promises, however splendid, when we have been tricked more than thirty times, misled so often and so openly.

Although the Turks had reached the Balkans, while Constantinople was still in Christian hands, there was an illusion of security; a walled bulwark still existed against the encroachment of Islam on Europe. The Second Rome with its Greek rite had endured four major sieges and blockades by the Ottoman Turks. There was still hope alive of the reforging of the Byzantine Empire with Western aid. A Burgundian knight, Betrandon de la Broquière, visited the Bosphorus on his return from a pilgrimage to Jerusalem and found the walls of the capital of the emperor John Palaeologos VIII repaired with new churches built. It seemed to him that a new Crusade was yet possible: . . . "the French, English and Germans are rather formidable, and, if they are united in sufficient numbers, they will be able to reach Jerusalem by land."

The emperor himself sought help against the overwhelming strength of the Ottoman Turks, sailing to Italy and conceding the supremacy of the Greek rite to the Latin one at the Union of Florence. The presiding pope, Eugenius IV, preached a crusade, which roused the menaced Poles and Rumanians and Hungarians to attack the Turkish armies. At Varna in 1444, their combined forces were massacred and scattered. Only the renowned Hungarian hero John Hunyadi managed to escape the remnants of his men. No further reinforcements of great significance would arrive to save Constantinople, where the citizens were already enraged by their emperor's deference to the Church of Rome.

Both the Byzantine emperor and the Turkish sultan died, to be succeeded by Constantine XI and the young Muhammad II, who was obsessed by the capture of the last great Christian stronghold towards the Near East. As the contemporary historian Michael Ducas recorded in his *Historia Byzantina*, the sultan day and night rehearsed his plans for taking Constantinople. And when in 1453 he brought up his hordes and his huge bronze cannon and siege engines, Ducas reported the despair of the Greek Christians. "Now the end of the city has come; now we see the signs of the ruin of our race; now the days of Anti-Christ are at hand; what is to become of us or what have we to do?" Although four Genoese vessels arrived with seven hundred soldiers under the command of Giovanni Giustiniani, the rest of Europe sat on its sword hand. There was no relieving crusade. The surrender to Rome at the Union of Florence seemed a sham. As a leading Byzantine, Lucas Notoras, declared in bitterness: "It is better to see in the city the power of the Turkish turban than of the Latin tiara."

By the extraordinary use of slaves and pulleys, Muhammad II bypassed the chain protecting the Golden Horn and had his galleys transported over a hilly promontory into the harbour of the Greek capital. A heavy bombardment of the city for several weeks terrorised the people, and was then followed by a triple assault. In the basilica of Sancta Sophia, the final Christian service was a requiem to the Greek civilisation of the past two thousand years. Although the first two assaults were repelled, the third broke through beside the St. Romanus Gate, where the last Byzantine emperor, Constantine, died fighting in the breach. Giustiniani was mortally wounded and died on the voyage to the island of Chios. The new sack of Constantinople lasted for three days and nights, and although some thought the Latin pillage of the city a quarter of a century before had been worse, the massacre and the plunder were extreme. Michael Ducas imitated the celebrated lament after the Latin rape of the capital of the last Greek Empire:

> "O, city, city, head of all cities! O, city, city, centre of the four quarters of the world! O, city, city, pride of the Christians and ruin of the barbarians! O, city, city, second paradise planted in the West, including all sorts of plants bending under the burden of spiritual fruits! Where is thy beauty, O, paradise? Where is the blessed strength of spirit and body of thy spiritual Graces? Where are the bodies of the Apostles of my Lord? . . . This was the enormous victory of the Turks, the extreme ruin of the Greeks, the infamy of the Latins; through it the Catholic faith was wounded, religion confused, the name of Christ reviled and oppressed. One of the two eyes of Christianity was

plucked out; one of the two hands was amputated, since the libraries were burnt down and the doctrines of Greek literature destroyed, without which no one considers himself a learned man."

Although the Church of Rome had long conspired against the Greek patriarchate of Constantinople, at the last resort, a Christian was a Christian was a Christian—and now nothing stood between Islamic Turkey and Europe. Three years later, Muhammad II took Athens from its Frankish overlords; where they had put the Church of the Holy Virgin Mary in the ancient Parthenon, he set up a mosque. Islam appeared both to have absorbed Hellenism and to have extinguished it with another religion. As the later pope Pius II wrote to the incumbent Nicholas V: "I grieve that Sancta Sophia, the most famous church in all the world, has been ruined or polluted. I grieve that saints' basilicas without number, built with wondrous skill, should lie beneath the desolation or defilement of Muhammad. What shall I say of the countless books, as yet unknown to the Latins, which were there? Alas, how many names of great men will now perish. Here is a second death for Homer and Plato too."

There were fears that Muhammad II would not stop at the conquest of Greece, but also coveted the First or Old Rome. Only Christian unity would stop this new scourge from the East. Yet paradoxically, it was the policy of Rome over supporting national rivalries among the Christian nations and in giving its supporters the indulgences of Crusaders that had driven more wedges into the cracks between the peoples and kingdoms of Europe. As the later pope Pius also observed, Christendom no longer had a leader:

Christendom has no head whom all obey. Neither the supreme pontiff nor the emperor is given his due. There is no reverence, no obedience. Like characters in fiction, figures in a painting, so do we look upon the pope and the emperor. Every city-state has its own ruler. There are as many princes as houses. How might one persuade the numberless Christian rulers to take up arms? . . . What order will there be in the army? What military discipline? What obedience? Who will feed so many people? Who will understand the different languages? Who will hold in check the different customs? Who will endear the English to the French? Who will get the Genoese to join with the Aragonese? Who will reconcile the Germans with the Hungarians and the Bohemians? If you lead a few men against the Turks, you are easily defeated. If you lead many, you are confounded.

What had been left behind by the third of the holy cities of Christendom after Jerusalem and Rome was its broken libraries and literature, fragments of which now passed across to educate the West, and the enduring legacy of its art and old being. To the Irish poet W. B. Yeats, "Sailing to Byzantium" would forever remain the denial of age, the voyage to paradise, as the pilgrimage to Jerusalem still was for so many other believers.

And therefore I have sailed the seas and come
To the holy city of Byzantium . . .

Once out of nature I shall never take
My bodily form from any natural thing,
But such a form as Grecian goldsmiths make
Of hammered gold and gold enamelling
To keep a drowsy Emperor awake;
Or set upon a golden bough to sing
To lords and ladies of Byzantium
Of what is past, or passing, or to come.

Three years after making Constantinople his new capital, the sultan Muhammad laid siege to Belgrade, the key fortress on the Danube that led up to Vienna itself. The new Pope, Calixtus III, however, was an aged Catalan who was committed to the crusading movement, even melting down ecclesiastical treasures "to use against the Turk." He gave a preaching mission to the Franciscan friar John of Capistrano, who raised many thousands of crusaders to march to the defence of Belgrade. This was the last of the people's crusades, and the only one which would prove a success. In the absence of most of the lords of Hungary appearing for the war, John of Tagliacozzo noted, "all those who assembled were commoners, peasants, the poor, priests, clerics, scholars, students, monks, mendicant friars of various Orders, members of the Third Order of Saint Francis, and hermits. Few of these people bore arms."

Reviewing these motley reinforcements, John Hunyadi despaired of defending Belgrade against the large Turkish army, which arrived in July with its formidable bronze cannon. His king and the court had fled to Vienna, while the nobles thought the defence of the city was a lost cause. He supported a capitulation; but John of Capistrano believed in divine intervention. First, the Turkish naval blockade of Belgrade was broken. Then a night attack on the walls by the mass of the Turkish forces was repulsed. Such fierce resistance discouraged Sultan Muhammad, and he decided to withdraw, fearing another crusading army was on its way. A sortie by Hunyadi's men captured the heavy artillery as it was taken off by the Turkish rear guard. A ragtag group of mainly peasant defenders with a war cry of "Jesus! Jesus! Jesus!" had routed the best army in eastern Europe. The hand of God was seen in such an unlikely victory. But the plague reached Belgrade and John of Capistrano and Hunyadi died, followed by Pope Calixtus two years later. And with their passing, all hope of recovering Constantinople and the Holy Land ended outside the dreams of visionaries.

For the forces of Islam were now ready to attack western Europe with more concentration than they had possessed since the seventh to the ninth centuries, when they had conquered North Africa and Sicily and most of Spain, and when they had even penetrated France. Muhammad II studied the words of Julius Caesar and foresaw himself as the ruler of a Mediterranean Empire, based on those of ancient days. "No one doubts that you are the Emperor of the Romans," the Greek George of Trebizond wrote to him. "Whoever is the legal master of the capital of the Empire is the Emperor and Constantinople is the capital of the Roman Empire." For the success of the Islamic religion in converting the tribes of central Asia and the Russian steppes would revive the idea of a vast cultural swathe cutting from Europe to China, where all practised the religious law of the Shari'a as interpreted by the international elite of the Ulama, where a continental federation was infused by the mystical thoughts about the divine spread by the Sufis, the missionaries of the spirit of Islam.

There seemed no limit to the expansion of the Ottoman Turks by land. Early in the sixteenth century, they overthrew the *mamluks* in Egypt and became the guardians of Mecca and Medina as well as Jerusalem. The sultan Suleyman I finally seized Belgrade in 1521 and eliminated the Knights Hospitaller from their bastion in Rhodes two years later. Christian influence in the Near East was reduced to the Greek Orthodox kingdom of

Georgia on the Black Sea and to some Aegean islands and Crete, which the Venetians still defended. And at the field of Mohacs in 1526, Suleyman destroyed the Hungarian army, opening the way to a conflict with the Catholic Habsburgs that would range for a hundred and fifty years from Malta to Sicily to the Adriatic and the Upper Danube, until Vienna itself would only be saved by the last Holy League against Islam put together by divided Christendom.

The Turks were also turning to the sea, where they were weak. Unfortunately, for them, they were adopting the wrong technology. The galley rowed by slaves appeared to be the best weapon of war. Venice had demonstrated its value as a battle platform and gun mount; but it was vulnerable to storms and heavy seas, once it left coastal waters. Already, the Arab *dhows* had proved their worth over long distances in the Indian Ocean, sailing from the Red Sea to garner the spice trade of the East, even encountering the cumbersome junks of China. But meanwhile the merchant *knorrs* of Scandinavia and the caravels of Portugal were adopting a lateen rig to increase their potential by sailing closer to the wind. Stern-post rudders, improved charts, and navigational techniques were to give to western Europe the sea power that it needed to surround the Islamic world by ocean trade and the occupation of strategic ports in Africa and Asia.

Yet the increasing galley fleets of the Ottoman Empire and the Barbary corsairs forced an accommodation on the West. Venice had to make peace with the Turks in 1479 and again in 1502, recognising the new naval supremacy of Islam in the eastern Mediterranean. Peace could not last, and the crusades had to be reviewed specifically against the new Islamic Rome of Constantinople. The war of the galleys against the Turks was enormously costly both to Venice and to King Philip II of Spain, who had become the chief defender of the Catholic faith in the western Mediterranean. The grant by the Curia of a tenth or even a fifth of church revenues for the defence of the coasts of Italy became essential to the lagoon republic, while Philip II depended on the sale of indulgences and a proportion of the tithe as well as the tenth, three necessary "graces" to subsidise the division of the western from the eastern Mediterranean. For that geography was what the sixteenth-century conflict between Christianity and Islam defined. As the French historian Braudel has written, each was a separate historical as well as climatic zone. The great naval conflicts took place in the frontiers of the separated sea, twice at Tripoli, three times at Djerba, and thrice at Tunis, and twice again at Bizerta. The siege of Malta in 1565, where the Knights Hospitaller clung on to their last stronghold, and the battle of Lepanto in 1571, when Don John of Austria and the Holy League destroyed the Turkish fleet in the Gulf of Corinth, were the last great defensive victories of the crusading movement. Cervantes was there at the fight and declared in *Don Quixote* that the struggle "revealed to all the nations of the world their great mistake in believing that the Turks were invincible by sea." They were not, and certainly outside the eastern Mediterranean, they were most vulnerable.

Yet the Portuguese and Spanish campaigns against Islam in North Africa failed. Although the Muslims and Jews were expelled from Spain unless they were converted to Christianity, the captured Moroccan and Algerian and Tunisian ports of Melilla and Mers el-Kebir, Oran and Velez de la Gomera, Cherchell and Tripoli, could not be held. And the final crusade of King Sebastian of Portugal into the hinterland of Morocco ended in 1578 in the disaster of Alcazar, which not only lost North Africa except for Tangier and Ceuta, but delivered his independent kingdom and the Portuguese Empire in Africa, Asia, and the Americas into the hands of his cousin, King Philip of Spain. His religious ambition had led to the loss of national freedom.

What was to destroy the supremacy of Islam in the Near East was not Christian attack, but exploration. Although the civilisations of the Mediterranean were to make a cultural and economic conquest in all the continents of the globe, the fleets of Europe would reduce the Mediterranean from being the cauldron of world trade into a begging-bowl held out to the Atlantic and Pacific Oceans. The colonisation of the Americas by the Spanish and the Portuguese was followed by ships and settlers from France and England and Holland. The process would be repeated across Africa and India and the islands of Asia. The bullion of Mexico and Peru and the spice trade of India and Java now flowed across the great oceans, with some of the wealth siphoned into the Mediterranean, which had previously served as the exchange and mart of the overland gold and silver herb and spice routes. Like a slower Puck, the European sea powers cast their girdle round the earth in eighty years or so, and they strangled their founding landlocked sea within the noose of the far-flung tackle of their voyages. "The opening up of the Atlantic," Braudel has written, "destroyed the age-old privilege of the Levant, which for a time had been the sole repository of the riches of the 'Indies.' From that point on, every day saw a widening of the gap between the standard of living of the West, which was going through a revolution in technical and economic progress, and the eastern world of low-cost living."

As the caravel and the carrack took the place of the caravan, and as the ocean superseded the desert, so the commercial centres of the Levant became less attractive for the new imperialist nations of western Europe. There was more profit to be had in the slave trade of Africa than of Circassia, and even more opportunity to convert the multitudinous infidels in the Gold Coast and Dahomey than in Beirut or Tripoli. The Near East was no longer the *souk,* where Asia bargained with Europe. Its commercial and industrial importance was in decline. As for Jerusalem itself, the cosmic axis became a blessed back alley. The expulsion of the Jews from Spain did increase the intellectual power of the small community of five hundred people there among some four thousand families. The Ottoman sultan Suleyman I first restored the walls and water supplies of the city and built the elaborate Damascus Gate. He also adorned the Muslim sacred area of the Haram esh-Sharif, particularly the most sacred Dome of the Rock. Although a poll tax was imposed on Christians and Jews, there was no persecution, for the Koran had forbidden violence against the other "people of the Book." And certainly, those who fled the anti-Semitism of many of the rulers of the rising nation-states of Europe preferred Turkish tolerance to a Dominican Inquisition.

Ironically for the Christian powers, their hounding of the Jews resulted in a reverse transfer of technology to Islam. As Venice was preparing to drive out its Jews after the victory of Lepanto, the Council of Ten was stopped from its intolerance by the arrival of its representative from Constantinople, who declared, according to the testimony of the physician Joseph Ha Cohen: "What pernicious act is this, to expel the Jews? Do you not know what it may cost you in years to come? Who gave the Turk his strength and where else would he have found the skilled craftsmen to make the cannon, bows, shot, swords, shields and bucklers which enable him to measure himself against other powers, if not among the Jews who were expelled by the Kings of Spain?"

After the Reformation and the Counter-Reformation, when the concept and mechanics of the Crusades were applied suicidally to the religious wars between Mediterranean southern Europe and Atlantic and Baltic northern Europe, the strangest suggestion was put to King Philip III of Spain for the reconquest of the holy places. Those Jews who had been forced to become Christians, the *conversos,* should be recruited as an army to retake their sacred city. This extraordinary proposal was a curious prophecy, which would have seemed impossible at the time. For within three hundred and fifty years, a Jewish army again converted to militancy would retake Jerusalem by the sword, an opportunity allowed by previous Christian reconquerors after their own unlikely return there. For with the religious wars of Europe, the Crusade towards Israel or Palestine appeared to be as distant as the coming of the Messiah, when Jerusalem would rise again as the City of God upon earth. Until then, it could only keep its importance in apocalyptic visions and imaginary maps, such as the Renaissance one showing it as the core of the three-petalled flower of Europe and Asia and Africa with America offshore beyond galleons and sea monsters—a chart still sold in the University Bookshop in modern Jerusalem.

TWELVE

IMPALPABLE VOIDNESS

Hide thou Jerusalem in impalpable voidness, not to be
Touched by the hand nor seen with the eye: O Jerusalem,
Would thou wert not & that thy place might never be found.

—William Blake, *Jerusalem*

As Europe plunged into centuries of religious civil war, the pilgrimage, or the crusade, towards Jerusalem was displaced. The journey had always been difficult; now it was nearly impossible. When Count Eberhard of Württemberg was consulted by Felix Fabri as a previous traveller to the Holy City, he replied that there was much in common between war and marriage and pilgrimage; they "may begin very well and end very badly." What happened during the Reformation and the Counter-Reformation was the building of many New Jerusalems within Europe to weigh against the alternative Holy City in Rome. This was both a secular and a spiritual reaction against the Catholic church, a reflex from the popular crusades and peasant revolts and Gnostic heresies of the Middle Ages.

The Brethren of the Free Spirit were the catalysts between the dissident Cathars and the Taborites and the Anabaptists of the Renaissance. They believed that every created thing was divine. A person who truly knew God carried his own heavenly city and personal Jerusalem within himself. On death, that speck or spark of God was reabsorbed into the essence of the everlasting. Throughout eternity, man was God and in God. There was no need of priest or Church or Jerusalem on earth to mediate in the salvation of a soul. Each had to seek out and find God, who already occupied the body of all beings.

To the doctrine of the Holy City within every living thing was added the myth of Eden. Humankind would return to the state of Adam and Eve in the Garden of Paradise, where there was no property or poverty or oppression, after the destruction of Orthodoxy and the victory of the Anti-Christ and the reign of Jesus for a thousand years. The adepts of the Free Spirit would enjoy that state of Paradise now and should rule the elect, the mass of the other believers. They could recall the Golden Age, which Jean de Meun had hymned in his popular *Roman de la Rose*. Such visions and egalitarian dreams had been behind the Peasants' Revolt in England, where the preacher John Ball had asked his famous question:

When Adam delved and Eve span,
Who was then a gentleman?

God's law meant that all authority should be overthrown and all goods held in common. Such doctrines inspired the extremists among the Hussites, after their victory in Bohemia. These Taborites believed in an Apocalypse in which only their towns would be spared, while the rest of the world was condemned. And from them broke off a more fanatical sect, the Adamites, who supported a holy war against the rest of humanity. They saw themselves as the angel with the fiery sword at the gates of Eden. They burned and massacred the inhabitants of all the neighbouring villages until the Taborite commander was forced to exterminate his own zealots, for fear that their message would subvert the whole of human society.

The most radical example of the building of a New Jerusalem was in Münster on the border of Holland and Germany. A city of fifteen thousand people, its powerful guilds were opposed to the tithes imposed by the monasteries and to the crusade taxes for fighting off the Turks. The workers there heard the millennial call of Thomas Müntzer, who predicted the imminent Second Coming after the rule of the Turks and the Anti-Christ; but he was beheaded by the princes. His follower, Bernt

Rothmann, was an apostate Lutheran preacher, who denounced Luther himself for cooperating with the authorities. He made Münster a magnet for the communards of that time, the believers in the Free Spirit who took the name of Anabaptists. In his footsteps followed Jan Bockelson, also known as John of Leyden, a charismatic young bully, who announced that in the coming catastrophe at Easter 1534, the whole earth would be destroyed and only Münster would be saved as the New Jerusalem.

The Lutherans and Roman Catholics within the walls were expelled or killed as the ungodly. The believers who remained were terrorised by armed bands of immigrants, the courtiers of John of Leyden, who now wore a crown and sat on a throne of gold and declared himself king of the millennial city of David. On his gold coins was printed the slogan: The Word Has Become Flesh and Dwells in Us. With his private death squads, which he commanded from the cathedral square now called Mount Zion, he requisitioned all the money and food and housing in Münster in the name of Jesus Christ; he used these resources to defend this centre of the Free Spirit against the German bishops and princes, who were resolved to extirpate such a pernicious heresy and outrage against their privileges. Other Anabaptist risings in Holland and Germany were quickly suppressed, while efforts to found still more New Jerusalems in Amsterdam and Minden ended in a slaughter of the radicals. A stringent blockade of Münster destroyed all resistance. Most of the elect were killed, and John of Leyden was paraded on a chain like an animal, and then tortured to death. It was the effective end of militant Anabaptism in the Reformation, although the dragon's breath of the creed smoked underground.

The Reformation opposed pilgrimages to holy places and the veneration of relics such as the True Cross. These stimuli to the crusading movement, however, did not prevent the Protestants from using religious zeal to mount their own crusades. Luther, indeed, supported the extermination of the Anabaptists and the rebellious peasants. To him, the pope was the Anti-Christ, and Catholics and Muslims were both heretics in alliance with Satan who should be pursued by war. As for the Jews, he anticipated their mass conversion, then turned on them in fury in his Wittenberg pamphlet, *On the Jews and their Lies,* the first popular work of anti-Semitism. He wanted all synagogues burned, prayer forbidden, Jewish homes razed, and forced labour inflicted on the people of that faith. He was instrumental in driving the Jews from Saxony and many German cities. Faced by Protestant persecution, the Jews looked for protection to the Catholic bishops and the Holy Roman Emperor, whose pogroms were intermittent. And grouping themselves in ghettos became the Jewish way of survival in the European city, beginning in Venice and spreading north and east, a forced segregation which would make their bunched communities even more vulnerable.

A Renaissance traveller and sceptic, Solomon Ibn Verga, now wrote in Hebrew *The Rod of Judah (Shevet Yehuda),* the first book for fourteen hundred years since the Jewish history of Josephus that questioned the destiny of his people. Ibn Verga told of more than sixty persecutions and pogroms and asked why they had happened. He criticised the Talmud and the obsession about the Torah. He found that the Jews were too proud and too resentful and yet too passive. They provoked the Christian poor into intolerance, although educated Christians did not hate Jews, who themselves dismissed any person who was not one of them. Prejudice lay within the ghetto as well as outside it. Reason and understanding were the only ways out of a historical trap of suspicion.

Such discrimination and fairness of judgement were rare in the many horrors and persecutions spanned by the Christian religious wars. The Reformation split Protestant Scandinavia, Germany, Holland, and Britain from southern Catholic Europe, and initiated centuries of strife by land and sea, in which national interest could hardly be distinguished from religious differences. For the Counter-Reformation proved as sanguinary and savage as the excesses of the Reformers against priests and nuns. The stake was now the fate not of Joan of Arc, but of the Protestant martyrs described by Foxe, and the captured sailors of the Elizabethan navy. The Inquisition was not used always against the Muslims and the Jews, but against the breakaway Christian religions—now identified with the conspiracies of the Devil, as in Olivier Maillard's medieval poem:

> *Cursed Satan, inventor of war,*
> *leader of a damned sect,*
> *took to the field of battle as a warrior,*
> *instigator of a deadly plot . . .*

As the Reformation incited the Counter-Reformation, so the fanaticism of the Reformers bred revenge. In 1544 the Council of Trent allied the removal of religious discord with the crusade against the infidel. And for the next hundred years until the end of the Thirty Years War in Middle Europe and the English Civil War, elements of the crusading ideology would surface in the propaganda of the conflict of the faiths. Notably, the year after the great Christian sea victory at Lepanto, the French religious wars began with the Massacre of St. Bartholomew's Day, when the Catholics turned on their fellow Huguenot citizens with the ferocity shown by the Crusaders when they first took Jerusalem. The mercilessness, maiming, and torture displayed by the French spiritual rivals towards those of another faith was as dreadful and inexcusable as in the crusade against the Cathars—a national self-mutilation in the name of nothing very much, but believed too much.

The crusading imagery was more credible in terms of imperial ambition. When the Spanish Armada left in 1588 to conquer England, red crosses billowed on its vaunting sails and the mission was blessed as if against the Turks at Lepanto. Its disaster was seen by the king of Spain as a divine judgement on him. And in effect, it was a perversion of the crusading faith, for the way to London was hardly towards another Jerusalem. Indeed, in Spain, a survivor of Lepanto would write the first modern novel of genius, *Don Quixote,* which would mock and translate the ideals of chivalry and crusading into the visions of an aged knight, tilting at windmills. What Godfrey de Bouillon had inspired, Cervantes pricked.

"The present heroism is bound to become grotesque," Georg Lukács wrote, "the strongest faith is bound to become madness, when the ways leading to the transcendental home have become impassable." So Cervantes transposed the mission of Don Quixote riding towards Jerusalem. The name of the Holy City is hardly mentioned in the book. The pilgrimage of the deluded knight is finally described as an interior journey into his own nature, opposed to the delusions of his age. If there is an infidel he fights, it is the misconceptions which he has. At his end, Cervantes is certain of the passing of the last of the Crusades. "Death came at last for Don Quixote, after he had received all the sacraments and once more, with many forceful arguments, had expressed his abomination of books of chivalry. The notary who was present remarked that in none of those books had he read of any knight-errant dying in his own bed so peacefully and in so Christian a manner. And so, among the tears and laments of all who were there, he gave up the ghost. That is to say, he died."

The burial of Don Quixote, however, did not inter the ideology of the Crusades towards the Holy City. The book endured, but changed the actual pilgrimage to a place on earth into the spiritual quest for the soul. No traverse of the Mediterranean was necessary now; the voyage lay through the individual brain and bowels towards redemption. This was made most clear among the Ranters and the Levellers and the New Model Army of the English Civil War; they saw Jerusalem and Mount Zion as their own path towards salvation.

The Levellers and the Diggers had their particular version of the Garden of Eden and of the holy earthly city, when the Catholic church was to be removed. As one of their ballads ran:

The Poore long
Have suffered wrong,
By the gentry of this Nation,
The Clergy they
Have bore a great sway
By their base insulation.

But they shall
Lye levell with all
They have corrupted our Fountains;
And then we shall see
Brave Community
When Vallies lye levell with Mountains.

The poem continued to tell that the "glorious Hate" which it related would bring "unspeakable comfort . . . and joy in our King." This was the vision of the Old Testament, which had inspired Joshua and his religious genocide. Driving behind the righteous and the elect was the chariot of the avenging God. Hatred was the prerequisite to Paradise, which still had its king. At this level, democracy and dictatorship fused, and Jean-Jacques Rousseau was predicted. However much the poor combined to grasp for their equality and prosperity, they could not conceive of progress without a chief; so the Anabaptists had found bitterly at Münster. The paradox of the millennial movements was their confusion of liberty with leadership. Heaven was ruled by a divine king. How to reach Jerusalem on earth without a Messiah?

The great Leveller Lilburne in 1645 discovered Jerusalem in Fleet Street in London, where printing was to continue for several centuries in the name of free speech. In the "fiery Furnace" of the *Sentinell,* night and day, Lilburne defended Zion, "the City of the Living God . . . desiring all my fellow brethren, that professe the same truth with me, as valiant and worthy soldiers of Jesus Christ to lend me their best corragious assistance." On this failed crusade, which was severed root and branch by Oliver Cromwell's Commonwealth, as the Hussites had exterminated the Adamites, Lilburne contended for an individual access to God's reign, not through any state or church. "This is the great Controversie, that God contends with the whole Earth for, and for which God will make the greatest of Princes and States to taste a Cup of trembling. . . . For Sir, let me tell you, it is the incommunicable Prerogative of Jesus Christ alone to be King of his Saints, and Law-giver to his Church and people, and to reigne in the soules and consciences of his chosen ones."

Despite the Puritan zealotry of Cromwell's New Model Army, it could not tolerate any radicalism against the state, when its leader was the state. All rebels become conservatives, when they are in power. They must conserve the fruits of the revolution. And thus, new rebels will be aroused. The cycle of change is a process, as Heraclitus recognised. The sun is new every day. And so it was with Jerusalem, which was refounded in the matter of Europe in the Reformation, far from its place. It now dwelt in the spirits of those who still believed in the heavenly city.

Already by the time of the English Civil War, eighty books and pamphlets had been published about an imminent Second Coming of Jesus Christ. Parliamentary soldiers discussed the theory that the earl of Essex was John the Baptist and King Charles I was the Anti-Christ. A sect called Fifth Monarchy Men believed that after the empires of Babylon and Persia, Greece and Rome, the rule of the saints would begin in England and dominate the world. They would destroy authority and property and bring a celestial government to earth, getting rid of want and even pain. But their abortive risings were crushed by Cromwell, and their millennial hopes were returned to dust. They had believed that the execution of King Charles I signalled the Resurrection and the reign of Christ the King. But their cosmic calendar was out of joint and time.

A certain reality, though, still pervaded Christianity. The opportunity presented by the suicidal religious wars of Europe was not missed by the sultans of Constantinople. Their particular *jihad* still extended as far as the conquest of the West. And in 1683, the Ottoman army reached the gates of Vienna. Given this poignard at the heart of Catholic Europe, Pope Innocent XI organised a final Holy League at the last ditch of the Habsburg Empire. He brought into the defence of the secular capital of Christendom the states of Bavaria and Saxony, Hungary and Poland, Russia and even Venice. The Cossacks fought the Ottoman cavalry; the combined forces of the League put the infidels to flight. And slowly the Turks were driven back towards the East until, at the end of the seventeenth century, the Peace of Karlowitz legitimised the fact that central Europe and some outposts in Greece remained in Christian hands. The counterattack of Islam on the West resulted in stalemate.

In a way, the triumph of the Turks in eastern Europe as well as in the Levant was a defeat for the cause of enlightened Islam. While western Europe was to progress in spite of its religious schisms, the Muslim Orient would tread water or begin to sink. The Ottoman Empire produced a benevolent and somnolent despotism over an original and enquiring urban civilisation, certainly in advance of any other at the time except in China. As was observed by the excellent historian of *The Crusades Through Arab Eyes:*

> Although the epoch of the Crusades ignited a genuine economic and cultural revolution in Western Europe, in the Orient these holy wars led to long centuries of decadence and obscurantism. Assaulted from all quarters, the Muslim world turned in on itself. It became over-sensitive, defensive, intolerant, sterile—attitudes that grew steadily worse as world-wide evolution, a process from which the Muslim world felt excluded, continued. Henceforth progress was the embodiment of "the other." Modernism became alien. Should cultural and religious identity be affirmed by rejecting this modernism, which

the West symbolised? Or, on the contrary, should the road of modernisation be embarked upon with resolution, thus risking loss of identity? Neither Iran, nor Turkey, nor the Arab world has ever succeeded in resolving this dilemma.

Under the rule of the various pashas of Syria, Jerusalem became a source of revenue and squabbles. In spite of the forcible conversion of the synagogue called the Ramban into a mosque, the population of the Jewish Quarter slowly increased because of immigration caused by western persecution. Yet the quarrels of the various Christian rites for space in the sacred places mirrored the factions and disputes in riven Europe. When the leading cleric Henry Maundrell made the pilgrimage to the Holy City in 1697, he noted an "unChristian fury and animosity, especially between the Greeks and the Latins." Several sects were disputing the command of the Church of the Holy Sepulchre. Arguments broke out about which party should celebrate its mass at what hour. "They have sometimes proceeded to blows and wounds even at the very door of the sepulchre, mingling their own blood with their sacrifices . . . in one of these unholy wars."

The dwindling of Jerusalem as a religious centre of pilgrimage was matched by its increase as a focus of mysticism. Some of the Jews led by Joseph Karo and Solomon Alkabaz migrated from Ottoman Greece to Safed in Galilee, preaching the redemption of Israel, which the prophets had foretold. These disciples of the Cabbala believed that their expulsion from the Promised Land was almost a proof of God's love of his Chosen People. The holiest of the Safed mystics, Isaac Luria, suggested that Creation had come from nothingness, an empty space caused by God's withdrawal. By implication, Israel was in that state after the destruction of the Temple and the exile of the Jews. Yet there was a transcendental hope that the void would be filled by the eventual return of the Messiah and his people to the Holy City, a process that might be aided by meditation and prayer. When a false Messiah, Sabbatai Zevi, did appear in 1666, he was seized by the Ottoman authorities and preferred conversion to Islam to the alternative of death—and so disappointed his supporters.

Although the eighteenth century was sometimes called the Age of Reason, it ended as an era of revolution. The belief in a millennium and the return of Christ to rule in his Holy City ran from the Puritan protests against Catholic practises through the English and French and German civil wars into the Industrial and American and French revolutions. In these different movements, five similar qualities were discovered in a scrutiny of popular millenarianism of this period. "First, the salvation is conceived as being for the faithful as a group—the saints, the true believers—and not as each individual seeking by himself to save his own soul. Next, this salvation is to be enjoyed in a kingdom on this earth, and it is to come soon and suddenly. It will be total in its effects: the present evil world will not be improved, but utterly destroyed, and replaced by a perfect society. Lastly the change will come about by divine agency, not by human efforts."

The quick material changes wrought by the Industrial Revolution were paralleled by the speedy social upheavals caused by the French Revolution. Such utter and instant transformations encouraged a belief in the Apocalypse soon. Many thought it already the time of the Anti-Christ, while the world was in the grip of Satan. In England, particularly, prophets arose who equated the Old Testament with national history and saw the previous Crusades for Jerusalem in terms of regenerating their native land. Richard Brothers was the most influential of these visionaries, and even his confinement in an asylum hardly affected his considerable influence on his dissenting contemporaries, including William Blake. From his example, the extraordinary group called the British Israelites would propose during the nineteenth century the return of the Jews to their homeland.

This policy was sought by Brothers in *A Revealed Knowledge* and later pamphlets. It had already been advocated to Cromwell's Commonwealth by the American Puritan group led by the Cartwrights, who thought that the Second Coming of Jesus Christ would be hastened when England and the Netherlands became "the first and readiest to transport Israel's sons and daughters on their ships to the land promised to their forefathers Abraham, Isaac and Jacob for an everlasting inheritance." Richard Brothers claimed that he was from the House of David and so a prince of the Hebrews with a mission to lead the Jews hidden among the English back to their homeland, for he had identified England with another Israel. His plans for the return of the Chosen People to the Promised Land were as specific as the logistics necessary for a Crusade. The leading states of Europe should provide twenty thousand tents and three hundred shiploads of timber and six hundred stone saws. Jerusalem should be rebuilt with the Garden of Eden at its centre according to the vision of the city in Ezekiel, where every courtyard and chamber and gate and arch was set in cubits and reeds over the nine obsessive chapters of the Bible, according to the words revealed to the prophet:

> "In the visions of God brought he me into the land of Israel, and set me upon a very high mountain, by which was as the frame of a city on the south.

> "And he brought me thither, and, behold, there was a man, whose appearance was like the appearance of brass, with a line of flax in his hand, and a measuring reed; and he stood in the gate.

> "And the man said unto me, Son of man, behold with thine eyes, and hear with thine ears, and set thine heart upon all that I shall shew thee; for to the intent that I might shew them unto thee art thou brought hither: declared all that thou seest to the house of Israel. . . .

> "And the glory of the Lord came into the house by way of the gate whose prospect is toward the east.

> "So the spirit took me up, and brought me into the inner court; and behold, the glory of the Lord filled the house.

> "And I heard him speaking unto me out of the house; and the man stood by me.

> "And he said unto me, Son of man, the place of my throne, and the place of the soles of my feet, where I will dwell in the midst of the children of Israel for ever, and my holy name, shall the house of Israel no more defile."

In his pamphlet *A Description of Jerusalem,* Brothers followed Ezekiel in the precision of his building measurements, stating that although he was no architect, God also was his instructor. The artist John Flaxman was actually asked by Brothers to design the reconstruction of the Temple, and plans of that original sacred shrine became common in millennial and

Masonic circles. These imaginations of Britain as the original Eden and Israel and Jerusalem, in spirit if not in place, were to stimulate the most
original and radical poet and artist of his age, William Blake, into producing his masterwork on the theme of the Holy City.

Blake's illuminated book *Jerusalem: The Emanation of the Giant Albion* and
his *Milton,* which also concerned Jerusalem, were written and illustrated
by 1804, when Britain was fighting Napoleon for the future of Europe. To
Blake, Jerusalem signified Liberty, the inspiration of both the American
and French revolutions. She was the divine vision of freedom in every person. She also represented, along with Shiloh, the heavenly city of peace
and communion with God, who had given her to mankind as his most precious gift, freedom of the soul. This liberty was not confined to the elect,
as other millenarians supposed. It was for every society and for all
mankind. And when the Last Judgement would come, Blake prophesied
in *The Four Zoas,* Jesus Christ would indeed descend from the celestial New
Jerusalem to reign on earth for a thousand years.

Blake declared that he wrote his *Jerusalem* "from immediate dictation,
twelve or sometimes twenty or thirty lines at a time; without premedita-
tion, and even against my will." As with Ezekiel, his vision of his Jerusalem
was personal, although said to be inspired by the divine. He declared its
material to derive from "persons and machinery entirely new to the inhabitants of earth." In the opinion of his seminal biographer, Alexander
Gilchrist, during the prose poem, "Jerusalem is once spoken of as Liberty;
she is also apostrophised as 'mild shade of man,' and must, on the whole,
be taken to symbolise a millennial state." That analysis of Blake's attribu-
tions of his Holy City was confirmed in his enduring poem *Milton,* which
has become an alternative English national anthem:

> And did those feet in ancient time
>   Walk upon England's mountains green?
> And was the holy Lamb of God
>   On England's pleasant pastures seen?
>
> And did the Countenance Divine
>   Shine forth upon our clouded hills?
> And was Jerusalem builded here
>   Among these dark Satanic Mills?

Bring me my bow of burning gold!
Bring me my arrows of desire!
Bring me my spear! O clouds, unfold!
Bring me my chariot of fire!

I will not cease from mental fight,
Nor shall my sword sleep in my hand,
Till we have built Jerusalem
In England's green and pleasant land.

That poem specifically linked Blake's fears of Newtonian science and the Industrial Revolution with millennial hopes of reintroducing a spiritual Eden and Jerusalem to his home country. As the giant Albion was early asked:

Where hast thou hidden thy Emanation lovely Jerusalem
From the vision and fruition of the Holy-one?

This concealment was a terrible loss. For Blake equated the disappearance of an English Eden with the advance of the factories and the machines, while in his vision the emanation of Jerusalem itself had once lived in London and in his country and in the whole known world.

Yet thou wast lovely as the summer cloud upon my hills
When Jerusalem was thy hearts desire in times of youth & love.
Thy sons came to Jerusalem with gifts, she sent them away
With blessings on their hands & on their feet, blessings of gold,
And pearl & diamond: thy Daughters sang in her Courts:
They came up to Jerusalem; they walked before Albion
In the Exchanges of London every Nation walkd
And London walkd in every Nation mutual in love & harmony
Albion coverd the whole Earth, England encompassed the Nations,
Mutual each within others bosom in Visions of Regeneration;
Jerusalem coverd the Atlantic Mounts & the Erythrean,
From bright Japan & China to Hesperia France & England.
Mount Zion lifted his head in every Nation under heaven:
And the Mount of Olives was beheld over the whole Earth:
The footsteps of the Lamb of God were there: but now no more . . .

This tragic sense of the loss of Paradise and the Holy City had also informed the first settlers in America and was a stand in their later revolution against the taxes and corruption of Europe, in the same way that previous Protestants had objected to the power of Rome. As Thomas Paine was to declare in his *Common Sense,* which had such an influence on the American Revolution: "The Reformation was preceded by the discovery of America: as if the Almighty graciously meant to open a sanctuary to the persecuted in future years." The Pilgrim fathers were fleeing oppression from the Church of England, and their pilgrimage to a New World in America was modelled on the wanderings of the tribes of Israel. Their settlements in New England were often given biblical names, Salem and Hebron, Bethlehem and Zion. A Jerusalem was later founded in Yates County in western New York, which would prove a warm pulpit for millennial and utopian preaching and scheming in the Burned-Over District. The seeds of the apocalyptic harvest were sown in Edward Johnson's historical tract of 1654, *Wonder-Working Providence of Sion's Savior in New England,* which saw the success of the Puritan colonies and the conquest of the Native American tribes in the terms of Joshua's and the Crusaders' victories: "Know this is the place where the Lord will create a new heaven and new earth in, new churches, and a new commonwealth together. Verily if the Lord be pleased to open your eyes, you may see the beginning of the fight, and what success the armies of our Lord Jesus Christ have hitherto had."

Both in England and in the American colonies, the Jews were granted full citizenship, and they began to identify with the body politic rather than with the lost Israel in Palestine. They were also not excluded from the rising Masonic orders with their cult of the ancient Temple at Jerusalem, reproduced after the eighteenth century in thousands of lodges across northern Europe and America. The myth of masonry was summarised in the *Dowland Manuscript,* said to derive from a Tudor original:

Long after the Children of Israel had come into the Land of Promise, that is now called amongst us in the country of Jerusalem, King David began the Temple that they called *Templum Domini,* and which is named with us the Temple of Jerusalem. And the same King David loved Masons well and cherished them much and gave them good pay. And he gave them the Charges and the manners as he had learned them in

Egypt, as given by Euclid, and still other Charges that you shall hear of afterwards. And after the decease of King David, Solomon, that was David's son, completed the Temple that his father had begun, and sent after Masons into divers countries and divers lands and gathered them together, so that he had fourscore thousand workers of stone, who were all named Masons. And he chose out of them three thousand who were appointed to be Masters and Governors of his work. Furthermore, there was a King of another region whom men called Hiram, and he loved well King Solomon, and gave him timber to his work. And he had a son who was called Aynon, who was a Master of Geometry, and Chief Master of all his Masons, and Master of all his engravings and carving, and of all kinds of Masonry that belonged to the Temple. . . . And Solomon confirmed both the Charges and the manners that his father had given the Masons. And thus was that worthy Science of Masonry confirmed in the country of Jerusalem, and in many other kingdoms.

This heritage from ancient Jerusalem was generally accepted by the millions of Freemasons, who were trying to recreate their own small Temples in their lodges. Although the Bible stipulated at length, particularly in Ezekiel, the dimensions of a Temple, such magnificence could not be rebuilt in the small rooms available. And so certain principles for these new sites of holiness were incorporated into the Mason's examination for an admission to the Third Degree. After giving the name of the local lodge, the inquiry proceeded:

QUESTION: *How stands your Lodge?*

ANSWER: *East and West, as the Temple of Jerusalem.*

QUESTION: *Where was the first Lodge?*

ANSWER: *In the porch of Solomon's Temple.*

QUESTION: *Are there lights in your Lodge?*

ANSWER: *Three, the North-east, the South-west, and the Eastern passage. The one Denotes the Master Mason, the other the Words and the Third the fellow-craft. . . .*

193

QUESTION: *Which is the Key of your Lodge?*

ANSWER: *A well-hung tongue.*

QUESTION: *Where lies the Key of your Lodge?*

ANSWER: *In the Bone Box. . . .*

The Freemasons were the heirs of the Templars and the Brethren of the Free Spirit in seeing the building of a lodge or a New Jerusalem as the symbol of dwelling within the temple of the individual body by cleansing it through the Holy Spirit. Each member was a living House of the Lord; the rites of purification of the private citadel were taught at the lodge or at prayer meetings. The Crusade for Jerusalem was translated to the inner quest for salvation. Self-knowledge and surrender to the will of God was the pilgrimage of the soul towards grace.

The part played by the millenarians and the Freemasons in the American and French revolutions and in the national revolts in Italy and the Habsburg Empire in the nineteenth century was significant, but hardly recorded. Certainly, the perniciousness led to their proscription by the Roman Catholic church. The American dollar bill still bears the Masonic device of the Great Pyramid surmounted by the All-Seeing Eye of Wisdom; it is inscribed with the date of 1776, when the Declaration of Independence began the *Novus Ordo Seclorum,* the "New Order of the Centuries." The capital of Washington in the District of Columbia was based by Major l'Enfant on the geometrical patterns that informed so many designs of ideal cities—circuses were imposed on a grid pattern, giving the variety of the curve within the regular pattern. The Capitol itself on its elevation lay under a dome on a flat rock. As the Pilgrims believed they were building a New Canaan in the wilderness, so the politicians and architects of the infant United States of America also planned a visionary form of city to head the New Order of the Centuries under the banner inscribed on dollar bills of higher note—In God We Trust.

In the French Revolution, two millenarian women, Suzette Labrousse and Catherine Théot, prophesied the coming Apocalypse. The groups which they influenced, the Masons of the Avignon Society with its Cathar legacy, and the Convulsionaries of Lyons, had their contacts with the

English Dissenters through Richard Brothers, who believed that he would lead the hidden Jews among the Gentiles in Europe back to the Holy Land and usher in the Second Coming of Christ. Currents of mysticism and occultism flourished among the Freemasons of the period and influenced its greater thinkers and scientists, such as Isaac Newton and Joseph Priestley.

Many modern historians trace a line from the medieval abbot Joachim of Fiore through John of Leyden at Münster and the communal American sect the Shakers, on through the French Revolution to early Marxism with its millennial visions stolen from anarchism of the state withering away to usher in a material paradise, where the proletariat might enjoy the fruits of production in a factory heavenly city upon earth. In later industrial and agricultural revolts from the Luddites to Captain Swing and the Agrarian Riots in East Anglia in 1816, the uprisings of the poor and the dispossessed were often expressed in terms of the medieval Crusade. As the Sons of Liberty declared to the property owners of Ashill: "Gentlemen, these few lines are to inform you that God Almighty have brought our blood to a proper circulation; that have been in a very bad state a long time, and now without an alteration of the foresaid, we mean to circulate your blood with the leave of God." Wherever Jerusalem was now held to be and whatever it was said to be—liberty or Paradise or a place in Palestine—a holy war might still be the way to get there.

THIRTEEN

REACHING ZION

"By the rivers of Babylon, there we sat down, yea, we wept,
when we remembered Zion."

—The 137th Psalm

The British engineered the return of the Jews to Jerusalem, although the French Revolution led to their just treatment in much of Europe. In 1791 the National Assembly voted a decree for the total emancipation of the Jews, and in gratitude, some Jews became Jacobins and began an identification with radical change. In London, the extraordinary mob leader Lord George Gordon was converted to the Jewish faith and called himself in prison the Hon. Israel bar Abraham Gordon: Edmund Burke referred to him as the Protestant rabbi. Napoleon's victories across Europe further confused revolutionary progress with Jewish freedom, so that certain clerical and conservative elements began to perceive—as they had in the Middle Ages—a Hebrew plot to subvert settled society. Curiously, as the Jews were given the rights of other citizens, so they were seen in some quarters as the hidden enemies of the modern state.

Before his expedition to Egypt, Napoleon had courted the Jews of Africa and Asia in his declaration of 1799, The Rightful Heirs of Palestine. The Israelites were a "unique nation, which in thousands of years, was deprived only of its ancestral lands by lust of conquest and tyranny, but not of name and national existence." Napoleon then referred to the prophecy of Isaiah, that "the ransomed of the Lord shall return, and come to Zion with songs and with everlasting joy upon their heads." They would soon enjoy the undisturbed possession of their heritage. "Arise, then, with gladness ye exiled!" Napoleon's efforts to conquer Palestine from Egypt, establish himself in Jerusalem, and hand over the defence of the Holy Land to the rebellious Jews were aborted by his defeat at the hands of the British and the Turks, followed by his return to France. But his call for liberty and nationalism still sounded in the ears of the Near East.

In western Europe, conversion remained the quick way to success in Christian society, for many disabilities still blocked the advance of the Jews, still barred from universities and professions such as the law. The Jews who were converted from their faith in the nineteenth century, however, were to change the perception of their people in England and Germany as well as in France. Benjamin Disraeli's father had written an essay on "The Genius of Judaism," but he had his son baptised into the Church of England. Karl Marx's grandfather had been a rabbi in Trier, but his father had become a Christian to practise at the bar. And Heinrich Heine was a child of the Napoleonic Wars, educated on the Lutheran Bible and in a French lycée. The Byron of the German language, he was to turn against his Jewish heritage as Karl Marx would, while Disraeli would become almost a Zionist after a pilgrimage to Jerusalem.

Before Disraeli was to become prime minister, the return of the Jews to Palestine was supported by Lord Palmerston, much influenced by the British Israelite views of the seventh earl of Shaftesbury, who believed that the Second Coming of Jesus Christ would not happen until his people had returned to their Holy Land, and that Palmerston was "chosen by God to be an instrument of good to His ancient people." By the end of the 1830s, the tiny Jewish population of Palestine had increased ten times over to ten thousand settlers, half of whom now lived in Jerusalem—a migration encouraged by the British government and the Rothschild family, who refused, however, to back the scheme of the German rabbi Zevi Hirsch Kalischer to buy Jerusalem and part of Israel from the Turkish sultan as part of a homeland. But the first English vice-consul, W. T. Young, appointed by Palmerston to the Holy City "to afford protection to the Jews generally," was soon followed by French and Prussian and American and

Armenian and Russian and Spanish representatives. Christianity was again taking interest in the site of the death of Christ. Life began to awaken in a sacred place that Chateaubriand had seen in 1806 as full of prisons and sepulchres rather than houses, "the distorted monuments of a cemetery in the middle of a desert. Go into the city, nothing will console you for the bleakness outside. You lose your way in little unpaved streets which rise and fall over uneven ground, and you walk along in dust clouds or over large pebbles. . . . There is no one in the streets, no one at the gates of the city." Chateaubriand also saw himself rather as a new Crusader, when he entered the Holy Sepulchre, an enlightened Christian come to rescue benighted Islam, which stood for "neither hatred of tyranny nor love of liberty."

To Disraeli, however, Jerusalem was still the spiritual centre of a proud and distinguished faith and an "unmixed blood" and race that adhered to the law of Moses—terms used by him with pride in this new age of imperialism. His novel *Alroy* spoke of his hero, the Prince of the Captivity, trying to restore Jerusalem to the Jews in the twelfth century. His first vision of the city was it standing "like the last gladiator in an amphitheatre of desolation," while the red cross of the Christians waved over its battlements. This mission also informed *Tancred*, subtitled *The New Crusade*, in which the aristocratic hero married a Jewess and reconciled British ambitions in the Near East with Arab hopes, so that the three religions might unite in a vast Alexandrian Empire against the Turks and the French. To Tancred, all the great things had been done by the little nations and cities, by "an Arabian tribe, a clan of the Aegean . . . Athens and Jerusalem," which was the cradle of the holy past, set in its barren hills. As Tancred saw it:

> What need for nature to be fair in a scene like this, where not a spot is visible that is not heroic or sacred, consecrated or memorable; not a rock that is not the cave of prophets; not a valley that is not the valley of heaven-anointed kings; not a mountain that is not the mountain of God!

> Before him is a living, a yet breathing and existing city, with Assyrian monarchs came down to besiege, which the chariots of Pharaohs encompassed, which Roman Emperors have personally assailed, for

199

which Saladin and Coeur de Lion, the Desert and Christendom, Asia and Europe, struggled in rival chivalry; a city which Mahomet sighed to rule, and over which the Creator alike of Assyrian kings and Egyptian Pharaohs and Roman Caesars, the Framer alike of the Desert and of Christendom, poured forth the full effusion of his divinely human sorrow. . . . The eye seized on Sion and Calvary; the gates of Bethlehem and Damascus; the hill of Titus; the Mosque of Mahomet and the tomb of Christ. The view of Jerusalem is the history the world; it is more, it is the history of earth and of heaven.

The rebirth of the Jewish presence in Jerusalem and the interest of Palmerston and Disraeli and Queen Victoria herself in Palestine had largely been the doing of Sir Moses Montefiore, a broker in the City of London for the Rothschilds, also the president of the Board of Deputies of the British Jews. He made seven pilgrimages in all to the Holy Land, the last at the age of ninety-one. He helped to rescue the Jewish community in Damascus from a blood persecution, and when Britain was allied with Turkey against Russia during the Crimean War, Montefiore travelled to Constantinople to petition the sultan for the purchase of land for the Jews outside the walls of Jerusalem. A plot was bought across the Hinnom Valley opposite Mount Zion, a windmill was built along with a large House of Tranquillity, where some twenty families might live. Medical help and water supplies were brought to the Jewish Quarter within the walls, and by 1896, three-fifths of the population of the city was Jewish, one-fifth Muslim, and one-fifth Christian to the number of forty-five thousand souls. Once more, the Jews were in a majority in Jerusalem.

To Disraeli's cast of mind, there should be no conflict between the British Empire and the Jews. He saw the Church of England as a Jewish institution, which kept alive Hebrew history and literature, while the three greatest legislators and administrators and reformers were all Jewish— Moses and Solomon and Christ, and their teachings moulded English beliefs and practises. "The life and property of England are protected by the laws of Sinai." In *Tancred,* Disraeli also described a supremely gifted power broker, Sidonia, who was superior to all other men because of the heritage of Israel, applied in Europe. And he proselytised his political colleagues such as Lord Stanley about the return of the Jews to Palestine, backed by financiers such as the Rothschilds. Any man who would carry out these plans would seem to be "the next Messiah, the true Saviour of his people."

His views were echoed and publicised later by George Eliot in *Daniel Deronda;* she also sought a bridge between the Bible and the Talmud, and through her Zionist character Mordecai, she voiced the hope of another paradise of peace which might flower in Canaan. "The world will gain as Israel gains." A community could be established in the Levant which contained the culture and sympathies of every great nation of Europe. "There will be a land set for a halting-place of enmities, a neutral ground for the East as Belgium is for the West." A restored Jerusalem in the hands of the Jews would be the centre of civilisation and concord upon earth. This became Deronda's final mission after his Jewish marriage, although he remained a Christian, and after the dying of Mordecai. As he declared to the unsympathetic Gwendolen Grandcourt, who told him that "*you* are just the same if you were not a Jew":

> "I am going to the East to become better acquainted with the condition of my race in various countries there," said Deronda, gently— anxious to be as explanatory as he could on what was the impersonal part of their separateness from each other. "The idea that I am possessed with is that of restoring a political existence to my people, making them a nation again, giving them a national centre, such as the English have, though they too are scattered over the face of the globe. That is a task which presents itself to me as a duty: I am resolved to begin it, however feebly. I am resolved to devote my life to it. At the least, I may awaken a movement in other minds, such as has been awakened in my own."

The influence of *Daniel Deronda* on the cause of Zionism was immense. In the words of Lucien Wolf, the novel gave "the Jewish national spirit the strongest stimulus it had experienced since the appearance of Shabbetai Zevi." Already in England, the Palestine Society and the Palestine Exploration Fund were constituted to survey the biblical sites. The officers of the Royal Engineers seconded there included Captain (later Lord) Kitchener, and Lieutenant Charles Warren, who made archaeological digs at Jerusalem in an endeavour to discover the exact locations of the Temple and the Holy Sepulchre. He later proposed that the sultan in Constantinople should permit the colonisation of Palestine by the Jews in return for a British assumption of some of the Turkish national debt. "It is written over and over again, in the word of God [that] Israel are returned to their own land." This approach was followed by the exhaustive topographical and geological efforts in the Holy Land carried out by Lieutenant Charles Reignier Conder. And with the publication of the excavations of Austen Henry Layard at Nineveh and the travels of Sir Richard Burton in Arabia, British interest in the culture of the Near East rose until Disraeli could solve the "great Asian mystery" suggested in *Tancred* by acquiring the passage to the Pacific Ocean through the Suez Canal, and translating Queen Victoria into the empress of India.

Among the Germans, Judaism provoked mixed feelings. The mastery of Heine over the German language led to a confusion in national opinion, which saw in him something of the alien. Heine himself could have taken French citizenship; but he preferred to remain a German. He once declared that there were three evils—poverty, pain, and Jewishness, which he found too full of censure and hatred. Full of ambition and self-loathing, he was baptised as a Protestant, although the Rothschilds continued to support him; members of the Heine family married into the European aristocracy. An *arriviste* as well as a genius with social as well as poetic aspirations, he despised Zionism and vaunted the values of the French Revolution. The French were the chosen people of the new religion of liberty, which William Blake had called Jerusalem. And Paris was the New Jerusalem, while the Rhine was "the Jordan that separates the consecrated land of freedom from the Land of the Philistines."

As with Heine, so with Marx. Immensely influenced by his rabbinical legacy and the Torah and the Talmud, his reaction from his heritage was incorporated into his radicalism. His Messiah was the means of production, which would lead to a material Promised Land. His vanguard and dictatorship of the proletariat was a Sanhedrin, an elite of the party rather than of the faith, the governors of the masses rather than the Jewish people. His classes were a retold parable of the sheep and the goats. His Jehovah was dialectical materialism, the will and the Word of God changed into the determination of a version of history which he called science. His millennium was as imminent as that of John of Leyden: he predicted the workers' revolution that would usher in a material paradise nine times in ten years in the mid-nineteenth century. Yet his laws of the processes of social change were to prove no more true in the long run than the fairy tales of the Brothers Grimm.

Marx's debt to his tradition made him renounce his influence. He turned on any idea that his powers of reason could be touched by his family's past religion. For him, Judaism was not so much the opium of its people, but the serpent in his scientific garden of determinism. Paradoxically, as he inspired thousands of young Jews to cast aside their faith and join in his messianic dream of an industrial Eden upon earth, so he turned on the Jews, particularly in eastern Europe, which Germany had coveted ever since the Crusades of the Teutonic Knights. To him, the Jews of Poland were the dirtiest of all races, particularly vile because they lived among the despised Slavs. Marx equally loathed the Jewish intelligentsia, although he was one of them. They had sold out to Mammon, not to Jehovah. "Money is the jealous God of Israel, besides which no other god may exist." This primitive resurrection of the medieval Crusaders' attack on the financiers among the Jews in the early German cities—those early pogroms based on fear and superstition—were vile obsessions in the mind of the most important revolutionary of his century, whose false analyses and conversion of the militant sermon into economic jargon were to spark a revolutionary revival across Europe that would have been the envy of Peter the Hermit or Martin Luther.

Another paradox converted a disciple of Marx into an apostle of Zionism. As Heine had been, Moses or Moritz Hess was a product of the ideas that Napoleon carried across to Germany. His grandfather was also a rabbi, although his father was a merchant in Cologne. Influenced by the sceptical Jewish philosopher Spinoza, he wrote *The Sacred History of Mankind,* a confused and anarchistic work that ran from the Creation to the French Revolution. He became a collaborator with Marx, who despised him intellectually; but his vehemence did much to convert Engels and Bakunin finally to socialism. Disillusioned after his rejection by his former comrades, he took the opposite direction to Marx and reverted to his Jewish tradition, reacting from the revolutionary ideas that had separated him in his youth from his faith. As his remarkable book *Rome and Jerusalem* declared, after an estrangement of twenty years, he had come back to his people. A buried thought was revived in him, "the thought of my nationality, which is inseparably connected with the ancestral heritage and the Holy Land, the Eternal City, the birthplace of the belief in the divine unity of life, as well as the hope in the future brotherhood of men."

Hess saw the restoration of the Jews to Palestine as "the Sabbath of history." His enemies were the sophisticated Jews, who wanted to be assimilated in Germany rather than found a new nation under the command of the Turks. Surely Frankfurt and Berlin were oases of culture and civilisation compared to Haifa and the actual Jerusalem on the ground. They would not listen to Hess's denunciation of them. "The 'new' Jew who denies the existence of Jewish nationality is not only a deserter in the religious sense but is also a traitor to his people, his race and even his family. If it were true that Jewish emancipation in exile is incompatible with Jewish nationality, then it is the duty of the Jews to sacrifice the former for the latter." Hess was to die a disappointed man. For it was too early in the growth of German anti-Semitism for such a transfer to Palestine to appear desirable to more than a few.

The contagion of messianic materialism was caught in the new industrial cities of Europe, where the Jews were now congregating, and occasionally in the Habsburg and the Tsarist empires, where eight million Jews would be living by the outbreak of the First World War, with five million dwelling in the rest of Europe. Increasing anti-Semitism in Russia, which led to intermittent pogroms, encouraged radicalism among some Jewish communities, which saw in socialism a means of overthrowing the Tsars, their persecutors. Emigration was another solution, not so much to Palestine, which was still under Muslim control, but to the United States of America, where the Pilgrim Fathers had also gone in search of a Promised Land.

More than two million Jews crossed the Atlantic before the First World War, displacing the Irish and the Italians in New York City as the largest immigrant group. Echoing the identification of the New Jerusalem with the quest for freedom, the Zionist poetess Emma Lazarus hailed the building of the Statue of Liberty as if a torch were being lit by a modern Moses to lead the way to another Israel in America before a return to Palestine might be possible.

Give me your tired, your poor,
Your huddled masses yearning to breathe free . . .

Indeed, when the State of Israel would be created after the Second World War, the descendants of those voyagers to the New World would give back to their ancestral homeland the resources and the sinews of war necessary for survival against the surrounding Muslim Old World.

The lights of reason were flickering even in France. When Captain Alfred Dreyfus was put on trial as a traitor, he was the only Jew serving on the general staff of the French army. He was accused on forged evidence of passing military intelligence to Germany. At the ceremony of his public stripping from rank, so similar to the humiliation suffered by the scapegoat in ancient Judea, a young Viennese journalist was present, Theodor Herzl, who had also seen the verdict pronounced in court against Dreyfus before he was sent to imprisonment on Devil's Island. The unjust sentence was to polarise French society and to set conservatives against radical opinion, causing riots and duels. It was also to inspire Herzl to write *Der Judenstaat,* the founding document of Zionism. Although he had supported assimilation into Habsburg society, he now saw that the refuge from the rising tide of anti-Semitism in Europe lay in the re-creation of Israel. The first excerpts from his pamphlet—hardly longer than *The Communist Manifesto*—were published in 1896 in the London *Jewish Chronicle,* then in Vienna, then in eighty editions across the Jewish Diaspora. "We are a *people, one* people," he declared. "We have everywhere tried honestly to integrate with the national communities surrounding us and to retain only our faith. We are not permitted to do so."

To Herzl, there were many roads to Jerusalem. He was prepared to colonise a new Israel where politics allowed and where resources were already allocated. The Rothschilds and Montefiore were backing settlements in Palestine, but Baron de Hirsch was supporting Jewish migration to Argentina. Wishing for the aid of the influential, Herzl said that he would take any site that might be offered. A Society of Jews should be formed, also a Jewish Company in the City of London, so financially secure that his scheme for resettlement should become "not a Panama but a Suez." He failed, however, to gain the goodwill of the richest Jews and the leading rabbis of western Europe, who thought him flamboyant and a dreamer like Disraeli's Alroy, the Prince of the Captivity with his long Assyrian beard. But his Zionist pamphlet attracted the support of the persecuted poor of eastern Europe and of powerful friends in one country free from the swelling of anti-Semitism, England.

Preceding Herzl's plans were those of Laurence Oliphant, a journalist and a utopian who approached the foreign secretary, Lord Salisbury, with a scheme already submitted to Disraeli, now Lord Beaconsfield. Oliphant set out the details for a development company in Palestine on a land concession leased from the Turkish government. Money could easily be raised from those who believed that the Second Coming and the millennium would be hastened by the return of the Jews to Israel. Assured of support from the government, Oliphant proceeded to Constantinople, where he made no progress, then he retired to Haifa, where he reported on the progress of the four Jewish agricultural colonies now established near the city. His writings inspired a British army colonel, Albert Goldsmid, to fund a Hovevei Zion society that desired slow colonisation, and when Herzl visited him, Goldsmid declared that he was Daniel Deronda, baptised a Christian, but reconverted to Judaism and the gradual return to Jerusalem.

Because the changes of government at Westminster and the caution of his initial English friends set back Herzl's enthusiastic progress, he decided to approach Germany, which had increasing investments and influence in Turkey. He met Kaiser Wilhelm II three times in Constantinople and even in Jerusalem, where the kaiser appeared in a white uniform on a white horse as the reincarnation of Frederick Barbarossa and Hohenstaufen. He had assumed the title of the Most Christian Sovereign, and he demanded to ride into the city through the Jaffa Gate, which was widened to give this new Teutonic Knight a more glorious entrance. His negotiations with Herzl, however, came to nothing, because Germany had no wish to jeopardise its excellent relations with Turkey, however much the kaiser himself wanted to return many of the German Jews to the Orient.

So Herzl still had to look on England as the point on which Archimedes had once rested his lever. His status had been enhanced by the calling of the First Zionist Congress in August 1978, in Basel. There, as Herzl confided in his diary, he "founded the Jewish State. . . . Perhaps in five years and certainly in fifty, everyone will know it." His true prophecy was certainly recognised by the delegates from sixteen countries, mainly from the poorer districts of eastern Europe. His appearance in formal dress was greeted with the ancient Jewish greeting *"Yechi Hamelech!"* or "Long live the king!" He was declared the Messiah by the chief rabbi of Sofia. The Second Zionist Congress opened two years later to the strains of Wagner, and among the delegates was Chaim Weizmann, born in Russia but then a student in Berlin who was destined to take Herzl's place. For the Zionist leader had a weak heart, and his incessant diplomacy did not improve his condition. If he was becoming a new Messiah to the ghetto, he had little physical chance of leading them back to Jerusalem.

His last successes lay in England, where he achieved recognition for the proposed Jewish state. An influx of east European Jews occasioned the appointment of the Royal Commission on Alien Immigration. Herzl was called as a witness by conservatives, who hoped he might support their case for an early exodus of the recent Jewish arrivals. This worried the leader of the English Jews, Lord Nathaniel Rothschild, who feared that Zionism could be used as an aid to anti-Semitism, a method of ridding European nations of their Jewish populations. Herzl carefully spoke for free asylum without any restrictions, then he stated his case for a new Israel, where the Jews would be recognised as citizens of their legal homeland, and where they might escape from persecution. He did not press for a solution to Palestine, but only the need to direct Jewish emigration elsewhere. Lord Rothschild pressed Herzl on Zionism, whether the fresh homeland for the oppressed Jews "be in Palestine itself or whether it be on the road to Palestine or elsewhere." Herzl responded that while the original Israel was the goal, an alternative refuge for the persecuted Jews of eastern Europe would be acceptable.

Herzl now suggested a compromise which Lord Rothschild approved, a Jewish colony in Cyprus or Sinai, both of which were under British control. At the Colonial Office, Joseph Chamberlain also approved of the scheme for a Jewish colony in general to be set up through a Colonial Trust, although not in the places mentioned. He liked the idea of giving the ten million Jews then in the world a rallying point, where they could become what Herzl called "secret but loyal subjects active in all walks of life all over the world." Although Sinai proved too waterless to support colonisation, Uganda was now suggested by Chamberlain as a wayside halt on the road to Jerusalem. Even if Herzl was disappointed, it was a form of making matter out of his dream. The important lawyer and member of Parliament David Lloyd George was commissioned to draft a chapter for a "New Palestine" in British East Africa. The foreign secretary, Lord Lansdowne, accepted the draft, implicitly recognising that there should be a Jewish state—something which had not existed for eighteen centuries. His reply stated:

> If a site can be found which the [Jewish Colonial] Trust and His Majesty's Commissioner consider suitable and which commends itself to His Majesty's Government, Lord Lansdowne will be prepared to entertain favourably proposals for the establishment of a Jewish colony of settlement, on conditions which enable the members to observe their national customs.

When Herzl read the letter from the Foreign Office, to the Sixth Zionist Congress in 1903, there was applause at the generosity of the British. But then doubts crept in. What was East Africa to the Near East? Or Uganda to Galilee? The desire for the true Israel was particularly strong among the Russian delegates, and when the vote was taken, Herzl only won a narrow majority for appointing a committee of inquiry to examine the Ugandan situation. The minority were implacable in their resistance and the death of Herzl a year later ended the African solution, which was opposed anyway by the British settlers already farming there. At the end of the day, there was no substitute for Jerusalem.

Yet the need to find a Jewish homeland for those powers who wished to divert Jewish immigration was becoming more critical. Even the reactionary Russian interior minister von Plehve supported the emigration of the Jews to Palestine or elsewhere, because he thought that they staffed the socialist and revolutionary ranks of those opposed to the Tsar. It was not that the new ruler of Russia, Nicholas II, was unpopular. Maxin Gorky, indeed, recorded in his autobiographical novel *Bystander* how the Orthodox masses of Russia yearned to follow behind his imperial banner. On the occasion of his coronation, more than half a million people assembled in Khodynka Fields outside Moscow. Gorky's hero watched them from a rooftop through a telescope. "The countless throng reminded him of the Crusades. . . . A picture came to his mind: Were this mass to surge suddenly like a wave into the city, its streets would not be able to hold the pressure of the dark torrents of people. The people would overturn the houses, trample their roofs into dust, sweep the entire city away."

This popular "crusade" ended in a stampede, which left nearly fifteen hundred dead. The masses were leaderless and agitators were hunted by the secret police, who often incited pogroms on the old pretext that the ills of the people were caused by the usury and evil practises of the Jews. When von Plehve was approached by a Jewish delegation to halt the persecutions, he told them, according to another minister, Witte: "Make your people stop their revolutionary actions, and I will stop the pogroms." The secret police, indeed, incited hatred of the Jews by disseminating the infamous concoction called *The Protocols of the Elders of Zion*. This paranoic fantasy purported to describe a meeting between the leaders of the twelve tribes of Israel, although these no longer existed. Using moneylending and republicanism and socialism, the Jews would infiltrate and subvert all the institutions of Europe until these would fall under their control. They would even undermine the great cities by blowing up the new underground railways. Finally, a Jewish king would rule over a world government, a perverted version of the coming of the Messiah or the Second Coming of Christ.

This farrago of anonymous nonsense suited reactionary theories of conspiracy. Millennial forebodings were inciting Russian fears. With the publication in 1900 of *War, Progress and the End of History,* the philosopher Solovyov prophesied a war with the Japanese, which they would win, before they conquered most of the world. The remnants of Europe would drive them back, a Christian Messiah would arise, and Armageddon would take place near Jerusalem, with the reign of Christ following that of the Anti-Christ. Only the first part of the prophecy proved true. Incited into provoking a war against Japan to divert disaffection at home into imperial adventures, the Tsar sent the Russian army and navy into disastrous defeats in the Far East. There were abortive revolutions in St. Petersburg and Moscow, and the Tsar was persuaded to make some concessions to democracy. The supporters of the absolute monarchy were easily persuaded that the socialist Jews were behind the catastrophes. There were pogroms in

Tbilisi and Kiev, in Baku and Tomsk and Odessa, where the Jewish quarters were looted and more than five hundred people were killed. The Tsar pretended surprise, writing to his mother of his amazement at how the pogroms occurred simultaneously in all the towns of Russia.

Faced with this systematic persecution over three decades, what was called the Second Aliyah or Immigration to Palestine was begun. The First Aliyah had started in 1882, when a few hundred Ashkenazi Zionists had arrived from Russia and Rumania, supported by the Hovevei Zion movement. They distinguished themselves from the Sephardi Jews already living in Palestine, some for generations, and called themselves the New Settlement. They were reinforced by the second Aliyah; these families from the ghettos brought along a separatist mentality as well as different languages, Russian and German and Yiddish as against the Spanish or Italian or Greek or Arabic of the Sephardim, whose ways and manners were of the East, while the northern incomers were disoriented. Although not as sharp a schism as between the Sunnis and the Shi'ites, or between the Catholics and the Greek Orthodox church and the Protestants, the distrust of the first Sephardi settlers from their Mediterranean cultures for the new arrivals from northeastern Europe would bedevil politics in Palestine and the later State of Israel. How could the original settlers believe that the latecomers were creating Zion, when it was already theirs and there? They felt somewhat as the Native Americans had felt when the Pilgrim Fathers had arrived to build a Zion in New England.

For the Ashkenazim, there was not only the question of relationships with the established Sephardi Jews, but also with the Palestinian Arabs. They had been warned early by Asher Ginzberg, who also used the Arabic name of Ahad Ha-'Am. There was little untilled soil in Palestine, unless there were large irrigation schemes. Under Ottoman rule, there was no good done by provoking the Arabs. Yet what did the new settlers do? "Just the very opposite! Serfs they were in the lands of the Diaspora and suddenly they find themselves in freedom, and this change has awakened in them an inclination to despotism. They treat the Arabs with hostility and cruelty, deprive them of their rights, offend them without cause and even boast of these deeds; and nobody among us opposes this despicable and dangerous inclination. We think that the Arabs are all savages, who live like animals and do not understand what is happening around. This is, however, a great error."

The Jewish population of the Holy Land doubled between 1880 and 1905 from thirty to sixty thousand people. Then the Zionists established the Anglo-Palestine Bank to assist Jewish settlement. This financial institution derived from Herzl's Jewish Colonial Trust, which had been offered Uganda. Now the Jewish National Fund was formed to attract donations in order to acquire land held in trust in Palestine. Three agricultural settlements were added to the thirteen Jewish villages already established, two in the Judean Hills and one by the Sea of Galilee, which became the first communal farm there. By the outbreak of the First World War, the number of Jews in Palestine had risen to some hundred thousand, a sixth of the total population, but two-thirds of those who lived in and by Jerusalem. They had achieved some sort of local government and self-sufficiency, although they remained dependent on outside contributions, chiefly from the Rothschilds and the Jewish National Fund. In a real sense, Europe was supporting a return of some Jews to their ancestral land.

Among the Ashkenazim, Germany supplied the preponderant influence through its language. Although the charitable Hilfsverein der Deutschen Juden was not a Zionist charity, it supported thirty schools in Palestine, where Hebrew was also taught. When war broke out between Britain and Germany, the choice between the great powers would have further split the Ashkenazim from the Sephardim, if their oppressors the Turks had not joined the side of the kaiser and the Austrian emperor. Because of its eighty-five million Muslim subjects in India and Egypt and the Sudan, the British government was most careful not to declare a holy war against the sultan in Constantinople. "Nothing is further from our thoughts or intuitions," Prime Minister Asquith declared, "than to initiate a crusade against their belief." He even offered to defend Muslim holy places against all enemies. But these protestations did not prevent the sultan from declaring a *jihad* against Britain to his own army and navy. A one-sided revival of the sacred war of the Muslim Levant against western Europe had been called forth.

For the Zionists, another part of Asquith's speech had great significance. After declaring that the Ottoman government, as it had drawn the sword so would perish by the sword, he announced "the death-knell of Ottoman dominion, not only in Europe, but in Asia." A leader in the *Jewish Chronicle* picked up the statement and asked, "If, as a result of the War, the dominion of Turkey in Asia is to be ended, then what is to be the fate of Palestine?" That was, indeed, the burning question for the Zionists, who saw the fate of Israel now in British hands. This was not the reaction of the Jews in Germany, who mainly supported the kaiser's assault on the Russian tyranny which had persecuted them and had instigated the two Aliyahs to Palestine. After the Germans' victory at Tannenberg, their armies were welcomed as liberators by the Polish Jews, as Napoleon's had been. German culture now promised the emancipation that the French had brought in their knapsacks.

The future leader of Zionism, however, had renounced Germany to become a British citizen. Chaim Weizmann had settled in Manchester to teach biochemistry at the university and to cultivate influential friends for the Jewish homeland. Through the editor of the *Manchester Guardian,* he met and converted to his cause two Lancashire members of Parliament, Winston Churchill and Arthur Balfour, the leader of the Conservative party, as well as David Lloyd George, now chancellor of the Exchequer. Another covert Zionist, the Liberal member of Parliament and chancellor of the duchy of Lancaster, Herbert Samuel, furthered the enterprise, after Asquith's speech against the Ottoman government. He suggested a Jewish national refuge as the centre of a new culture to the foreign secretary, Sir Edward Grey, who favoured the idea sentimentally and practically thought it an ideal neutral state between British and French interests in the Levant, once Turkey was dismembered. But the prime minister was cool on the project, commenting in a private letter that Samuel's memorandum read "almost like a new edition of *Tancred* brought up to date."

No progress could be made by the Zionists until Asquith was replaced by Lloyd George at Ten Downing Street. Weizmann ingratiated himself further with the future makers of decisions by setting up an advisory office in London for sympathisers to his cause and by helping Winston Churchill in his new role in the Admiralty. Churchill asked Weizmann if he could arrange the production of thirty thousand tons of acetone for making explosives: His job was to assemble the scientists and the laboratories. "My work," Weizmann later wrote, "brought me into touch with all kinds of people, high and low, in the British Government. Balfour succeeded Churchill in the Admiralty, Lloyd George became Minister of Munitions, and I had much to do with his board, for a great many problems not connected with acetone flowed into my laboratories. When the first period of experiment and construction was over, I had a certain amount of leisure, as well as more opportunity, to see British statesmen. . . ."

Some of the munitions which Weizmann was helping to make would be used by the Mediterranean fleet and the Egyptian Expeditionary Force to liberate Jerusalem from the Turks. For a Near Eastern campaign was being opened to relieve the stalemate on the western front. The desert Arabs were in revolt against the Turks. Significantly, the descendant of the Prophet, King of the Hejaz and Keeper of the Holy Cities of Medina and Mecca, Sherif Hussein, refused the call of the sultan for a *jihad* against Britain. The Arab Revolt of 1916 was fomented by T. E. Lawrence to create guerrilla forces in Arabia on the borders of Palestine, while General Allenby was seconded from France to lead a European and colonial army to recapture the Holy Land in a campaign that was resolutely not called a crusade.

The Egyptian Expeditionary Force took no new road to Jerusalem. In the words of one war correspondent, who accompanied the soldiers and the camels, the horses and the armoured cars:

We fought on fields which had been the battlegrounds of Egyptian and Assyrian armies, where Hittites, Ethiopians, Persians, Parthians, and Mongols poured out their blood in times when kingdoms were strong by the sword alone. The Ptolemies invaded Syria by this way, and here the Greeks put their colonising hands on the country. Alexander the Great made his route to Egypt. Pompey marched over the Maritime Plain and inaugurated that Roman rule which lasted for centuries; till Islam made its wide irresistible sweep in the seventh century. Then the Crusaders fought and won and lost, and Napoleon's ambitions in the East were wrecked just beyond the plains. . . . When the Commander-in-Chief had to decide how to take Jerusalem, we saw the British force move along precisely the same route that has been taken by armies since the time when Joshua overcame the Amorites and the day was lengthened by the sun and moon standing still till the battle was won. Geography had its influence on the strategy of today as completely as it did when armies were not cumbered with guns and mechanical transport.

In his guerrilla campaign with the desert tribes, Lawrence used the camel as his long-range weapon; after the capture of Mecca, he helped to cut off Medina and take Aqaba on the Red Sea, thus creating a supply port for his roving warriors where ships could sail from Port Suez with gold and guns past the Crusaders' fortress on Faroun Island at the harbour mouth. General Allenby advanced near the coastline towards Gaza and beyond in the last great cavalry campaign of modern warfare, using the mobility and shock charge of his horsemen as Godfrey de Bouillon and King Richard III of England had done. The Australian Light Horse would gallop into the Turkish ranks with their sabres, shouting, "Allah, you bastards, we will give you Allah," in their version of the Templar battle cry of "Beauséant." At Huj, the Warwickshire and Worcestershire yeomanry charged mountain and machine guns, hacking the Turkish loaders into silence with fearful losses. The Dorset and Buckingham and Berkshire yeomanries repeated that suicidal assault to take the Mughar-Katrah Ridge. They were emulating the berserk gallops of the military orders into Muslim defences in the time of the Kingdom of Jerusalem. Lawrence had enlightened Allenby on how his mounted guerrillas could harass the Turkish flanks as the Crusaders had in the days of Saladin, while the general's favourite reading strategy of ancient campaigns in the Middle East was the Old Testament and the *Historical Geography of the Holy Land*. In those texts, there were many warnings against leaving the coastal plains for the Judean Hills, where manoeuvre was limited and ambush was probable. But finally the mountains had to be crossed to take Jerusalem, where the German commander von Falkenhayn had set up his headquarters in the German hospice on the Mount of Olives, while the Turkish headquarters were in the French hospice of Nôtre Dame. For the German and the Turkish forces had set up a defensive line at Nebi Samuel, where the prophet Samuel was now buried beneath the dome of a mosque, and where King Richard had turned back from reaching the Holy City on the Third Crusade.

Allenby did not intend to repeat the tragedies of the past. He would force the surrender of Jerusalem in December 1917 without an assault.

There would be no new massacre in the Holy City. The Allied cause could not stand such bad propaganda. As he instructed his commanders, "On no account is any risk to be run of bringing the City of Jerusalem or its immediate environs within the area of operations." He did not know that von Falkenhayn had orders not to be besieged in the Holy City and risk its sacred treasures. Hand-to-hand fighting on the ridges and a failed Turkish counterattack allowed Allenby's divisions almost to surround Jerusalem, leaving an escape route for the enemy forces, which abandoned their base, leaving the Turkish mayor to give up the keys to the new conquerors. At first, these were offered to a pair of lost mess cooks, who were looking for their officers and wisely refused such a signal honour. They ended in the hands of General Shea, deputed to enter the gates on behalf of Allenby. He drove into the city, where one witness wrote that he was met with "shrill cries of delight in a babel of tongues. Women threw flowers into the car and spread palm leaves on the road." The official report of the yielding of the keys read: "Thus at 12:30 the Holy City was surrendered for the twenty-third time, and for the first time to British arms, and on this occasion without bloodshed among the inhabitants or damage to the buildings in the City itself."

With the example of Christ to guide him, Allenby decided to make a humble entry, unlike the swagger of the kaiser. He walked on foot through the Jaffa Gate, leading a small procession of his staff and representatives of the Allies and Lawrence, who considered it to be "the supreme moment of the war." He proceeded into the Mount Zion Quarter and stopped on the steps of the Citadel, the entrance to David's Tower. There a proclamation was read to the citizens in several languages, promising that all the sacred places of Islam and Christianity and Judaism would be respected. At the adjacent old Turkish barrack square, Allenby met the Muslim leaders, the mayor and the mufti and the sheikhs who were the keepers of the Dome of the Rock, the al-Aqsa mosque, and the Mosque of Omar, as well as the remaining prelates of the Latin, Greek Orthodox, American, Coptic, and Syriac churches along with the rabbis of the Holy City. He confirmed his pledge of religious toleration. Guards were placed in all the sacred sites. Particularly careful of Muslim susceptibilities, Allenby's log repeated his orders:

The Mosque of Omar and the area round it has been placed under Moslem control and a military cordon composed of Indian Mahomedan officers and soldiers has been established round the Mosque. Orders have been issued that without permission of the Military Governor and the Moslem in charge of the Mosque no non-Moslem is to pass this cordon. . . . The Tomb of Hebron has been placed under exclusive Moslem control.

The hereditary custodians of the Wakfs at the Gates of the Holy Sepulchre have been requested to take up their accustomed duties in remembrance of the magnanimous act of the Caliph Omar who protected the Church.

Allenby refused to tell the world press that his capture of Jerusalem was a Crusade, although he was universally hailed as the Last Crusader. He was not only dependent on his Muslim troops from India, but on the Arab irregulars owing allegiance to Sherif Hussein and his son Feisal, whom Lawrence called the Armed Prophet. Jerusalem had fallen peacefully, all the holy places were protected. Now the military objective was to advance on Damascus and Aleppo. Again Allenby followed crusading strategy, using his cavalry supported by sea power to progress along the shoreline, taking Acre and Haifa on the way north.

There was no new defeat at the Horns of Hittin, for Tiberias was evacuated before the Christian advance. There was a final great cavalry battle over the ruins of Megiddo, or Armageddon, prophesied as the site of the millennial struggle. The three battalions of Jewish volunteers particularly distinguished themselves in the fight and became known as the Jewish Legion. Damascus was surrounded and fell almost without resistance; through Lawrence's diplomacy, control of the city was given to Feisal and remained in Islamic hands. But with news of the terms of the secret Sykes-Picot treaty, carving up the Levant between Britain and France, Lawrence asked Allenby for permission to leave for Europe, where he could struggle on the diplomatic front for the Arab independence, which he had promised Feisal and his father and the desert Arabs. Just before Aleppo fell, the armistice was announced on 31 October 1918, and the First World War had ended.

Although Sir Mark Sykes was a Zionist and acted as an intermediary between Chaim Weizmann and the British government, he was a Catholic and had sympathies with the church in France. The French, represented by Picot, insisted on maintaining their historical influence in Syria, while they were reluctant to concede the British influence over Palestine. A secret agreement gave France control as far south as Acre and the Sea of Galilee, thus cutting ancient Israel in two and denying independence to the Arabs in Syria and Palestine, while the position of allied Russia was left unclear. It was premature, anyway; as the director of British intelligence commented, "We are rather in the position of the hunters who divided up the skin of the bear before they had killed it." But this agreement did open the way for a British declaration on the future of a Jewish homeland in Palestine.

Weizmann pressed for the full Zionist programme. With the aid of Lord Walter Rothschild, whose father had recently died, he presented a list of basic aims, which included the recognition of: a Jewish nation in Palestine with full civic and political rights; the necessity for the Jewish resettlement of Palestine with the right of free immigration there; and the granting to the settlers of every facility for immediate naturalisation and land purchase. With the new prime minister, Lloyd George, and the new foreign secretary, Balfour, both Zionists, Weizmann thought he could achieve his objectives as Allenby was doing in his capture of the Holy Land.

Yet the political situation was changing all the time. The Kerensky government fell in Russia and the Bolsheviks came to power, thus ending any Allied wish to give them some influence in the Levant. And the United States of America joined the Allies; both its Democratic president, Woodrow Wilson, and its senior Republican senator, Henry Cabot Lodge, were sympathetic to Zionism. A Jewish national home seemed to Lodge entirely commendable, while he abhorred Muslim control of Jerusalem. And Balfour in his "Memorandum Respecting Syria, Palestine and Mesopotamia" was forthright about the future of the Holy Land: "The Four Great Powers are committed to Zionism. And Zionism, be it right or wrong, good or bad, is rooted in age-long traditions, in present needs, in future hopes, of far profounder import than the desires and prejudices of the seven hundred thousand Arabs who now inhabit that ancient land."

The letter known as the Balfour Declaration heralded the State of Israel. If the form of the announcement was not exactly what Weizmann wanted, it did make legitimate the aspirations of Zionism. The declaration was flawed, of course, because of British imperial ambitions in the Middle East, the wish to satisfy Arab demands for independence, the necessity of soothing Muslim fears, and the accommodation with France under the Sykes-Picot agreement. Guided by such considerations, Balfour sent a letter to Lord Rothschild, which was masterful in its ambiguity; it considered all the factors and gave something to all parties, though most to the Zionists. The important part of the text read:

> His Majesty's Government view with favour the establishment in Palestine of a National Home for the Jewish people, and will use their best endeavours to facilitate the achievement of this object, it being clearly understood that nothing shall be done which may prejudice the civil and religious rights of existing non-Jewish communities in Palestine, or the rights and political status enjoyed by Jews in any other country.

One month after the Balfour Declaration, Allenby entered Jerusalem by the Jaffa Gate. For the Jews, the timing was almost messianic. The Holy City was in the hands of the occupying power, which had granted the principle of a national homeland in Palestine. Although the governance of ancient Israel could not be solved until the Allied haggling at the Treaty of Versailles was over, British forces held the territory and would hardly be moved. Weizmann's good fortune was to find Zionists in control of the cabinet in London, although their Protestant fervour had Biblical rather than humanitarian motives. They saw the restoration of Jerusalem to God's Chosen People as affording a light to the Gentiles and a harbinger of the Second Coming of Christ. Even if British imperial interests lay more with good relationships with the Arabs, there was enough religious zeal left over from their Scottish and Welsh educations in Balfour and Lloyd George to give Weizmann the ground on which to plant his mustard seed. Through his work, the British were to fulfil Napoleon's promise of the century before in his quotation from Isaiah—"The ransomed of the land shall return, and come to Zion with songs and everlasting joy upon their heads."

FOURTEEN

INTOLERABLE
MANDATE

And now a word to the Jews in Palestine. I have no doubt that they are going about it the wrong way. The Palestine of the Biblical conception is not a geographical tract. It is in their hearts. But if they must look to Palestine as their national home, it is wrong to enter it under the shadow of the British gun. . . . They can settle in Palestine only by the goodwill of the Arabs.

—Mahatma Gandhi, 1917

"The Allied Powers . . . have entrusted to my country a Mandate to watch over the interests of Palestine, and to ensure to your country that peaceful and prosperous development which has so long been denied to you.

"You are well aware that the . . . powers have decided that measures be adopted to secure . . . a National Home for the Jewish People.

"I realise profoundly the solemnity of the trust involved in the government of a country which is sacred alike to Christians, Muhammedans and Jews, and I will watch with deep interest and warm sympathy the future progress and development of a state whose history has been of such tremendous import to the world."

This was the message of the first Christian king effectively to rule Jerusalem and the Holy Land for more than seven hundred years. The pious royal hopes of George V were drafted in 1920 by the British government, which was to be granted a mandate over Palestine. Before the peace conference in Paris, Lawrence had arranged a meeting between Feisal and Weizmann in London. Both the Arab and the Jewish leader were against the Sykes-Picot agreement, but according to Weizmann, Feisal remarked that "it was curious there should be friction between Jews and Arabs in Palestine. There was no friction in any other country where Jews lived together with Arabs." Feisal was then reported to say that the Zionist and the Arab causes were fellow movements, and that he would try to make Britain the trustee power for Arabia and Palestine, and if he did not succeed, he would try for action from America. To a British delegate at the peace conference, Feisal declared he wanted the Zionists to come to Palestine, which would be transformed. "It will become a garden; it will blossom like the rose. We shall borrow their experts; we shall work together. We shall do the same in all the countries which we Arabs turned into deserts." Feisal and Weizmann signed a concord that would allow Jewish immigration and settlement in Palestine, as long as the Arab farmers were protected. Yet Feisal added a rider that, if the Arabs did not attain their independence, he would hold his agreement with the Zionists null and void.

Unfortunately, the peace conference granted the whole of Syria and Lebanon as a mandate to the French, although a Syrian National Congress elected Feisal as the king of a united Syria. When the French insisted on their crusading "rights" in the Levant, Feisal did point out through Lawrence's interpretation that they had lost the medieval wars. Although they did not win the argument, the French still sent troops to Damascus and deposed Feisal. This was imperialism and no Crusade. Feisal then abrogated his agreement with the Zionists, declaring that both Syria and Palestine had been covered by his pledge. The British, however, found him another throne in Iraq, which was effectively under their control, and a Hashimite dynasty was established there. His father, King Hussein, did not do so well in Arabia, where he was forced to abdicate in favour of another son, Ali, who had to cede the throne in turn to Abdul Aziz ibn Saud, the prince of the fanatical Wahabis in central Arabia. He captured Mecca and Medina, establishing his own dynasty as the keepers of the two holier cities in Islam. Another son Abdullah, however, was made emir of Transjordan under the British Mandate, and he was to live to become in 1948 the Hashimite ruler of an independent kingdom. Although he was to be assassinated in the al-Aqsa mosque three years later, his grandson King Hussein has remained the last of the ruling Hashimite dynasty descended from the Prophet and the keeper of the Muslim holy places in Jerusalem guaranteed by General Allenby, the Dome of the Rock and the al-Aqsa mosque and the Mosque of Omar.

To plan a state is never to run a state. However much the Balfour Declaration appeared to reconcile Zionist and moderate Jewish opinion with Arab nationalism and the needs of the Palestine Muslims, British domination proved that there was no way to pacify the irreconcilable. Ruling ended friendship, administration bred enmity. As the military governor of Jerusalem, Ronald Storrs, declared, he was not wholly either for the Jews or the Arabs, but for both. "Two hours of Arab grievances drive me to the Synagogue," he wrote, "while after an intensive course of Zionist propaganda I am prepared to embrace Islam." The refusal of the British authorities immediately to allow a provisional Jewish government in Palestine led to the formation of the Hashomer, a first clandestine defence force, arranged by Vladimir Jabotinsky, who had inspired the recruitment of the three battalions of the "Jewish Legion," now disbanded by the British. His campaign was aided by Arab raids against the Jewish settlements of Tel Hai and Metullah in Upper Galilee, where the pioneer farmer Trumpeldor was killed, followed by a riot against the Jews in Jerusalem itself. Nine Jews and Arabs were murdered, two hundred injured, synagogues burned. Jabotinsky tried to intervene during the riots with a hundred armed volunteers, but he was turned away and arrested and sentenced to penal servitude, although he soon received an amnesty on the arrival of Herbert Samuel, the first British high commissioner, with his civil administration. On his release, Jabotinsky resolved to form a Haganah, a Jewish army ready to fight for a forthcoming State of Israel.

The Arabs were also organising for a future holy war. A secret group of militants named Al-Fatah, or the "Young Arabs," was started in Paris in 1911 and was transferred with French backing to Damascus to pursue its struggle against the British Mandate and Zionism. This group was later to develop into an Arab National Congress. As in the Crusades, the Christian powers were divided in their policies over the Holy Land. And Herbert Samuel made a fatal error in the pursuit of impartiality. Alongside Jabotinsky, he amnestied Haj Amin al-Husseini, who was fiercely opposed to both the British and the presence of the Jews in Palestine. He was allowed to become grand mufti of Jerusalem, a position which he used to foment riots in the cause of Arab independence, especially when he and his associates took over a Supreme Muslim Council set up by the British administration; the grand mufti also headed the Muslim religious courts and controlled the Wakf, extensive religious endowments given by the faithful. He was an instigator of various attacks on the immigrants to Palestine. Forty-three Jews were murdered in 1921 in Jaffa, one hundred and fifty in another assault eight years later. The grand mufti was to become a supporter of Hitler and his "Final Solution." He eliminated any hope of Weizmann's dream of cooperation between the Jews and the Palestinian Arabs in the Promised Land.

The riots provoked Herbert Samuel to initiate a British policy of stopping or slowing Jewish immigration, which was chiefly from Poland at the time. He declared that Britain could not have a second Ireland on its hands, another religious war of Catholics against Protestant immigrants. This policy turned the Zionists against the British, who had helped them so effectively back to their homeland. The Ashkenazi majority of the settlers was also anti-imperialist and loathed the British mandate; the ideology was chiefly socialist and the common languages were German and Yiddish with a future commitment to Hebrew. David Ben-Gurion from Plonsk in Russian Poland travelled round the Sephardi Jewish communities in the Near East, sailed to New York to help organise migration to Palestine, served in the "Jewish Legion," and became the secretary-general of the Histadruth, the Zionist trade-union movement, which enrolled during the 1920s a majority of the Jewish workers in Palestine. During the next decade, he and his comrades would capture the Zionist executive, which would be called the Jewish Agency. Also in Poland, Jabotinsky founded the Betar, a militant youth organisation which drilled and learned to shoot. One of its organisers was the young Menachem Begin, the later leader of an extremist underground movement in Palestine.

Numbers on the soil and in the cities were essential, if the Jews wished to reduce the large Arab preponderance. Fortunately for them, Winston Churchill was appointed colonial secretary and issued a White Paper in 1922, defending British aims. His Majesty's government did not intend to create a wholly Jewish Palestine, which would become "as Jewish as

England is English." The whole of the country would not be converted into a Jewish National Home, but "such a home should be founded *in* Palestine." The existing Jewish community should be developed where it was "as of right and not on sufferance." Churchill's wording seemed to imply a later partition of the Holy Land; for Jewish settlement was forbidden in Transjordan. Yet he did lift immigration restrictions; but the response was disappointing to the Zionists until the Great Depression and the rise of fascism in Europe. In the twelve years after 1920 during a Third and Fourth Aliyah, the average annual inflow into Palestine was ten thousand Jews, until they numbered one-sixth of the population; three-quarters lived in the cities and one-quarter on the land, where the socialist experiments in cooperative farming aided by a Labour Brigade were developing. The mother of the later *kibbutzim* was born in the swampland of the Jezreel valley.

A beacon in the return to Israel was the formal opening in 1925 of the Hebrew University on the heights of Mount Scopus overlooking Jerusalem. The aged Lord Balfour arrived with General Allenby and Dr. Weizmann to speak of the cultural heritage now being taught at the Holy City. It appeared a moment of truth for the vision of the British Israelites and Benjamin Disraeli and George Eliot, that a light for the Gentiles would shine forth after the return of God's Chosen People to their blessed country. Balfour visited Tel Aviv and the Jezreel valley, where he was astonished by the economic progress and proud demeanour of the people, so different from those he had met in his constituency in Manchester. His declaration seemed to have brought about progress in neglected Israel, and the last year when Herbert Samuel was high commissioner ended in some sort of peace, in spite of Arab revolts against imperialism in Baghdad and Damascus.

The next high commissioner, Field Marshal Lord Plumer, carried out Churchill's policies of slow and steady support for the growth of Jewish communities in Palestine, without antagonising the Arabs overmuch. When the grand mufti declared that he could not be responsible for law and order if a sacred Jewish procession was held in Jerusalem, Plumer was said to have replied, "You need not worry about law and order. That is my responsibility." During the next four years, however, the grand mufti incited Muslim passions against the infidels, particularly over the sacred sites in his care, the Dome of the Rock and the al-Aqsa mosque, so near to the Western Wall, where the Jews made their devotions under various restrictions, as it lay within the Arab holy quarter of the Haram esh-Sharif.

In the summer of 1929, the young Jews of the Betar organised a demonstration at the Western Wall, demanding free access and worship, and hoisting a Zionist flag. A week later, the Muslim crowds at prayer on Mount Moriah were told of a Jewish plot to destroy the al-Aqsa mosque and the Dome of the Rock in order to rebuild the Temple of Solomon. An orchestrated riot began with pogroms carried out by young Arabs in the Jewish Quarter in Jerusalem, in Hebron and in Safed and other towns; one hundred and forty Jews were killed, many more wounded. The only retaliation was in Jaffa, where an *imam* was killed by Betar members from Tel Aviv along with six more Arabs. British forces were sent into action by the new high commissioner, Sir John Chancellor, and the riots were put down with the loss of more than a hundred further Arab lives.

The following commission of enquiry endorsed the fears of the Arabs and recommended restrictions on Jewish immigration and land purchase, while excusing the grand mufti of promoting a religious conflict. The Labour government now in power in England was split in its sympathies for the Histadruth socialist union policy as well as for the Arab victims of imperialism. Nothing was done to bind the wounds that had broken open in Jerusalem. The policy of impartiality had become one of refereeing a stalemate. The British were not pursuing a strategy of dividing and ruling. They could not rule or bridge the religious divide.

The rise to power of Hitler in Germany and the beginning of the worst persecution of the Jews in history led to the floodgates opening for immigration. In the three years after 1932, one hundred and fifty thousand Jews entered Palestine; the following year, they numbered three in ten of the population. Arab opinion could easily be inflamed at such a sudden increase. Nazareth became the centre not of worship of the birth of Christ, but of an underground movement led by a Syrian, Izzed Din al-Qassem, which sabotaged rail tracks and oil pipelines. Equally, the Haganah was being developed as a Jewish defence force, responsible for organising illegal immigration and acquiring weapons for a future conflict. It was advised by an extraordinary young British officer, Orde Wingate; he organised "night squads" for quick response and came to be called the Lawrence of

Judea. The Betar followed the path of Al-Fatah and formed a group of militant secret cadres known as the Irgun Zvai Leumi, or the National Military Organisation. The fuse and the powder were laid for a conflagration that only needed a spark.

Fresh anti-Jewish riots occurred in 1936 with the formation of the Arab Higher Committee under the leadership of the grand mufti, who called a general strike until Jewish immigration was suspended and a National Arab Government was instituted. The British sent in another division of troops; a thousand Arabs fell in the subsequent civil strife, and a hundred Jews. Another investigating commission was announced under Lord Peel. It recognised the implacable hostility between the Zionists and the Arab nationalists, saying that "neither community believes in its heart that it will be safe unless it is master in its home." It recommended what Churchill had implied, the partition of Palestine into three parts, Jewish and Arab and a British Mandate responsible to the League of Nations with a proposed jurisdiction similar to that of the last Kingdom of Jerusalem—an enclave including the Holy City and Bethlehem and Nazareth and stretching to the sea. The Jewish state would be given the coastal plain from Tel Aviv to a point south of Haifa, the Valley of Jezreel, and most of Galilee. Chaim Weizmann, the president of the World Zionist Organisation, saw merit in the scheme because a Jewish state was actually to be created; but he could not persuade his fellow Zionists to accept it. Then a Pan-Arab Congress in Syria wholly rejected the proposal, and although the grand mufti and the Arab Higher Committee were deported or fled to Syria, Arab militance in Palestine broke out into sporadic hostilities. No partition was acceptable, which appeared to give "the richest land to the Jews, the holiest to the English, the most barren to the Arabs."

Before the outbreak of the Second World War in Europe, both religious groups in Palestine were preparing for a holy, as well as a civil, war. Jabotinsky kept on splitting the Zionists into Revisionist or New Zionists. "Zionism is a colonising adventure," he declared, "and it therefore stands or falls by the question of armed force. It is important to build, it is important to speak Hebrew, but unfortunately, it is even more important to be able to shoot." Such principles had inspired Joshua and the tribes of Israel. They must be revived. Judea had fallen in blood and fire, according to Jabotinsky, and in fire and blood it would rise again. Although he was increasingly put out to grass as Ben-Gurion rose in power to lead the Jewish Agency, his influence over the nascent Jewish army and underground squads was immense. There had to be a fight at some time to create and then expand a Jewish state. As even Weizmann had said cryptically, when he advised the acceptance of a minimal Israel under the plan of the Peel Commission, "The Kingdom of David was smaller, under Solomon it became an empire. Who knows?"

Searching for an impossible compromise, the Chamberlain government in England came up with a proposal almost as ill-starred as the Munich agreement with Hitler—and certain to bring no peace at any time. Apparently forgetful of the Balfour Declaration, a new government White Paper in 1939 advocated the creation within ten years of a binational Arab and Jewish state in Palestine, while Jewish land acquisition was halted and immigration restricted to seventy-five thousand people over the next five years—such a solution, when there was the threat of the Holocaust. Ben-Gurion went to the high commissioner of the time, Sir Harold MacMichael, in anger, saying: "This attempt to frustrate the age-long aspirations of the Jewish people to become rooted again in the soil of its ancient homeland is made at a time when millions of Jews are being mercilessly persecuted by a cruel enemy. The Jewish people will not submit to the conversion of the National Home into a ghetto!"

This scabby British policy was rejected by both the Arab Higher Committee in exile and the Zionists, who now perceived Britain as their enemy. Yet the outbreak of the Second World War between the Allied and the Axis powers, between democracy and fascism, was to make Zionists consider England again as a necessary and temporary friend against the worst of evils, the Third Reich, dedicated to the extermination of the Jews. As Ben-Gurion again declared, "The Jews of Palestine happen to be the only community in the Middle East whose very survival is bound up with the defeat of Hitler. We shall fight in this war as if there were no White Paper, and we shall fight the White Paper as if there were no war."

Initially, in the period of what came to be known as the Phony War, when Germany was carving up Poland with Russia and holding its attack on France, the British were uninterested in the Jewish offer of help. The Jews in Palestine themselves were demoralised by the Stalin-Hitler alliance. Communism in Russia had been practising a form of anti-Semitism, particularly after Trotsky had been forced into exile. Many of the Ashkenazi immigrants, however, were nostalgic for the early socialism of their home-land before it was tainted by the horror of the *gulag,* a civil genocide that was to exceed the Holocaust in the numbers of the dead. The alliance of the Communists with the Fascists to partition Poland was too cynical to ex-cuse and the consequences of that conspiracy too dreadful to contemplate. The Ashkenazim were also imbued with German culture, and its perver-sion by the Nazis was another slow death to body and soul. Yet these Euro-pean betrayals of the ideals of socialism and civilisation were fuel to the Zionist fire in creating a new Israel, where the Jews could forge their own identity and community in Asia.

With belligerent Europe even more dependent on their oil supplies, the Arabs saw their opportunity as well as their disability. Although Turkey was deterred from again supporting Germany, it exercised a benevolent neutrality, while certain nationalist Arabs such as the grand mufti and some politicians in Iran and Iraq saw the Italian and German advance on the Nile through North Africa as a chance of overthrowing the hated Anglo-French hegemony in the Middle East. The patchwork of artificial national bound-aries in the Near East had only been a European imposition after the First World War. Moreover, the Palestinian Arabs considered that they were suffering from Europe's sins against the Jews, whom Islam had generally treated with tolerance. The Germans were responsible for genocide, not them. The concentration camps and the policy of extermination, which was initiated by a cultured and officially Protestant power, carried the pogroms of the Crusades into the nightmares of mass murder, far worse and more deliberate than the massacre perpetrated at the fall of Jerusalem. Yet this was the sin of Christianity against Judaism. Islam had nothing to do with it. Why then should Europe encourage the institution of a State of Israel in Palestine, where the Arabs had dwelt for more than a thousand years and still held a large majority? Europe appeared to be another Pilate, washing its hands of the murder of Christ's people by exporting its col-lective guilt into the Muslim world.

This European civil war began separately from Japan's war against China in Asia. Only as it developed did it become a Second World War. Even Nazi Germany tried to revive the ideology of the Crusades, but without Christ. Hitler was depicted in shining armour with the white banner of the

Templars and the Teutonic Knights flying behind him. He had rebuilt the grand master's fortress and headquarters at Marienburg for his eastern crusade against the despised Slavs and the Jews. The Allied powers certainly saw Hitler and Mussolini as the forces of darkness, if not of the Anti-Christ. Although this was not a religious war, as those of the Protestants against the Catholics had been, it was in the eyes of the British people a struggle of good against evil, perhaps the last just war, preached by St. Augustine. And in this, the Jews agreed, united at last in the call for their homeland by the genocide of the Nazi regime.

The first offer of forming a Jewish Brigade for the British forces in Egypt was refused. This was the result of Ben-Gurion building up the resources of the Haganah; caches of armaments were continually being discovered by the British Palestine Police. The situation, however, was ambiguous, because by the end of 1940, there were fifteen thousand armed Jews officially forming the Jewish Settlement Police, but also unofficially members of the Haganah. Yet the underground movements, the Irgun and the even more extreme Stern Gang, were beginning reprisals against the Arabs and attacks on British military bases. Although Jewish commandos were used by the British in an attempt to quell the rebellion in Iraq, the raid failed. Now prime minister, Winston Churchill favoured the formation of a Jewish Brigade, but he was blocked by his chief of the Imperial General Staff and his foreign secretary, Anthony Eden, who courted Arab favour. Only with the Japanese attack on Pearl Harbour and the belated entry of the United States into the war after Britain had fought long and almost alone, did Weizmann and Ben-Gurion have the chance to harness the peace aims of the greatest industrial power in the world to the cause of Zionism. A declaration of the American Zionists at the Biltmore Hotel in 1942 demanded all of Palestine as a Jewish commonwealth.

The American president, Franklin D. Roosevelt, was careful to play down to the Arabs the significance of the Zionist lobby; but it was an important factor in Allied diplomacy. For fear of appearing to permit the recruitment of a Jewish army, the British did not allow a separate brigade, but they did recruit twenty-six thousand Palestinian Jews and nine thousand Palestinian Arabs into their armed forces. The grand mufti, now deposed, was also recruiting from his headquarters in Berlin. Although Lord

Moyne was assassinated in Cairo by Zionist terrorists in 1944, under American pressure Churchill accepted a plan from Weizmann that the serving Jews should be able to sew the Star of David on their tunics. Their religious fight against fascism was recognised by that symbolic action, and in the closing months of the world war, a Jewish Brigade of five thousand men was formed at last.

When the invasion of Normandy by the Allied forces eventually took place on D Day in June 1944, the American general Eisenhower deliberately called it the Great Crusade. He used biblical language, invoking the need to "beseech the blessings of Almighty God on this great and noble undertaking." President Roosevelt also preached a divine message. "Almighty God: Our sons, pride of our Nation, this day have set upon a mighty endeavor. . . . They will need Thy blessings. Their road will be long and hard." In the counterinvasion from Normandy of 1066, William the Conqueror had also embarked on a successful crusade, flying the papal banner. Some nine hundred years later, the largest sea-borne invasion in history began the liberation of France and western Europe, while eastern Europe fell to the Soviet Red Army and totalitarian control. Although the long and hard road mentioned by Roosevelt seemed to lead to Berlin— to be partitioned among the conquering powers—it also led indirectly to Jerusalem, which would also be split between Muslim and Jew.

Hitler had tried to exterminate all the Jews in Europe in the Holocaust, the attempted genocide of a whole people. A million and a half survivors, some from the concentration camps of Auschwitz and Belsen and Buchenwald and Treblinka, had only one sure refuge left in a murderous continent. For outside the safe havens of America and Britain, they had suffered unspeakably in Christian Europe, usually handed over to Nazi annihilation. When Ben-Gurion was asked by a United Nations special committee why the Haganah was encouraging illegal immigration into Palestine, he pointed to what the British had done at Dunkirk. They had saved their expeditionary force in small boats, turning a military disaster into a moral triumph. "We suffered a greater disaster in Europe than the British Army," Ben-Gurion said. "Not a few thousands, not tens of thousands, but millions—six million were put to death. Can anybody realise what that means to us?"

It meant the hatred of most of the worldwide Jewish community for British efforts to stop the refugees arriving in old hulks in Palestine. The Royal Navy turned most of the ships back, including the *President Warfield,* renamed the *Exodus 1947.* When its suffering passengers were finally discharged in a camp in a West Germany under Allied military occupation, the Zionists had won their Dunkirk. That refugee odyssey gave them a moral victory that could no longer prevent free immigration to Palestine, which was rapidly descending into chaos and civil strife and becoming what Arthur Koestler called "John Bull's other Ireland."

Weizmann and his British supporters had expected the Labour government, after its mammoth triumph against Winston Churchill in 1945, to be even more sympathetic to the formation of a State of Israel than the great British war leader had been. They were cruelly deceived. The foreign secretary, Ernest Bevin, had been a union chief, but without much sympathy for the Histadruth in his insular fashion. Relationships with America and Russia and the Arab oil states were more important to him than with the Jews, whom he bluntly said were not at the head of the queue. The continuing British delay at turning into fact the recommendations of the Balfour Declaration and the Peel Commission drove Ben-Gurion into action. The Palmach, the commando wing of the Haganah, cooperated with the Irgun in a series of attacks on British air force bases, military camps, port installations, and even the Tel Aviv radio station. The British drafted more troops into Palestine, and they suggested an Anglo-American Commission to examine the future of the Mandate. Its recommendations were that one hundred thousand Jews should immediately be admitted to Palestine and that all restrictions on the sale of land should be lifted; these were anathema to the British government, which had given other undertakings to the Arabs, particularly to King Abdullah of Transjordan, whose British-officered Arab Legion of four thousand five hundred men was the best national standing army in the Levant.

As Jewish militance increased, so did British repression. Twenty-seven hundred Jewish leaders were interned for some months after a massive snatch by British intelligence. The reprisal was the Irgun's bomb explosion at the King David Hotel in Jerusalem, where ninety-one lives were lost, Jews and Arabs among the British. The revulsion from this atrocity polarised the enmity between the Zionists and the British, who now had less stomach for supporting a disintegrating situation without much strategical importance, for there were no oil wells in the Promised Land. Bevin announced in the House of Commons that the problem would be submitted to the United Nations, which would give its decision.

On 31 August 1947, its Special Committee on Palestine published its report, recommending that the British Mandate should be ended within a year, that Palestine should be partitioned into sovereign Arab and Jewish democratic states, that the rights and interests of all minorities should be protected, that the two independent bodies should unite economically, and that the city of Jerusalem itself should become a demilitarised and neutral zone, while both new states guaranteed the protection of all holy places and freedom of conscience and worship. The Jewish state was to include western Galilee, the coastal plain, and the Negev down to the Red Sea, while Arab Palestine would incorporate the rest of the country outside international Jerusalem. In spite of Arab opposition, the report of the Special Committee was passed by the United Nations to create the State of Israel. There were scenes of extraordinary joy in Jerusalem, where rams' horns were sounded, and according to its future military governor, Dov Joseph, "even the most agnostic confessed that at that moment they felt the hand of God was upon them."

With celebration came renunciation and fear. The Arab states would have nothing to do with the partition proposals. They would only accept a plebiscite in a united Palestine, which would lead to an Arab agreement with a Jewish minority. And as for the Jews, they had lost their primary reason for coming home to Israel—Jerusalem, which was to be administered by an international trustee who was neither an Arab nor a Jew. As Dov Joseph was to write in his account of the siege of Jerusalem in the war of 1948, *The Faithful City*, ". . . the Jerusalem to which Jews have wished to return since the Diaspora began in the ancient city, the true heartland of Zion in the Judaean hills. For hundreds of years, our holidays have featured the greeting 'Next year in Jerusalem.' A patch on one wall of every orthodox Jewish house has been left unattended for the sake of Jerusalem. The bridegroom at a Jewish wedding feast still crushes a glass under his right foot to show his grief at the destruction of the Temple. The climax of the most important prayer recited thrice daily by religious Jews is: 'And to Jerusalem Thy city shalt Thou return in mercy, as Thou has promised.' For Jews, it has always been the one Holy City."

The British government did not approve of the United Nations' resolution, but it declared that it would evacuate Palestine in time. The interim of the Mandate became a vacuum with the British forces hardly able to enforce their authority and staying out of the cross fire between the emergent Jewish and Arab armed groups, preparing for the inevitable battle for the land. "If troubles begin," the last British high commissioner, Sir Alan Cunningham, told Ben-Gurion, "I fear that we shall not be able to help you. We shall not be able to defend you." The Haganah could protect the coastal strip around Tel Aviv, but it was difficult to assist the majority Jewish population of Jerusalem, particularly those in the Old City. And here the outrages began, two explosions which destroyed the *Palestine Post* building and the commercial centre of the New City, Ben Yehuda Street, with the loss of fifty-three lives. The Zionists accused the British of responsibility, denied by them and the Arabs. The Irgun and the Stern Gang then executed ten British soldiers, followed by the horrific slaughter of the Arab village of Deir Yassin beside the Jaffa road. Two hundred and fifty men and women and children were killed and mutilated in a ghastly reenaction of what the Nazis had done to the Jews at Lidice and other European villages. This calculated massacre was a deliberate instrument of terror, aimed at making the Palestinian Arabs flee from Jaffa and Judea, although they hoped to return behind the advancing Arab regular armies from the south and the east. In the end, six hundred and fifty thousand Palestinian Arabs became refugees; only a quarter of that number stayed where they were. Deir Yassin was the worst atrocity of the struggle for Palestine, and it provided the Arabs with propaganda for decades to come, especially when the terrorist leaders Menachem Begin and Yitzhak Shamir would both become prime ministers of the State of Israel. The Irgun and the Stern Gang, however, seemed to most moderate Jews such as Dov Joseph "dagger men who believed in 'the holy lie' and 'the holy murder.'"

The former grand mufti had now reached Cairo and still preached a *jihad* for the recovery of Jerusalem. Yet what would save the nascent State of Israel was what had saved the Kingdom of Jerusalem for two centuries, the divisions among the Arab countries. The Arab Legion of King Abdullah of Transjordan was certainly the most efficient fighting force ranged against the Haganah, and the king intended to expand his influence into Palestine and Jerusalem; this policy put him at odds with the former grand mufti, who was supported by Egypt and Syria, and whose family was a powerful clan in Jerusalem, probably responsible for the retaliatory attack known as the Hadassah massacre, when seventy-seven doctors and university teachers, nurses, and patients were killed in a convoy from the Hebrew University and hospital on Mount Scopus. Abdullah was responsible for no atrocities with his well-disciplined forces, although he did declare to his troops: "It is our duty to join in the holy war, a war in which the neighboring Arab states will participate." In fact, only Iraq and Lebanon joined Egypt and Syria in the fighting: Saudi Arabia sent one company of soldiers. Yet such were the potential numerical odds against the State of Israel that the British field-marshal Montgomery said that the Arabs would "hit the Jews for six" and push them into the Mediterranean.

The reverse was the truth. The Haganah prevailed everywhere, especially on the old crusader battlegrounds. Haifa was taken, along with Safed and Jaffa and Acre. The road was opened to Tiberias and eastern Galilee. The exception was the Old City of Jerusalem, which proved indefensible after the intervention of the Arab Legion. The two thousand Jews in their quarter were hardly fighting men and women; many were aged rabbis or holy scribes or Yeshiva students, while the members of the supremely orthodox Neturei Karta sect believed that a State of Israel would be blasphemy. Only two hundred serving soldiers defended the whole area from assault, and the situation was hardly improved when the Palmach mounted a relief operation. As at Masada, there were too few defending the core of their faith against too many, for King Abdullah was determined to become the keeper of the Muslim holy places in Jerusalem.

In spite of American and British efforts in the Security Council to impose a trusteeship on Palestine in order to stop the war, Ben-Gurion read in Tel Aviv Museum a Scroll or Declaration of Independence, which included these words:

> The State of Israel will be open to the immigration of Jews from all countries of their dispersion; will promote the development of the country for the benefit of all its inhabitants; will be based on the

principles of liberty, justice and peace as conceived by the Prophets of Israel; will uphold the full social and political equality of all its citizens, without distinction of religion, race or sex; will guarantee freedom of religion, conscience, education and culture; will safeguard the Holy Places of all religions; and will loyally uphold the principles of the United Nations Charter. . . .

Our call goes out to the Jewish people all over the world to rally to our side in the task of immigration and development and to stand by us in the great struggle for the fulfilment of the dream of generations for the redemption of Israel.

The American and the Russian governments recognised the new State of Israel, thus ending any equivocation on the part of the United Nations. But the existence of the new state did not save the focus of its faith, the Old City of Jerusalem. Although there were still ammunition and some supplies, the garrison surrendered to the Arab Legion, on the pledge of a safe-conduct of the whole Jewish population to the new Jerusalem of the western city suburbs, still held by the Haganah. The terms were scrupulously observed by the Muslim troops, and none of the Jews was harmed in the evacuation. The Holy City passed back under Muslim control. King Abdullah was its effective ruler along with the areas west of the Jordan River occupied by his soldiers. After the breakdown of the first truce between the opposing Jewish and Arab forces, the troops in the Haganah secured the corridor from Jerusalem to the sea, as the Crusaders had once done. They took Lydda and Ramleh and Nazareth, where the Israeli soldiers were strictly ordered to refrain from doing any damage to the Christian holy places. They eventually advanced to Beersheba, incorporating four-fifths of the area of the old Palestine, more than their grant under the terms of the partition.

They failed to recapture the Old City, although the Haganah twice broke through the Jaffa Gate and established a bridgehead at the New Gate, but there was no dislodging of the Arab Legion from its control of the rest of the city before a final cease-fire and armistice with the five hostile Arab nations, which still refused to end their declared state of holy war. They and the Arab League, however, did give up supporting the former grand mufti with his shadow government of Palestine, and they recognised the result of the fighting; the territories that Jordan had annexed, including the Old City of Jerusalem, were to remain "a trust in its hands until the Palestine case is finally solved in the interests of its inhabitants."

The mediator for the United Nations, Count Folke Bernadotte, had his own plans for the partition of Palestine, later posthumously published in his book, *To Jerusalem*. He asked the French foreign minister, Georges Bidault, whether his country would agree to Jerusalem as an Arab centre. Bidault replied that such an action would make the whole Christian world join in a new Crusade. A similar suggestion to the provisional government of the State of Israel provoked another sharp response to such a "disastrous" scheme which ignored the past, including "the historic associations of Judaism with the Holy City; the unique place, occupied by Jerusalem in Jewish history and present-day Jewish life; the Jewish inhabitants' two-thirds majority in the city before the commencement of Arab aggression—a majority greatly increased since then as a result of Arab evacuation; the fact that the whole of Jerusalem, with only a few minor exceptions, is now in Jewish hands; and not least, the fact that after an exhaustive study of the problem and as a result of an overwhelming consensus of Christian opinion in its midst, the General Assembly resolved that Jerusalem be placed under an international regime."

Faced with such implacable opposition, Bernadotte returned to old proposals for the whole of Jerusalem to be placed "under effective United Nations control, with maximum feasible local autonomy for its Arab and Jewish communities and safeguards for access to the Holy Places." The Stern Gang demonstrated against the Swedish count's presence with posters declaring, Stockholm Is Yours; Jerusalem Is Ours. Then he was assassinated in the Holy City, and the mediation came to an end. His killers were never brought to book. And what had been won by the gun in Jerusalem remained in the hands of the victors, with the Holy City partitioned between Jew and Muslim, as Berlin and Vienna were divided between the occupying Allied powers. The United Nations' resolution, which had effectively created the State of Israel, was negated in its call for an international trusteeship over Jerusalem on behalf of the three great faiths that revered its sacredness—Judaism and Christianity and Islam. Any lasting peace was murdered with Bernadotte. Even Dr. Chaim Weizmann, now become the first president of Israel, recognised the iron facts in a speech from his first visit to the citizens of Jerusalem after the War of Liberation:

> "Where are all those who spoke high-sounding phrases about the spiritual significance of Jerusalem to the entire civilised world? Did they raise a finger to protect Jerusalem, its men, women and children, its buildings and houses of prayer, against the shells of the Arabs who for months, day and night, rained death upon your homes? Did they do anything when the Jewish quarters of the Old City with their revered synagogues were turned into rubble heaps by Arab cannon and were desecrated after the surrender? . . .

> "Fear not, my friends—the old synagogues will be rebuilt anew and the way to the Wailing Wall will be opened again. With your blood and sacrifices you have renewed the covenant of old. Jerusalem is ours by virtue of the blood which your sons shed defending it."

FIFTEEN

IRREVOCABLE CAPITAL

"The United Nations saw fit this year to decide that our eternal city should become a corpus separatum *under international control. Our rebuttal of this wicked counsel was unequivocal and resolute: The Government and Knesset at once moved their seat to Jerusalem and made Israel's crown and capital irrevocable and for all men to see."*

—David Ben-Gurion, 1949

The new administration of Israel named Jerusalem as the seat of its government. Prime minister Ben-Gurion declared the Holy City to be Israel's Eternal Capital. He said that it was not necessary for the parliament of the new state, the Knesset, to confirm the decision, although this was done. For King David had already set the precedent. With such deeds, Israel was committed to a continuing war against Islam. The General Assembly of the United Nations had just affirmed in December 1949 the original proposals to make Jerusalem a neutral zone under internal trusteeship, but with the Israeli action and opposition from all the Arab states except for Jordan, the Security Council and the General Assembly shelved the matter. A new building for the Knesset was completed in West Jerusalem in 1966 with funds contributed by the British Rothschild family, while a new campus was built for the Hebrew University and a new Hadassah medical centre. Although most European embassies remained in Tel Aviv, Jerusalem was restored as the heart of Israel.

A form of militant archaeology led by Israeli generals aimed to change the present and reclaim the past of the new state. After the mass flight of the Palestinian Arabs from their villages, four hundred of these were demolished: Not a stone was left in place. "Jewish villages were built in the place of Arab villages," the future general Moshe Dayan declared. "You do not even know the names of these Arab villages . . . because their geography books no longer exist." New Jewish settlements were given biblical names. Dayan himself dug obsessively to excavate the past of ancient Israel in order to prove the rights of its modern existence, as did the chief of staff, Yigal Yadin, in charge of the great historical excavations at Masada. That resistance centre of the revolt against the Romans became the focus of Israeli army ritual, where the defence forces swore to fight to the death as they had done so long ago.

The idealism of the early pioneers to Israel with their vision of Jerusalem as the head of a theocratic state was tempered by the need for security. It had been exactly the same for the Franks on the First Crusade, which captured the celestial city, only to discover that the Kingdom of Jerusalem could only be maintained by remaining on a permanent war footing with resources brought from abroad. As the Italian maritime states had supplied the Crusaders with their reinforcements and munitions, so the United States of America would do for Israel, sending it Hawk missiles and Patton tanks and Skyhawk jet bombers for its defence forces, subsidised by the billions of dollars raised by international Jewish charities. No wonder that the increasing fundamentalism and nationalism of the Muslim powers saw in Israel another colonial excrescence from Europe and America. This was no Jewish return to an ancestral homeland, but an instrument of Western imperialism against Islam. In terms of the Cold War between capitalism and communism, Israel was America's aircraft carrier that was docked in the Levant. The humiliation of the Arab defeat in the war of 1948 was as searing as the catastrophe of the First Crusade, when Jerusalem had wholly been lost and a foreign invader installed in Palestine.

The Arabs were further embittered by the refusal of the United Nations to achieve repatriation and compensation for the million refugees now clustered in camps in Jordan and on the Egyptian border. As the commissioner-general of the United Nations Relief and Works Agency said of them, "In their own eyes they are not refugees at all in the sense in which that term is used to describe persons who have uprooted themselves and broken with their past in order to seek a new life in new surroundings and in a new country. The Palestine refugees regard themselves rather as temporary wards of the international community whom they hold responsible for the upheaval which resulted in their having to leave their homes. As they see it, the international community has a duty to enable them to return to their homes and meanwhile, to provide for their maintenance and welfare." Their frustration at worldwide inaction would lead to the formation in June 1964 of the Palestine Liberation Organisation with the blessing of the Arab League "as a vanguard for the collective Arab struggle for the liberation of Palestine." Continual holy warfare was now provoked.

Even the conglomerations of Palestinian Arabs who had remained in Israel lived in three security zones in Galilee and the border of the West Bank of Jordan and the Beersheba district of the Negev. These areas were subject to emergency regulations and military law under various restrictions for the Arabs almost as complex as the Tsarist law against the Jews in Russia before the revolution. While the Israelis felt justified in protecting themselves from potential enemies, the Arabs within their borders suffered from discrimination and persecution inside their own land, although the country was becoming predominantly Jewish after the Knesset had passed in 1950 the Law of Return, guaranteeing entry into Israel and full civil rights to any Jew from anywhere on earth. More than half a million immigrants came to the Promised Land during the next six years.

The second war between Israel and the Arab states was certainly instigated in Europe. The charismatic Colonel Gamal Abdel Nasser had taken power in 1954 in Egypt. Two years later, on the withdrawal of British troops from the Suez Canal Zone, and on the refusal of America to finance the monumental Aswan Dam project, Nasser nationalised the Anglo-French Suez Canal Company, saying that the dues from its operation would now finance his great project on the Nile. He had already barred Israeli shipping from using the canal, which had once been Britain's vital link to its Indian Empire. The British prime minister,

Anthony Eden, confused Nasser with Hitler and believed that acceptance of the Egyptian seizure of the strategical waterway was equivalent to Chamberlain's appeasement of the Nazi dictator at Munich before the Second World War. The Egyptian colonel was putting his thumb on the "windpipe" of Europe's economy. The situation was worsened by the dismissal by Jordan's King Hussein of Sir John Glubb Pasha, the British commander of the Arab Legion, following riots in support of Nasser and against imperialism in Amman. Britain appeared to be losing its essential hold on the oil of the Middle East, much of which had passed through the canal to the west.

In the circumstances, the British and French governments decided to use Israel's wish to cripple Nasser and rectify its southern frontier in their own interests. If Israel would invade Sinai, the understanding was that the two European powers would destroy the Egyptian air force and navy and reoccupy the Canal Zone on the pretext of separating the combatants. Secrecy and hypocrisy were the watchwords of the day. All was conditional upon the Security Council of the United Nations failing to pass a resolution which would take action against Egypt. This was prevented by the Soviet Union, which approved of Nasser's seizure of the old imperial canal company.

Israel's commitment was still uncertain. It launched a diversionary attack on the Jordanian police fortress at Qalqiliya, using artillery and airborne units. King Hussein asked for reinforcements from the Royal Air Force and the help of an Iraqi division, while the British chargé d'affaires in Tel Aviv told Ben-Gurion that if Israel attacked again, Britain would assist Jordan. Moshe Dayan confessed to the feeling that, "save for the Almighty, only the British are capable of complicating affairs to such a degree." At the very moment they were preparing to topple Nasser, they were ready to take part in a war against Israel. But there were no more attacks on Jordan, and Dayan advised his general staff to take advantage of the Anglo-French proposals and to invade Sinai. "We should behave like the cyclist who is riding uphill when a truck chances by and he grabs hold."

With the Anglo-French military preparations complete in Cyprus and the secret assistance of French Mystère jets, the Israelis dropped paratroopers at the Mitla Pass near the Suez Canal, destroyed the *fedayeen* guerrilla bases in Gaza, and freed the Gulf of Aqaba and the Strait of Tiran in a series of easy victories over the surprised Egyptian forces. The British and the French bombed Egyptian targets after dropping warning notices. Then the United States Sixth Fleet permitted an amphibious landing near Port Said, which was soon occupied. The invaders were ready to push south to El Qantara and Ismailia in order to secure the length of the canal. President Eisenhower had not been informed and was at the close of his re-election campaign to the White House. The British had miscalculated that his need for the Jewish vote in New York and California would prevent his censure of the deception practised by the aggressors on Egypt.

The Russians took advantage of the division of the Western powers to send in their troops to suppress independence movements in Poland and Hungary. But Eisenhower's election victory and anger at the duplicity of Britain and France and Israel made America join Russia and virtually the whole of the United Nations to condemn the attack on Nasser. Mass demonstrations in London showed huge English opposition to its government's intervention; while the selling of sterling by the United States Federal Reserve Bank depleted the reserves of the British Treasury, which was also blocked from drawing on the International Monetary Fund. Financial pressure and nearly universal censure forced Anthony Eden to accept an immediate cease-fire as a preliminary to a general retreat.

Threatened with sanctions, Israel also had to agree to withdraw from Egyptian territory, although its minister Abba Eban stressed the great paradox that Egypt behaved to Israel as though there were war, but expected Israel to behave to Egypt as though there were peace. When the Israeli forces pulled back from Sinai, however, they destroyed buildings and roads and railways. "God had scorched the Sinai earth," General Burns of the United Nations noted, "and His chosen people removed whatever stood above it." And a United Nations expeditionary force occupied the border zone of the Gaza Strip, preventing any *fedayeen* attacks on Israel from there for the next decade.

In 1967 on Independence Day, Israel decided to hold its usual military parade in Jerusalem, although its armistice agreement with Jordan only allowed specific weapons there. To the Arabs, this was a provocation and perhaps a declaration of imminent hostilities. There had been many guerrilla attacks from Syria, which appeared to back the Palestine Liberation Organisation, formed in East Jerusalem in 1964, although soon at odds with Jordan. The usual Middle Eastern condition for war, a quarrel over scarce water supplies, had already begun, with Israel using irrigation from the Jordan River, while its tributaries were threatened with diversion by an Arab decision to build a dam across the Yarmuk River. Egypt built up its forces in Sinai and demanded the withdrawal of the United Nations forces from its frontiers and its soil. This was followed by the closing of the Gulf of Aqaba to Israeli cargo ships. The grounds were that Israel was preparing to attack Damascus and overthrow the Syrian government. "The Jews threatened war," Nasser said. "We tell them: You are welcome, we are ready."

Nasser believed that Israel was wholly backed by America and Britain, while the Soviet Union would support the Arab cause. In point of fact, although President Lyndon Johnson and Prime Minister Harold Wilson were on the side of Israel, both advised against going to war. The British suggested an international naval force to keep open the Strait of Tiran, an unlikely suggestion that was known as the regatta. In Israel, the divided political parties formed a national coalition, and the key post of the defence ministry was given to the hawkish General Moshe Dayan. Mobilisation now escalated in Israel and the front-line Arab states. The Jewish general staff decided to eliminate the Egyptian war force on the ground in a preemptive strike. Nine in ten of the three hundred and fifty Soviet-made combat aircraft were destroyed at dawn. Attacks on Syrian airfields then knocked out their capabilities. Jordan was drawn into the conflict and Amman was bombed. It was the opportunity for Israel to take all of Jerusalem.

Both the Arab Legion and the Israeli troops advanced on the United Nations compound in Jerusalem; all its occupants were finally expelled by the Israelis, who wanted no peacekeeping attempts within the Holy City. Their commander, Uzi Narkiss, had been one of the last Palmach commandos to evacuate the Old City when it had been taken by Jordan nineteen years before. An armoured unit helped sappers to clear the three defended ridges to the north and Nebi Samuel, so important in Allenby's capture of Jerusalem, while troops swung east to cut off the Jericho Road and south to straddle the way to Bethlehem. Three battalions of paratroopers advanced through the northern suburbs towards the Mandlebaum Gate. After two days of the assault, the Arab Legion still held the

Old City and the Mount of Olives, which fell to an assault on the third day of battle. Most of the Jordanian troops withdrew, and Colonel Mordechai Gur's Third Battalion, supported by tanks, broke through St. Stephen's Gate. The Lion's Gate was blown up, and armoured vehicles ground into the Via Dolorosa. The paratroopers reached the Western Wall and prayed: They were joined by General Dayan. There was no damage to the Temple Mount or to the Church of the Holy Sepulchre, nor to Bethlehem or Hebron or the other holy sites on the West Bank of the river Jordan, rapidly captured by the Jerusalem and other brigades over the following days. The Egyptian army disintegrated on the Gaza Strip and Sinai and fled home. A final attack on the Syrian forces on the Golan Heights, which might threaten Damascus, was also successful. Having seized all its objectives, Israel accepted a cease-fire after a Six-Day War, the worst defeat suffered by combined Muslim forces since the Mongols' and Allenby's invasions.

A million resentful Arabs lived in the occupied areas of the Gaza Strip, Sinai, the West Bank, and the Golan Heights: They would constitute a never-ending threat. These areas were put under military government, but the Old City and East Jerusalem were annexed. All barriers were removed. The Israeli government announced that the process of integration was irreversible and not negotiable. The population of seventy-five thousand Arabs, of which one-sixth were Christian, would be protected: Muslim courts would still function alongside the Jewish High Rabbinical Court. While Israel complained that several synagogues and the Jewish cemetery on the Mount of Olives had been desecrated, the Muslim *imams* pointed to damage on one gate of the al-Aqsa mosque. General Dayan had the Israeli flag removed from the Dome of the Rock and Abraham's shrine near Hebron. Calls by extreme religious groups among the Jews to rebuild the Temple on the Mount were resisted, and access to the sacred places of the Holy City was guaranteed to all faiths. Members of the future Gush Emunim, who believed in their right to settle in all of biblical Judea, did conspire to blow up the mosques on the site of the Temple of Solomon in 1984; but they were thwarted by Israeli intelligence. They believed that a rebuilt Temple would pave the way, after a terrible Arab war of fire and blood, for the advent of the Messiah. But no Israeli government would dare risk a full *jihad* by tampering with the

Rock, from which the Prophet, Muhammad, had declared his ascent to heaven, even though it was the site of King David's Holy of Holies. Although the Jews again held Jerusalem, they could not impose their most ancient past on the intervening architecture of history.

The World Council of Churches appreciated the care which the new authorities took over the biblical areas, blessed to Christendom. The Roman Catholic church, however, had still not forgotten the power it had held during the Latin Kingdom of Jerusalem; and so the Vatican asserted that the only solution which held out "a sufficient guarantee" for the protection of the holy places was international supervision under the United Nations of the city and its vicinity. When the General Assembly voted on the matter, a large majority refused to recognise the annexation of East Jerusalem. Thus, outside Israel, the legal position of the Holy City was not proven, but within its walls, as always, it was ruled by its conquerors.

After five months of discussion and diplomacy, the Security Council of the United Nations did pass unanimously Resolution 242, which expressed some general principles, such as the inadmissibility of the acquisition of territory by war, the right of every state to live in peace within secure and recognised boundaries, and the necessity for free navigation through international waterways. But a resolution is not a solution: These were only guidelines for a settlement between Israel and the Arab states, which should be negotiated by a special representative. In the absence of sanctions or any form of compulsion, there was no reason for Israel to hurry over the terms for peace, if she thought her security was helped by holding on to the occupied areas, which were already in her hands. But her interminable delays in accepting any withdrawal led to a war of attrition across the Suez Canal, now closed to shipping. Another million refugees were forced to leave the port cities. A fourth major conflict became all but inevitable.

As well as fighting across the canal from its Bar-Lev fortified line, Israel faced guerrilla raids from Lebanon and particularly from Jordan, where Palestinian guerrillas took over large areas of the country. After an attempt to assassinate King Hussein as his grandfather had been in the al-Aqsa mosque, and after the hijacking of four passenger aircraft belonging to the Western powers, the Palestinian guerrillas were expelled by the king from Jordan in spite of Syrian military intervention, which was halted by the threat of Israel's entry into the crisis. No sooner was this done than Nasser died, leaving Egypt in the hands of his deputy Anwar Sadat, who would try to initiate a peace settlement in the Middle East as well as move his country from the Russian to the American sphere of influence.

Dismissing his Soviet military advisers, Sadat found his efforts to reach a bilateral agreement with Israel also dismissed. Rebuffed, he mobilised Egyptian armed forces and concerted plans for an attack on Israel in early October of 1973 with the Syrian president, Hafiz al-Assad. Israel was continuing to put settlements in the occupied territories and appeared ready to remain fighting a series of skirmishes that stopped just short of outright war. An unusual failure by Israeli military intelligence allowed for a surprise assault across the Suez Canal on the Bar-Lev line on the afternoon of the celebration of Yom Kippur. Ninety thousand Egyptian soldiers and twelve thousand tanks and other military vehicles crossed the waterway and destroyed the Israeli fortifications, pressing on to the Sinai passes. The operation was named Badr, after the Prophet Muhammad's first victory against his enemies in Mecca, while the troops shouted the holy call "Allah Akhbah!" Simultaneously, two Syrian armoured columns of five hundred tanks each, supported by missiles, broke through the defences of the Golan Heights and threatened to descend to attack Galilee. Jordan was mobilising its forces, as was Iraq, to come to the aid of Syria. The situation was the most serious yet faced by Israel.

Its military command decided to retaliate first against Syria. Damascus and other cities were bombed. The Syrian armour was destroyed by expensive air attacks. The ground lost on the Golan Heights was recaptured. Then the Israeli tank commander, Arik Sharon, found a gap between the Egyptian Second and Third Armies in Sinai, thrust between them to the canal, and crossed it, encircling the Third Army and opening the way to Cairo itself. While the United Nations was split on the terms for a ceasefire, Israel agreed one with Egypt and another with Syria. All three countries had their forces in dangerous and extended positions and were short of munitions and supplies. None could claim victory, only stalemate. But Israel had finally begun to learn the bitter lesson of the crusading Kingdom of Jerusalem: how vulnerable it was to a sudden combined pincer attack from the Arab countries surrounding it; how the victories of its far-flung mobile columns did not ensure a lasting enemy defeat; and how impossible it was to hold occupied territory with a hostile population of an antagonistic faith.

The Arabs also learned some lessons to their profit despite their casualties. Their threat to cut off all oil supplies to Western Europe and America had ensured little support for Israel. Although both superpowers, the United States and Russia, had been asked to intervene, they did not, fearful of igniting the Cold War into an atomic blaze. And although the Arab powers lost some seventy thousand men, killed and wounded and taken prisoner, the significant Israeli losses of more than eight thousand in similar categories was a severe blow to a nation so short of manpower. Even worse for Jewish morale was the end of the legend of easy victory and invincibility, for both the Syrians and the Egyptians had fought well and hard, both in retreat and in early triumph.

All the same, the United States, through its presidential envoy, Henry Kissinger, had limited the conflict by controlling the supply of American arms to Israel in order to match those of the Russians to the Arabs; by forestalling any Soviet intervention in warning Moscow of American naval and airborne preparations in the Mediterranean; and by incessant shuttle diplomacy between the warring parties which ended in talks in Geneva. To one observer, Kissinger was both the composer of the music and the conductor of the orchestra. Although President Nixon's fall from grace and office over the Watergate scandal and President Carter's election to the White House prevented peace in the Middle East from emerging under the aegis of the Republican party, the remarkable Anwar Sadat broke the logjam in Arab relations with Israel. He decided to go to Jerusalem to address the Knesset and pray in the al-Aqsa mosque and even visit the Church of the Holy Sepulchre. He would speak of Jerusalem as a city of peace and open his address with the words: "We all love this land, the land of God, we all, Muslims, Christians and Jews all worship God." He was absolutely aware of the significance of this religious visit to the Muslim world and of its probable consequences. To Kissinger, Sadat was a great man because he understood the importance of intangibles, while he told President Carter, "Some things in the Middle East are not logical or reasonable." The problem of Jerusalem never was nor would be.

When Sadat went to Jerusalem, his foreign minister resigned, telling him that if he went, he would play all his cards "for nothing and lose completely the support of the Arab countries." Arab summit meetings had already recognised the Palestine Liberation Organisation under its new leader, Yasser Arafat, as the sole representative of the Palestinian people. Although he told the United Nations that he carried a gun in one hand and an olive branch in the other, the weapon was more in evidence in guerrilla raids on Israel than the green leaves of peace. Yet Sadat ignored this decision by opting for direct negotiations between his country and Israel and the United States, which were to culminate in 1979 in the Camp David Accords.

These agreements set a framework for a peace treaty between Egypt and Israel, which would withdraw from Sinai over three years, if the Suez Canal and the Gulf of Aqaba became international waterways open to all shipping. On the legitimate rights of the Palestinian people and the status of Jerusalem, there could be no meeting of minds. The Israeli delegation, now led by Menachem Begin, nearly packed its bags at Camp David and went home when it heard that the United States intended to issue an open letter opposing the illegal annexation of the Old City and East Jerusalem. At the end of the day, President Carter only sent a private letter to Sadat that there had been no change in the American position on Jerusalem as declared before the United Nations. For as a devout Southern Baptist brought up on reading the Bible as the revealed Word of God, he declared his fundamental belief and bias at that time: "Israel is a return at last to the Bible land from which the Jews were driven so many hundred years ago, the establishment of the nation of Israel is the fulfilment of Biblical prophecies and the very essence of fulfilment."

In failing to insist on a firm agreement on Palestinian rights as well as the Holy City, Sadat knew that he had condemned himself with the rest of Islam. By making a separate peace, Egypt found itself suspended from membership of the Arab League, which transferred its headquarters from Cairo to Tunis. As befell so many radical Arab leaders before him, Sadat would go down before the rising forces of Muslim fundamentalism and the assassins' grenades and bullets. His killers called their sect Al-Jihad, the Holy War. His dealings with the West seemed blasphemy to many

Muslims as well as treachery to the United Arab cause. He had offended against the three negatives of the Arab summit of 1967 in Khartoum: "no peace with Israel, no recognition of Israel, no negotiations with Israel." His efforts for peace were his death warrant.

In their obduracy over dealing with the rights of the Palestinian refugees and Jerusalem, the Israelis condemned themselves to twenty more years of border warfare, exacerbated by their invasion of southern Lebanon, which provoked a new Shi'ite *jihad* against them, including suicide bombing missions. Their retaliation to terrorist attacks was always more than biblical—ten eyes for an eye, a jaw of teeth for a tooth. They miscalculated the fervour and spread of Muslim fundamentalism, which would find a revolutionary base in Iran after the *mullahs* overthrew the Shah and the "Great Satan" of American imperialism in the same year of the Camp David Accords. Initially welcomed by the Russians, this radical recall of the *jihad* against infidel influences would make the Soviet Empire lose its colonial war to the *mujahideen* in Afghanistan before the unexpected and sudden collapse of Marxism and the Union of Soviet Socialist Republics. If Egypt and Israel had correctly selected the sole victor of the Cold War, their reliance on the United States put them even more at odds with radical Islam, reverting to the concept of a holy war against Western materialism.

Equally, many of the Muslims underestimated the power of Christian orthodoxy and fundamentalism. They had not done so in the days of the Kingdom of Jerusalem defended by the knights of the military orders. The Crusades remained in popular memory as the primary invasion of the West. When the Turkish fanatic Mehmet Ali Agca tried to murder the pope in 1981, he wrote: "I have decided to kill John Paul the Second, supreme commander of the Crusades." Curiously enough, many Catholics were to ascribe the beginning of the downfall of Russia and its Eastern European empire to this Polish pope, whose support allied Catholicism with resistance in Poland, a national faith as strong as that of the Hussites, which now led to a form of people's crusade against the godless materialism of the Soviets.

When the astute Egyptian commentator and friend of Sadat, Muhammad Heikal, tried to explain to his Arab readers how Westerners such as Kissinger thought, he wrote that they believed that "the truth is what we see at this moment, and not what we think or believe as a consequence of what has happened before." His analysis was confirmed by a leading Muslim historian of the Crusades, who noted the surprising extent to which the attitude of the Arabs towards the West was still influenced by events of seven centuries ago:

> Today, on the eve of the third millennium, the political and religious leaders of the Arab world constantly refer to Saladin, to the fall of Jerusalem and its recapture. In the popular mind, and in some official discourse too, Israel is regarded as a new Crusader state. Of the three divisions of the Palestine Liberation Army, one bears the name Hittin and another Ayn Jalut. In his days of glory, President Nasser was regularly compared to Saladin, who, like him, had united Syria and Egypt—and even Yemen! The Arabs perceived the Suez expedition of 1956 as a Crusade by the French and the English, similar to that of 1191. . . . It is not difficult to think of President Sadat when we hear Sibt Ibn al-Jawzi speaking to the people of Damascus and denouncing the "betrayal" of al-Kamil, the ruler of Cairo, who dared to acknowledge enemy sovereignty over the holy city. It is tempting to confound past and present when we read of a struggle between Damascus and Jerusalem for control of the Golan Heights or the Bekaa Valley. It is hard not to daydream when we read *Usama*'s reflections about the military superiority of the invaders.

Such attitudes would inform the most recent conflict between the Muslim Middle East and the Christian West—the Gulf War. The eight-year conflict between Iran and Iraq in the late 1980s had been more nationalist than religious, although Shi'ite Iran had presented itself as the rescuer of the Shi'ite majority in Iraq, ruled by the Sunni minority through the dictatorship of Saddam Hussein. A wounding stalemate in the fratricidal war that had resulted in a million or more casualties allowed Saddam to turn his attention south to oil-rich and indefensible Kuwait, perhaps as a preliminary to striking at Saudi Arabia and taking over the custodianship of Mecca and Medina, the core of the Muslim faith. Already in November 1979, radical Islamic fundamentalists had stormed the Great Mosque at Mecca in protest at the pro-Western regime.

The Kuwaiti and Saudi dynasties were forced to call upon the former imperialist powers to protect their religious role as well as the oil fields vital to the world economy. Thus, in his aggression, Saddam could claim that he represented radical Islam in its *jihad* against imperialist Israel, the creation of the infidel West. His rape of Kuwait was presented as a necessary advance in a holy war, while Jordan's heavy reliance on Iraq's economy made that strategic state a covert ally, however much King Hussein wished to remain a friend of the United States. During the American buildup of its force in the Persian Gulf along with contingents chiefly from Britain and France, Saddam countered massive bombing and missile attacks by launching his own missiles on Tel-Aviv and Israel, which was restrained by the United States from riposting as it had in a previous sortie against Iraq's nuclear programme. For the Americans feared to offend the susceptibilities of their Arab allies, Arabia and Egypt and Turkey, which would hardly tolerate the Jews joining the struggle against their Arab enemy.

The "mother of all battles" ended for Saddam in total defeat with another quarter of a million casualties. Western technology with its laser-guided shells and smart bombs destroyed the superior Iraq numbers and capacity to fight, leaving Saddam with a Kurdish rebellion in the north and a Shi'ite revolt in the south. The Iraqi dictator, however, claimed victory in the face of catastrophe. When he announced the forced withdrawal of his troops from Kuwait, he declared:

"Everybody will remember that the gates of Constantinople were not opened to Muslims from the first attempt and that the cause of dear Palestine which has been neglected by the international community is now again knocking at the closed doors to force them to solve it, no matter how hard the aggressors tried to obstruct this. . . .

"Shout for victory, O brothers; shout for your victory and the victory of all honourable people, O Iraqis. You have fought thirty countries, and all the evil and the largest machine of war and destruction in the world that surrounds them. The soldiers of faith have triumphed over the soldiers of wrong, O stalwart men. Your God is the one who granted your victory."

While Richard Chency, the American secretary of war, pointed out that "the mother of all battles turned into the mother of all retreats," he was careful not to follow the path of the Assassins. "The last thing we want to do is to turn Saddam into a martyr." And yet, the immense victory was not to be the finish of the interminable *jihads* and crusades. "It is the war of the next five hundred years," a citizen of Baghdad said in 1992. "It is to say what everybody in the Third World will say—I am independent." But as the Kuwaiti roving ambassador said after Saddam's destruction of his homeland, "They saw a paradise next to them, and they cannibalised that paradise. They destroyed the peace of that land of their dreams."

Yet the split in the Arab states appeared to be significant, now that they were no longer united against imperialist threats to their independence, something which Saddam had hardly guaranteed to Kuwait. Even radical Syria had joined conservative Saudi Arabia against Iraq, while King Hussein was forced to change tack and beat a path back towards the Western star. A new chance for a permanent peace was born, because the United States had demonstrated that it was the only superpower left that could destroy all opposition, while Israel was frightened into some sort of accommodation by the proof of its vulnerability to Arab missiles, even though it had already acquired a nuclear capacity of its own in collaboration with another pariah of the United Nations, the Republic of South Africa. The Palestine Liberation Organisation had also backed the losing side, Iraq, and so it was threatened with the curtailing of funds and bases by other leading Arab countries. "New friendships and hatreds were forged in war and the old fault lines of the region were shattered forever," a leader in the London *Sunday Times* declared. "It is not the firmest basis for peace; but it is the best we have had in half a century of Arab-Israeli conflict."

Through assiduous American diplomacy by James Baker, the secretary of state for President George Bush, Syria agreed to enter into peace negotiations with Israel, which also agreed to treat with the Palestine Organisation at last. Jordan was also coming back into the fold of Western approval. The first step was for Israel to admit that it would cede occupied territory for peace. This was what Sadat had asked the Knesset to do, when he had addressed it in Jerusalem. He had reminded the Jews of their common ancestor Abraham and had asked them to sacrifice land to the Palestinian Arabs as Abraham had been prepared to sacrifice his son to God.

The first cession was to be minimal, but the basis of a sovereign state for the Palestinian Arabs. They would receive the Gaza Strip and an enclave around Jericho as a taster to the West Bank, the areas which were becoming ungovernable because of the continuing uprising called the *intifada* incited by the extremist Hamas and Islamic *jihad* groups, who were clients of radical Iran. That little state, to be run by Yasser Arafat and his police, would have to prove it was a competent government and could prevent the attacks of *fedayeen* on Israel over the border. Then more land might be conceded, once Israel was assured of its security. "In general," the Israeli leader, Yitzhak Rabin, declared, "peace is not made with your friends. Peace is made with enemies, some of whom—and I won't name names— I loathe very much."

What stood against this inching towards peace were the Jewish settlements in the occupied territories, declared by religious extremists such as the Gush Emunim to be the inalienable parts of biblical Judea and Samaria, and the annexation of Jerusalem. As the Kibbutz Dati, representing the religious communities, addressed God in its prayer on Independence Day: "Extend the boundaries of our land, just as You have promised our forefathers, from the river Euphrates to the river of Egypt. Build Your holy city Jerusalem, capital of Israel; and there may Your Temple be established as in the days of Solomon." Time and again on the question of the settlements and Jerusalem, the peace talks stalled, for none of the parties could satisfy the demand of the fundamentalists in their differing faiths.

For the radical religious movements of the Jews and the Muslims were very much the same. Ancient Israel was the focus of the Hebrew militants as the land promised exclusively to the Jews, where they would create an ideal society, while the Islamic believers who preached the *jihad* also wished to create a just community in their traditional places of settlement for more than a thousand years after the coming of the Prophet of Allah. The extremists of the two religions wanted to replace secular with religious law and policy, the Jews with the Torah, the Muslims with the Shariah. Both feared Western materialism because it obscured the Will of God, and both had millennial visions that the reign of justice upon earth was imminent after the coming of the Messiah or the last *imam*. A fervour for the total destruction of their enemies was a common factor among these zealots. It almost seemed a Christian crusading legacy. The point was, however, no longer to kill one another, but to arrive at a necessary tolerance between the poles of behaviour, at the golden mean of the classical Greeks.

On intractable Jerusalem, there was a strange agreement between radical religion and political finesse. The Temple Mount was occupied by the Muslim shrines, the Dome of the Rock and the al-Aqsa mosque. Any attempt to tear them down and rebuild the Jewish Temple of Solomon would ensure an insoluble *jihad*. Yet the area had been so sacred to the ancient tribes of Israel that few had been allowed to enter the Holy of Holies. And the bulk of rabbinical opinion now declared that believing Jews must not climb onto the Temple Mount. If they did, they would suffer *Karet,* the loss of the afterlife. The purpose of the rabbis may have been to draw a line between the capture of Jerusalem and messianic hopes. In the case of the Neturei Karta—indeed, "the Guardians of the City"—the secular state of Israel was immoral and its victories were the work of Satan. Only the Torah should rule in Israel. Such idealism and fanaticism must be kept from Muslim sacred places, even if they had also been those of Israel. For the government, such an avoidance of rioting and war was a blessing. And as for the building of another Temple, most of the rabbis also declared that it should only be built according to the specifications of Ezekiel by God's intervention through the coming of another Prophet, not yet in view. For once, religious thoroughness and delicacy suited state policy in a country where the faith so often conflicted with the cautious security of the state.

Religious radicalism on the right of Israeli politics was often an American import along with material values. When President Carter had addressed the Knesset in 1979, he had stressed his country's special concern for Israel. Seven presidents had already shown that the relationship was indestructible, "because it is rooted in the consciousness and the morals and the religion and the beliefs of the American people themselves. . . . Israel and the United States were shaped by pioneers—my nation is also a nation of immigrants and refugees—by peoples gathered in both nations from many lands." This religious concept of the common destiny of Israel and America had also been that of the British Zionists such as Josiah Wedgwood, who saw the Jewish pioneers as "the Pilgrim Fathers of Palestine." Such vision and acceptance allowed the welcome of Jewish militant groups to New York and London, although Arab religious extremism was unwelcome, as it was held to lead to the terrorism which culminated in the destruction of an American aeroplane over Lockerbie in Scotland and the bombing of the World Trade Centre in New York. When the supremely Arab-hating Rabbi Meir Kahane, whose followers were rabid opponents of any land concessions to the Palestinian Arabs, was assassinated in New York, his disciple Baruch Goldstein did his best to wreck the peace negotiations by massacring more than twenty Arabs at prayer in the Hebron mosque. He failed, the peace process continued. "You are a foreign import," Yitzhak Rabin said of Kahane's followers. "You are an errant weed. Sensible Judaism spits you out."

Other messianic trends in Judaism were more welcome. On the death in New York of the aged Rabbi Menachem Schneerson, Rabin declared it a loss for all of the Jewish people. "A great sage is gone." The seventh of the Lubavitcher rabbinic dynasty, Schneerson was thought to be the new Messiah by many of his disciples, forty thousand of whom lived in Israel. An ardent supporter of the Jewish right to occupy Judea and Samaria, he opposed the Camp David peace treaty with Sadat, and yet he withheld any religious recognition of the State of Israel because the new Messiah had not yet come. He himself refused to leave Brooklyn and set foot in Israel, where he was awaited as that Messiah. His death ended the speculation and did not bring a millennium.

One remarkable man, Theodor or Teddy Kollek, born near Budapest and the founder of a kibbutz in the 1930s on the Sea of Galilee, had kept the peace in Jerusalem for twenty-eight years. This mayor was driven by an extraordinary energy allied with a genius for diplomacy and a passion for the Holy City. He knew of its divisions. As he has testified, there are in Jerusalem one hundred and four groups of Jews with cultural differences. There are forty groups of Christians, while the Protestants have only been there for one hundred and fifty years. There are many Muslim sects, all differing over the religious law of the Koran, the Shariah, as against the common law, which is also opposed by the Torah of certain Jewish groups. All these sects differ over human rights as well as religious law set against common law. Of the Jews, Kollek has said, "We were all minorities everywhere against the Government. Now we are the majority." The only

solution in Jerusalem between the differing sects was long-term education. Jerusalem would otherwise become "a mixture between Beirut and
Belfast," which it was not yet.

Without offence to the Muslim and Christian minorities, one hundred thousand people out of five hundred thousand, Kollek ringed the
walls with new apartment buildings and monuments, film institutes and
music centres and parks, museums and campuses and convention halls and
tourist hotels. Aided by a Jerusalem Foundation heavily subsidised from
Europe and the United States, he modernised the Holy City while retaining the aura of the ancient religious sites. He respected the Muslim shrines
on the Temple Mount, which were restored by their keeper, King Hussein
of Jordan, from the proceeds of the sale for more than eight million pounds
of his London mansion on Palace Green. Although Kollek considered the
unity of Jerusalem "an irreversible historic fact," his autobiography testified to the resilience and continuity of his people over the millennia. Even
if Jerusalem were divided again, "We are like ants building the most beautiful ant hill that was ever created, and we hope it will continue to exist
undisturbed. But who knows? Maybe a man with a stick will come along,
poke into our masterpiece, and part of it will be destroyed. If so, here
we are, like ants. And we will build it again and again as well and as beau-
tifully as we know how."

Unfortunately, in the elections of November 1993, which took place
at the start of the process of the Israeli withdrawal from Gaza and Jericho,
Kollek was ousted by Ehud Olmert, a former health minister and right-
wing Likud party politician. Olmert scared the voters by warning them
that if the Likud were not brought to power, East Jerusalem would be given
back to the Arabs along with the Western Wall. He promised more Jewish settlement in the Old City including its Muslim Quarter, where the
extreme nationalists of Ateret Cohanim were already establishing themselves. "We are told to settle the Land of Israel everywhere," a sympathetic
rabbi said, "so most certainly in the Old City." Announcements by Arafat
that Jerusalem would become the capital of the Palestinian state were followed by Israeli reluctance to allow him to pray at the al-Aqsa mosque because his security could not be guaranteed. He also delivered a harangue
in the Great Mosque of Johannesburg to Muslim South Africans, promis-

ing a *jihad* to retake Jerusalem; later he lamely excused this outburst by claiming that the word *jihad* meant a *peaceful* campaign— "an Orwellian oxymoron," as *The Jerusalem Post* called it.

Moreover, Arafat had referred to the peace agreement with Israel as no more than that "signed between our Prophet and the tribe of Kuraish," a treaty which had allowed him to pray at Mecca although based in Medina. The terms were broken two years later on a pilgrimage to Mecca, when the Prophet and his followers seized the Muslim shrine. Such historic references boded ill for a lasting accord with Israel, particularly as King Fahd of Saudi Arabia, also the keeper of holy Medina and Mecca, had defined a *jihad* as "a united, comprehensive, integrated Arab-Islamic confrontation in which we place all our resources and our spiritual, cultural, political, material and military potential in a long and continuing holy war." Moreover, the fate of the Bawi Quraiza, a Jewish tribe allied to the Prophet Muhammad which betrayed the original Muslims, was not forgotten, for after its defeat, no tolerance prevailed any more than in the time of Joshua. The males were beheaded, the women and the children enslaved. Was there ever to be an end to the lessons of history?

Although Arafat did take up the strings of government after arriving at Gaza and Jericho, he did not reach Jerusalem, even if he had told cheering crowds of Palestinian Arabs that he was going to pray there after being kissed in welcome by Jewish leaders of the Neturei Karta sect. Using tactics modelled on the *intifada*, a hundred thousand right-wing demonstrators blocked the streets leading to Zion Square in Jerusalem; they were addressed by the Likud leader, who said, "What Arafat really wants is not an Arab state next to Israel, but an Arab state instead of Israel." While refusing Arafat access to the Temple Mount, the Israeli government made overtures to King Hussein of Jordan, already the keeper of the Dome of the Rock and the al-Aqsa mosque, who declared that only God could have sovereignty over Jerusalem's holy places. As it was, full diplomatic ties had recently been forged between Israel and the Vatican for the first time, and the foreign minister, Shimon Peres, now offered extraterritorial status for Christian and Muslim sites. "I have said Jerusalem is closed politically and open religiously," Peres declared in a rebuff of Arafat's hopes. "This means that it will remain unified, and only as Israel's capital, not two capitals. It will remain under Israeli sovereignty. However, when it comes to the needs and rights of various believers, we are open to proposals." After further militant Muslim murders of Jewish citizens, the prime minister, Yitzhak Rabin, confirmed Israel's hold over Jerusalem, saying to a student, "The supreme thing is a united Jerusalem as the capital of Israel under Israeli sovereignty."

Adroitly confirming the split between Jordan and the Palestine Liberation Organisation, the Israelis permitted King Hussein to fly in an honour guard of Israeli fighters over Tel-Aviv and then over Jerusalem. He would be the first Arab monarch to pray there again, as he was the last before its seizure from his control in 1967. In response to the Palestinian pressures within Jordan, the crown prince, Hassan, promised that the holy places within Jerusalem would eventually fall to Palestinian authority, but this hope appeared more of an indefinite olive branch than a deal. The Arab disunity evident during the Gulf War was emphasised as Jordan, followed by Syria, prepared to sign bilateral peace accords with Israel, prodded by American diplomacy. For there was only one superpower now, the United States, and Israel was its protégé. When a shrunken Russia asked for a role in the forthcoming peace talks on the future of Jerusalem because of its church holdings in the Holy City, it was rebuffed. It had lost its influence in the Middle East and had more to fear from holy wars closer to home in central Asia.

A paradox of the dissolution of the Soviet Union was that the *jihad* it had encouraged against Israel was now imported into the newly dependent Asian republics with Muslim majorities. The failed war in Afghanistan persuaded the guerrillas there to export their religious influence over the borders. In Azerbaijan and Turkmenistan, Uzbekistan and Kyrgyzstan, Kazakhstan and Tajikistan, orthodox Sunni Islamic diplomacy backed by Turkey and Saudi Arabia and Pakistan rivalled radical Shi'ite overtures from Iran to capture the hearts and minds of the fifty million Muslims of central Asia, now ready to be whipped into religious reprisals against the godless Russian minorities, which had been installed among them by the Tsars and Bolsheviks, rather as the Ashkenazim had come to Palestine. They also had the capacity to smuggle some nuclear weapons to radical Islam. In the summer of 1994, the leader of the breakaway republic of Chechenia in the Caucasus did threaten a *jihad* against Moscow that would make the war in Afghanistan pale into insignificance, and Moscow began the ceaseless conflict. The Russian government had learned nothing. The lost war in Afghanistan had changed the Pakistani city of Peshawar into a capital of militant Islam, ready to export terror and violence not only towards Kabul, but also towards Kashmir, where another *jihad* was declared against India's occupation of part of that divided province.

Another paradox was that once peace in the Middle East appeared possible because of the global dominance of capitalism after the collapse of communism, so Muslim fundamentalism gained strength in many of the Arab states that had been colonial before independence, but had since become friendly with the West. After a coup, Sudan became ruled by the Shari'a and pursued the rebel Christian south with a vengeance, while the outlawed Muslim Brotherhood became the alternative power in the land in Egypt. The religious Muslim parties were banned in Algeria by the ruling revolutionary party after apparently winning an election there. The underground attacks of the Armed Islamic Group with popular support on French aid workers and European businessmen threatened a *jihad* in North Africa that would engulf the conservative regimes in neighbouring Morocco and Tunisia.

As Western technology and materialism won, so Islam protested in search of justice and purity. No threat was posed to Jerusalem, however, except from an occasional terrorist attack. Only if a radical Islamic power were to acquire missiles with a nuclear capability would the Holy Land now be threatened with annihilation as dreadful as the Holocaust, but even that fanatical retribution had to be the order of a deranged mind, given the effective American hegemony over the world with fearful powers of retaliation, a dominance that would last beyond the millennium into the next century.

The fundamentalists in Israel also appeared unlikely to take over a Jewish government, which they found immoral and even blasphemous. However strong the national faith, reason and considerations of security had always ruled the various political coalitions, Labour and the Likud and smaller parties, which administered the state. Moreover, the third Christian force that had always been concerned in the strike for Jerusalem, the Catholic church and various Protestant sects and Masonic groups deriving from the Templars, was also unlikely to seize the reins of power in the United States or any of the previous European medieval crusading states. While some British governments and most American postwar administrations had been sympathetic to the State of Israel, which would not have come into existence or continued without their backing and resources, a Protestant persuasion derived from Old Testament sources had never superseded strategical considerations. An Arab oil embargo had always proved a greater deterrent than the Laws of Moses.

In the internal politics of the United States, the influence of the Jews on the communications system and in the professions counterbalanced the efforts of Southern populist Protestant preachers to translate what they called a moral majority into pressure on the president to carry out the literal words of the Bible and build another Temple for Jesus in Jerusalem. Those millennial sects usually built profitable biblical Temples of their own on commercial ground, which was then said to be sacred. Some of these ended in total destruction or disappointment. The final immolation practised in Guyana by the American People's Temple of Jim Jones and in Waco, Texas, by the Branch Davidians of David Koresh, was a fatal answer to the inadequacy of their messiahs, who ordered mass suicide as a revenge for their failure to build a New Jerusalem. Another extensive self-murder by the disciples of the Russian Maria Devi Khristos, who pronounced herself to be the Messiah and the reincarnated Christ, did not take place in her designated New Jerusalem—St. Sophia's Square in Kiev—when nothing much happened on the date of her forecast Apocalypse. The Jehovah's Witnesses had revised their original prophecy of Armageddon and the Second Coming of Christ from the outbreak of the First World War to the millennium after the year A.D. 2000 when Jesus would descend again to rule in Jerusalem.

As yet, no American president has shown any signs of the delusions of messianic grandeur and the apocalyptic assumptions that afflicted Adolf Hitler. The best hope in the nuclear age of preserving life on earth is that the democratic system with its checks and balances in the United States and Europe and Israel may prevent any elected leader fulfilling his temporary megalomania. Few restraints, however, apply to the military dictators of some Islamic countries such as Iraq, where President Saddam's call for a false *jihad* led to national catastrophe and Arab disunity.

There is no probable strike now for Jerusalem. If wisdom prevails in the Israeli government, the Muslims and the Christians will achieve a kind of international zone that covers their most sacred places, even though Israel will never yield the sovereignty of the Holy City without an almighty struggle. Construction of apartments as fortified blockhouses has continued to serve as an outer wall to East Jerusalem. Supported in essence by the Christian powers and her own stubbornness, Israel will prevail in her sense of historical possession in the coming decades. She is the mother of Jerusalem: Christianity and Islam later discovered their Holy Places there. Although the conqueror has always declared a divine right to the Holy City, the founder staked the first claim. And with the announcement of celebrations for the three thousandth anniversary of the founding of Jerusalem, Israel has demonstrated to all the world its original and immovable title.

ENVOI

In my Exchanges every Land
Shall walk; & mine, in every Land,
Mutual shall build Jerusalem,
Both heart in heart & hand in hand.

—William Blake, "To the Jews," from *Jerusalem*

Modern politics bows to economics, not to history. The lessons of the past are oblivion, the mistakes a daily repetition. Yet this is not true of Jerusalem. Among the Jews, ancient Israel is today and tomorrow and forever. Among the Muslims, the Prophet who stepped into heaven from the Rock, now under its Dome, he lives everlastingly. Only the Christians of the West have ignored much of their heritage in the pursuit of a higher standard of living rather than being. Their New Jerusalem lies as much in the supermart as in the heart. But for the last contenders for the Holy City on earth, few of the acts of three thousand years have been forgiven, and none forgotten.

As a holy city of pilgrimage, Jerusalem is common to all the three leading religions of the Near East, but one sense of pilgrimage is mainly the heritage of Jews and Muslims—the sense of going to Jerusalem in order to be buried there in the belief that when the dead are resurrected, those buried in Jerusalem will first be made alive. This idea is conceived so literally that the grave plots on the Mount of Olives nearer to the Golden Gate, through which the Messiah is expected to pass, are more expensive than those farther away. The nearer a body is to the gate, the closer the body will be to the head of the line at the time of the Resurrection. Jerusalem is surrounded by a huge necropolis, and the dead cannot be ignored in any decision of the living about Jerusalem's future.

Jerusalem also served as a holy city for Islam in its claim to be the successor of Judaism and the rival of Christianity. Jerusalem was an important city for religious studies and contained large seminaries—it was a holy city in the sense that the Vatican is for Catholics and Qum is for the Shi'ites in Iran. Jerusalem was also a city that attracted many mystics, "holy men," apparently under the influence of the Christian monks that lived in and around it. They saw Jerusalem as a place for the purification of the soul and, above all, as the city of the Resurrection. And so Jerusalem became three religions wrestling over God's little plot.

The search for a new and positive identity has been crucial in the ideology of holy wars. It is part of the monotheistic tradition shared by all three of the religions of Judaism, Christianity, and Islam. It was also central in the ideology of the Sunni extremists in Egypt at the time of Sadat, the Muslim Brotherhood. So was the concern for social justice and equality. So too, Shi'ite Iranians, who were indifferent to Marxist analyses of the situation in their country under the Shah, could understand exactly why he was a bad ruler when the principles of Abu Bakr or the Imam Ali were applied to that regime. They had been unmoved by a nationalist explanation of why they should throw off the shackles of the United States and take control of their own destinies. Yet the call to action was deeply embedded in the Islamic tradition. When the Ayatollah Khomeini said that "faith consists of this form of belief that impels men to action," they could understand exactly what he meant.

Islam had always championed the cause of the poor and had encouraged them to stand up for their own rights. Neither the United States nor the Soviet Union had been a real friend to the poor, Khomeini argued. There was no reason why there should be abject poverty in Iran, which was an oil-rich country; the imperial powers had simply exploited this resource so that the people had never benefited from it themselves. Filled with an apocalyptic vision that had inspired other holy wars, Khomeini argued that the poor must take their destiny into their own hands and initiate change by declaring war against the *mostakberin,* the ruling classes.

Muslims must lead the way and be a vanguard for all the poor people of the world who had been damaged by the imperialism of the superpowers. The Islamic revolutionary *jihad* would bring about a new world order.

The leadership of the Christian world had, however, passed from Europe to the United States. America's approach towards the Arabs and the Jews was bound to be different. Many of the old crusading attitudes reached America together with the immigrants from Europe. But from the days of the *Mayflower,* the Americans had identified with the Jews and had given their new Canaan a biblical identity, before the arrival of the millions of Jews who fled persecution in Europe. Today some American Jews argue either that New York is the new capital of Judaism or that, together with Israel, they will create something new for themselves and the world, which will replace the Jewish culture that was lost in Europe. Americans can rightly be proud of this achievement. They have established a strong emotional bond and even an identification with a people whom Europeans have persecuted and massacred ever since the Crusades. Yet, in a sense, both America and Israel are creations of Europe. For most Americans and Israelis, the bond is strong because each recognises the other at a deep level. People who have suffered oppression have a strong bond and empathy that others, who have not suffered in this way, cannot understand. Yet this does not mean that either of these countries of refugees should be able to oppress other people and drive them into permanent exile.

A strong kingship, such as America feels for Israel, means that objectivity can be very difficult. A threat to Israel could be seen as a threat to the identity of America itself and as a wound in her integrity. Certainly the United States saw Israel as her alter ego in the Middle East. They were in the same camp. For example, the American bombing of Tripoli in Libya in April 1986 in the war against international terrorism caused considerable revulsion throughout Europe and actually occasioned some Arab sympathy for Colonel Qaddafi, who had hitherto been seen rather as a maverick in the Arab world and had not been taken very seriously. When moderate Arab leaders like President Mubarak of Egypt and King Hussein of Jordan heard that America had been selling arms to Iran, the leading terrorist state in the region, they felt outraged and insulted. They had put themselves in some danger in their own countries by trying to curb extremism and supporting American policies. They felt this dubious Irangate initiative as a slap in the face, although it must be said that their response was restrained and controlled. On 3 July 1988, Iran Air Flight 655, a civilian flight, was shot down by mistake by the American peacekeeping fleet in the gulf. It was, perhaps, not surprising that the Arab and Muslim population of the Middle East sometimes felt that the American peace mission in the area was double-edged and aggressive, even more so after the Gulf War.

That conflict was tragic for the cause of Arab unity and split the Muslim states irreparably from each other. The division largely reflected the gap between Sunni orthodoxy against Muslim fundamentalism and Shi'ite radicalism. It also signalled, as the acute Kanan Makiya noted, a retreat into silence and "from the public realm into the comforting but suffocating embrace of smaller and smaller units of identity like tribe, religion, sect, and family allegiances. Silence is a synonym for the death of compassion in the Arab world; it is the politics of not washing your laundry in public while gruesome cruelties and whole worlds of morbidity unfold around you. Silence is choosing, ostrichlike, not to know what Arab is doing to fellow Arab, all in the name of a knee-jerk anti-westernism which has turned into a disease."

Crusading Christianity had developed as a response to a long period of humiliation and impotence during the Dark Ages. It was a radical departure, having nothing whatever to do with the pacifist religion of Jesus; but it provided the people of Europe with an ideology that restored their self-respect and made the West a world power. The Iranian Revolution, with its theme of hatred of the Western world, was born of the humiliation and impotence of the colonial period, when Britain and America were felt to have exploited the people of Iran and to have supported the tyrannical regime of the Shah. Similar to crusading in some ways, the Iranian experience was a radical departure from established Muslim tradition. In January 1988, the Ayatollah Khomeini issued a *fatwa* which shocked the *mullahs* of Qum. He claimed that his regime had the same authority as the Prophet Muhammad and that it had the power to stop "any religious law if it feels that it is correct to do so," even religious practises like prayer, fasting, or the *Hajj* pilgrimage. No Muslim leader had ever claimed parity with the Prophet or asserted the power to abolish any of the five pillars of Islam. Like the Crusaders, the ayatollah had departed dramatically from the spirit of the religion for which he had fought. When the Salman Rushdie *fatwa* was pronounced, the official Muslim response in the Arab world was far more restrained and had more in common with the cautious policies of Saladin. The ayatollah's form of Islam had, over the years of his rule, acquired a tendency more in common with the fanatical Crusaders than with mainstream Islam.

The endless holy wars have continued. It was because of the medieval blood-libel of the Jew that six million Jews were exterminated by the Nazis in the Final Solution, more horribly than when they were burned alive in their synagogues after the First Crusade took Jerusalem in blood and fire. The Polish pope unleashed a crusade in Eastern Europe against material- ism and Marxism and triumphed. The anti-Christian Marxist regimes col- lapsed with surprising ease. The eighteenth-century Age of Reason had given way to a strong and fundamentalist resurgence of Christianity in the nineteenth century. Similarly, the secularism of the twentieth century gave way to a renewed religious passion in many faiths. It was very hard to live according to the bleak light of the atheistic or agnostic day, which had ra- tionally disposed of belief in the divine. In Judaism, Christianity, and Is- lam, which all insisted that their myths were historically true, people had a religious geography which gave them a sense of their place in the world and a tangible connection with the unseen and the hereafter. So strong was this desire to believe in a Holy City on earth and in heaven that the polit- ical reality inevitably faded from view.

Yet peace in Jerusalem remained a vision over the centuries and a prac- tical possibility, when the United States established itself as the only su- perpower on earth for a decade or two. In an important article on "The Dream of Co-existence," the Mediterranean historian Bernard Lewis stressed the common heritage of the three great Levantine religions from the ancient Middle East, from Greco-Roman antiquity, and from Jewish revelation and prophecy. While the Jews kept to Judaism, they were not exclusive, for anyone might join them, and other monotheists were not excluded from Paradise. Traditional Christianity and Islam, however, claimed to possess both universal and exclusive truths. There was no sal- vation outside their particular creeds, although conversion to the true faith was possible: Missionary activities were encouraged across the world. Yet the Christians took over the Hebrew Bible and added a New Testament as a final revelation, changing ancient Israel and Jerusalem for various churches and New Jerusalems that replaced the original Holy Land and City. The Muslims, however, conquered Israel and Jerusalem, and so absorbed the Jews with general tolerance within their various empires for thirteen hundred years.

The conversion of the Jews was no priority to Islam, while in Europe, their separate faith appeared damnable to a militant medieval Catholic society. It took the view of Haman in the Book of Esther and of the Greeks and Romans, that the Jews were to be hated because they lived apart and followed their own customs and would recognise no God but their own. Their stubborn aloneness led to their persecution and anti-Semitism, the bane of Western religion. The Jews were held to live in unpardonable error, in a continuous conspiracy against the truth of God. And yet out of European philosophy in the Enlightenment came the solution to the co-existence of the three great Mediterranean faiths, whatever their civil wars and differences. That was the separation of Church and state, summed up by John Locke in his *Letter Concerning Toleration* of 1689, when he declared that "neither Pagan nor Mahometan, nor Jew, ought to be excluded from the civil rights of the Commonwealth because of his religion."

Only in Turkey has the Western example been fully followed, the separation of religion from the state and the institution of a civil law opposed to the Shari'a. Although both Judaism and Christianity had largely adopted the secular state, Islam only rarely has effected the division between the rule of God and man. Indeed, the chief danger of a final holy war in the Middle East lies in Muslim fundamentalists taking over a state armed with Western technology, missiles and nuclear weapons. As Bernard Lewis pointed out, the Muslim radicals and militants are fighting the enemy within as well as the enemy without. "Sometimes he is the Jew or Zion-ist—the terms are more or less interchangeable; sometimes the Christian or missionary or crusader, again more or less interchangeable; some-times the Western imperialist, nowadays redefined as the United States; occasionally—though not much of late—the Soviet Communist. The pri-mary enemy and immediate object of attack among many of these groups are the native secularisers, those who have tried to weaken and modify the Islamic base of the state by introducing secular schools and universities, secular laws and courts, and thus excluding Islam, and so also the professional exponents of Islam, from two major areas which they had previously dominated, education and justice."

Across the world approaching the second millennium, the secular state had already triumphed over the religious state. Orthodox Islam was fighting the last ditch. A brilliant Jewish examination of idolatry after the age of Freud equated it with ideology. It was a form of collective illusion which became an absolute devotion, an attitude that transferred a feeling into a divine being, named "nation" or "class" or "race" or "blood and iron" or "earth." These were idols in an age of apparent materialism. Absolute values could now be conferred upon many things and causes, particularly money, along with "institutions such as the state, persons, goals, ideologies, and even a football team." These objects of worship were given a transcendental goal, a form of earthly success hailed as a divine mission or a heavenly victory.

These gross crusades were perversions of the holy wars and *jihads* that depended on religious zeal. Such abiding and aggressive faith is still an element in Judaism and Christianity and Islam, however much their secular rulers wish to rule it out of their diplomatic considerations. From the strike for Jerusalem, which was certainly the founding Holy City of God upon earth and the focus of the three continents of Europe and Asia and Africa, a solution is emerging. The original believer and settler in the city of the Temple Mount is sovereign, although not on the Temple Mount. The later religions of Christianity and Islam may now control in perpetuity their holy palaces upon the fundamental Jewish sacred site. If not, they should build their each and every Jerusalem elsewhere, the vision of peace in their own lands, as William Blake once suggested, "to the Jews" in London:

> *The fields from Islington to Marylebone,*
> *To Primrose Hill and Saint John's Wood,*
> *Were builded over with pillars of gold;*
> *And there Jerusalem's pillars stood.*

SHORT BIBLIOGRAPHY
AND NOTES

ONE HEAVEN'S GATE

The quotations from William Blake are taken from his poem *Jerusalem: The Emanation of the Giant Albion,* republished by the William Blake Trust/The Tate Gallery (London, 1991). The quotations from the King James Bible come from Deuteronomy, chapter 7, verses 1–6: Joshua, chapter 8, verses 24–28, and chapter 10, verses 36–37:2 Chronicles, chapter 4, verses 11–18: Kings, chapter 7, verses 13–46: and Nehemiah, chapter 4, verse 17. Two wise and balanced books on the Holy Land and City, Colin Thubron's *Jerusalem* (London, 1969) and Teddy Kollek and Moshe Pearlman, *Pilgrims to the Holy Land: The Story of Pilgrimage through the Ages* (London, 1990) have much informed me. While *Jerusalem: Song of Songs* (New York, 1981) by Jill and Leon Uris is full of remarkable insights, it is too much in favour of the Jewish faith and too much an attack on the Christian and Islamic faiths to appear a work of true history. Alexander Horne, *King Solomon's Temple in the Masonic Tradition* (London, 1972), remains the most useful recent work on that theme. John Michell, *The Dimensions of Paradise: The Proportions and Symbolic Numbers of Ancient Cosmology* (London, 1988) is visionary in the measurements of the New Jerusalem. St. John the Divine's vision of the Holy City is described in Revelation, chapter 21. Helen Rosenau, *The Ideal City: Its Architectural Evolution* (New York, 1972) is admirable in its scope and insight; so is John Passmore's analysis of *The Perfectability of Man* (London, 1970) and his explanation of the doctrines of St. Augustine. See also the stimulating thesis by Norman Cohn, *Cosmos, Chaos and the World to Come: The Ancient Roots of Apocalyptic Faith* (Yale University Press, New Haven, 1993).

TWO THAT WHICH STRIKETH

The text from Isaiah, chapter 66, verse 14, inscribed in Hebrew on a Jerusalem wall in the fourth century A.D., and the words of Mukaddasi are cited in *Pilgrims to the Holy Land,* work already mentioned. The rise of Islam is well-analysed in Bernard Lewis, *The Arabs in History* (rev. ed., London, 1970). He quotes Ibn Khurradadhbeh on Jewish merchants and the Jewish and Christian opinions of the Muslim occupation of Jerusalem. Most useful for the continuing doctrine of the *jihad* is Karen Armstrong, *Holy War: The Crusades and Their Impact on Today's World* (rev. ed., New York, 1991). Illuminating also is John L. Esposito's *The Islamic Threat: Myth or Reality?* (Oxford, 1992). Important for the Byzantine influence is Henri Stierlin, *Orient Byzantin* (Fribourg, Switzerland, 1988). And brilliant in its geopolitical interpretation is Archibald R. Lewis, *Nomads and Crusaders: A. D. 1000–1368* (Bloomington, Indiana, 1988). Important generalisations on the period may be found in Daniel J. Boorstin, *The Creators* (New York, 1992), and in Theodore Zeldin, *An Intimate History of Humanity* (London, 1994).

THREE THE ROCK OF PARADISE

I have written before on the origins of Paradise and the Garden in *The Sword and the Grail* (London, 1993). The Song of Solomon is quoted from chapter 4, verses 12–16. L. J. Ringbom, *Graltempel und Paradies* (Stockholm, 1951) is invaluable on the connections of the Grail Castle with Oriental thought and architecture. There is an excellent introduction to *The Song of Roland* by its translator, D. D. R. Owen (Woodbridge, New Hampshire, 1990). Richard F. Cassady is most useful on *The Norman Achievement* (London, 1986). Nobody may try to understand the Crusades without reading Sir Steven Runciman's seminal work, *A History of the Crusades* (3 vols., Cambridge, 1951–54).

FOUR THE CROSS OVER JERUSALEM

Amin Maalouf, *The Crusades Through Arab Eyes* (London, 1984) is an admirable corrective to the Christian chroniclers and quotes the opinions of Arab historians of the time. Zoé Oldenbourg in *The Crusades* (London, 1965) is second only to Runciman in her understanding of that religious phenomenon. The quotation from Exodus comes from chapter 23, verse 22. Most valuable in his analysis is Hans Eberhard Mayer, *The Crusades* (Oxford, 1972). Most important on the Crusades and European colonisation is Robert Bartlett, *The Making of Europe: Conquest, Colonization and Cultural Change 950–1350* (London, 1993).

FIVE   SURVIVAL BY DISUNION

Jonathan Riley-Smith is admirable on the motives of the Crusades in *The First Crusade and the Idea of Crusading* (London, 1993); also useful is his edition of *The Atlas of the Crusades* (London, 1991) and L. and J. Riley-Smith, *The Crusades: Idea and Reality 1095–1294* (London, 1982). The quotation on the Knights Templar by St. Bernard of Clairvaux comes from his *De laude novae militiae,* contained in *Patrologia Latina,* CLXXXII, pp. 923–6. Farhad Daftary puts the revisionist case in *The Assassin Legends: Myths of the Isma'ilis* (London, 1994). The quotations from Ibn al-Qalanisi and from Abu al-Faraj Basil come from *The Crusades Through Arab Eyes,* work cited. I am again indebted to Zoé Olden-bourg's *The Crusades* for the significant comparisons of the Kingdom of Jerusalem with the modern State of Israel and for Fulcher of Chartres' statement about Westerners becoming Orientals.

SIX   MANY THE TEMPLE

For St. Bernard's views on the Crusades, see G. Constable, "The Second Crusade As Seen By Contemporaries," *Traditio,* 9 (1953) and J. Leclercq, "L'encyclique de St-Bernard en faveur de la croisade," *Revue bénédictine,* 81 (1974). Essential reading remain the quoted works by Sir Steven Runciman, Zoé Oldenbourg, Hans Eberhard Mayer, and Amin Maalouf, who quote Nur al-Din, and the leaders with the chronicler of Damascus, and William of Tyre and Ibn al-Athir and Saladin and Abu Shama.

    Parentalia, or Memoirs of the Family of the Wrens; but Chiefly of Sir Christopher Wren was compiled by his son Christopher and published in London in 1750. The leading researcher on *King Solomon's Temple in the Masonic Tradition* (London, 1972) is Alexander Horne, a Thirty-third Degree Mason. I am deeply indebted to his scholarly inquiry and have quoted from him. The Question and Answer of the Masonic catechism are taken from *Jachin and Boaz,* a London Lodge catechism of 1762. The creed of the Templars is examined in the significant book by A. Bothwell-Gosse, *The Knights Templar* (London, 1910). J. N. Casavis, *The Greek Origin of Freemasonry* (New York, 1955), tells of Dionysian roots. The poem on the Four Crowned Martyrs is the medieval *Ars Quatuor Coronatorum*. D. Knoop, G. P. Jones, and D. Hamer edited the *Cooke MS* in *The Two Earliest Masonic MSS* (Manchester, 1938). The quotation from Cyril of Alexandria derives from his *Contra Julianum*.

SEVEN   THE FALL OF THE HOLY CITY

For the quotations from Ibn al-Athir and Baha al-Din and al-Fadel and the *Estoire d'Éracles,* I am indebted to the major sources summarised in the notes for Chapter Six as well as Francesco Gabrieli's admirable *Arab Historians of the Crusades* (London, 1969) and P. H. Newby's stimulating *Saladin in His Time* (London, 1983).

EIGHT   GOD'S OWN

Zoé Oldenbourg again wrote a classic study, *Massacre at Montségur: A History of the Albigensian Crusade* (London, 1961), in which William de Puylaurens, William de Tudela, and the *Chanson de la Croisade* are mentioned. Also stimulating is Jonathan Sumption, *The Albigensian Crusade* (London, 1978). The main sources given in the previous two chapters brought me to the quotations from Niketas Choniates, Saladin, Emperor Alexius III, Pope Innocent III, Robert of Clari, the Chronicle of Norvgorod, Villehardouin, Mesarites, and Imad al-Din, along with the important two volumes of A. A. Vasiliev, *History of the Byzantine Empire* (Madison, Wisconsin, 1952).

NINE   SAVIOUR OR ANTI-CHRIST

Georg Lukács, *The Theory of the Novel,* was first published in 1920 in Berlin, and a translation in 1971 in London. I am particularly indebted to Karen Armstrong for her interpretation of the popular crusades in *Holy War,* work cited, and to Jonathan Riley-Smith, ed. *The Atlas of the Crusades,* work cited, for his section on "Critics of Crusading." Also important for understanding the heresies of the eleventh to thirteenth centuries are R. I. Moore, *The Origins of European Dissent* (London, 1977) and *The Birth of Popular Heresy* (London, 1975), as is Jeffrey B. Russell, *Dissent and Reform in the Early Middle Ages* (New York,

1982). Nahmanides's letter is quoted in the excellent book already cited, *Pilgrims to the Holy Land* by Teddy Kollek and Moshe Pearlman. The quotation from James of Vitry was from Régine Pernoud, *The Crusaders* (London, 1963): The words in italics are mine. The correspondence between Emperor Frederick II and Sultan al-Kamil as well as the Qadi of Nablus's account of the emperor in Jerusalem and Ibn al-Jawzi's detestation of him and the lament of Ibn al-Athir over the Mongol invasion are noted in Amin Maalouf's *The Crusades Through Arab Eyes,* work cited. Sir Steven Runciman has particular insights on this period of internecine strife in the third volume of his classic *A History of the Crusades.*

TEN   FINAL LOSS

Isaac ben Joseph ibn-Chelo is quoted in the excellent *Pilgrims to the Holy Land,* already cited. Sultan Baybars' letter to Bohemond VI of Antioch is quoted by Robert Payne in his stimulating *The Dream and the Tomb: A History of the Crusades* (New York, 1984). Sir Steven Runciman's seminal *A History of the Crusades* is especially informative on the analysis of the Crusades for Pope Gregory X, *Collectio de Scandalis Ecclesiae.* The Templar writing from Acre is quoted by Stephen Howarth, *The Knights Templar* (London, 1982), while Maalouf's cited *The Crusades Through Arab Eyes* gives the text of the accord between the sultan Qalawun and the Kingdom of Jerusalem as well as the account by Abu al-Fida of the sack of Tripoli and Acre.

Nahmanides and his pupil are presented by Joshua Prawer in his important *The Latin Kingdom of Jerusalem: European Colonialism in the Middle Ages* (London, 1972). A full account of the aftermath of the fall of the Knights Templar may be found in Andrew Sinclair, *The Sword and the Grail* (London, 1993).

ELEVEN   FALSE DIRECTIONS

Norman Housley's book on *The Later Crusades, 1274–1580: From Lyons to Alcazar* (Oxford, 1992) is definitive. I am particularly indebted to him for his analysis of crusading calls after the fall of Constantinople, as well as pointing this author to quotations from Pope Boniface VIII, the *Lollard Conclusions,* Luther, the marquis of Cadiz, Betrandon de la Broquière, Pope Pius II, John of Tagliacozzo, and George of Trebizond. Peter W. Edbury, *The Kingdom of Cyprus and the Crusades, 1191–1374* (Cambridge, 1991) is perceptive on the expedition to

Alexandria of King Peter of Cyprus. On the origins of Christian pacifism, Peter Brock is interesting in his *Freedom from Violence: Sectarian Nonresistance from the Middle Ages to the Great War* (Toronto, 1991). The *Consultatio* of Erasmus comes from P. S. Allen and other editors, *Opus epistolarum Desiderii Erasmi Roterodami* (12 vols., Oxford, 1906–58).

The second volume of A. A. Vasiliev, *History of the Byzantine Empire,* already cited, is excellent on the fall of Constantinople, and it quotes Lucas Notoras and Michael Ducas. W. B. Yeats's poem "Sailing to Byzantium" was first published in London in *The Tower,* 1928. Fernand Braudel, *The Mediterranean and the Mediterranean World in the Age of Philip II* (2 vols., London, 1972) remains seminal. Joseph Ha Cohen is quoted in E. Carmody, *Archives Israelites de France* (12 vols., Paris, 1857), while the Crusade of the *conversos* towards Jerusalem comes from S. W. Baron, *A Social and Religious History of the Jews,* XV, *Resettlement and Exploration* (2 ed., New York, 1973).

TWELVE   IMPALPABLE VOIDNESS

The count of Württemberg's advice to Felix Fabri is quoted in H. F. M. Prescott, *Jerusalem Journey: Pilgrimage to the Holy Land in the Fifteenth Century* (London, 1954). A significant school of history on the millennial cults and later revolutions was headed by Norman Cohn, *The Pursuit of the Millennium* (London, 1957). Most important in this field also were Eric Hobsbawn, *Primitive Rebels* (rev. ed., New York, 1965) and with George Rudé, *Captain Swing* (London, 1969); Christopher Hill, *Antichrist in Seventeeth-Century England* (Oxford, 1971); Henri Desroches, *The American Shakers: From Neo-Christianity to Presocialism* (Amherst, Univ. of Massachusetts Press, 1971); E. P. Thompson, *The Making of The English Working Class* (rev. ed., London, 1968); Sylvia L. Thrupp, ed., *Millennial Dreams in Action* (The Hague, 1962); Gordon Leff, *Heresy in the Later Middle Ages* (2 vols., Manchester, 1967); Howard Kaminsky, *A History of the Hussite Revolution* (Berkeley, 1967); Robert E. Lerner, *The Heresy of the Free Spirit in the Later Middle Ages* (Berkeley, 1972); and J. L. Talmon, *Political Messianism* (New York, 1960).

Olivier Maillard's poem on Satan is quoted in Larissa Taylor, *Soldiers of Christ: Preaching in Late Medieval and Reformation France* (Oxford, 1992). Georg Lukács, *The Theory of the Novel,* has already been cited. The translation from *Don Quixote* by Miguel de Cervantes is by Samuel Putnam (New York, 1949). The Diggers' ballad is quoted in Eduard Bernstein, *Cromwell & Communism: Socialism and Democracy in the Great English Revolution* (London, 1930), while William Haller, *Liberty and Reformation in the Puritan Revolution* (New York, 1955) is good on Lilburne's beliefs. Important for an understanding of the prophecies of the times is Keith Thomas, *Religion and the Decline of Magic* (London, 1971). Amin Maalouf, *The Crusades Through Arab Eyes,* has already been cited, as has *Pilgrims to the Holy Land,* which quotes Henry Maundrell. The analysis of the qualities of millenarianism comes from Clarke Garrett, *Respectable Folly* (Baltimore, 1975) and J. F. C. Harrison, *The Second Coming: Popular Millenarianism 1780–1850* (London, 1979), while Michael Barkun, *Disaster and the Millennium* (New Haven, 1974), takes the story of apocalyptic prophecy to modern times.

The chapters in Ezekiel dealing with the rebuilding of the Temple and Jerusalem are from 40–48. William Blake's *Jerusalem: The Emanation of the Giant Albion* has been admirably reproduced by the Tate Gallery in 1991 in conjunction with the William Blake Trust. For an understanding of Blake's meaning in using the word *Jerusalem,* S. Foster Damon, *A Blake Dictionary: The Ideas and Symbols of William Blake* (London, 1973) is recommended. Alexander Gilchrist, *Life of William Blake,* was published in 1880 in two volumes in London. On millenarianism in the United States of America, Alice Felt Tyler, *Freedom's Ferment* (Univ. of Minnesota, 1944) and Whitney R. Cross, *The Burned-Over District* (Cornell Univ., 1950) are informative. Essential to an understanding of the importance of the Temple and Jerusalem among the Freemasons is Alexander Horne, *King Solomon's Temple in the Masonic Tradition* (London, 1972); it quotes the *Dowland Manuscript* and the Mason's admission to the lodge at Kilwinning. The threat of the Sons of Liberty to the gentlemen is contained in A. J. Peacock, *Bread or Blood: A Study of the Agrarian Riots in East Anglia in 1816* (London, 1965).

THIRTEEN   REACHING ZION

Barnet Litvinoff, *Road to Jerusalem: Zionism's Imprint on History* (London, 1965) is excellent on the subject, particularly on Herzl and Weizmann. Paul Johnson, *A History of the Jews* (London, 1987) analyses with perception the impact of Zionism on British politics, while Ronald Sanders, *The High Walls of Jerusalem: A History of the Balfour Declaration and the Birth of the British Mandate for Palestine* (New York, 1983) is perceptive on Disraeli's and George Eliot's contribution to Zionism as well as on the Balfour Declaration. Chateaubriand published his *Journey from Paris to Jerusalem and from Jerusalem to Paris* in France in 1811.

Disraeli's novel *Alroy* was published in a new edition in London in 1862 and *Tancred* in a new edition in London in 1894, while George Eliot's *Daniel Deronda* was first published in 1876 in London. For Disraeli's conversation with Lord Stanley, see *Disraeli, Derby and the Conservative Party: The Political Journals of George Stanley* (J. R. Vincent, ed., London, 1978). Lucien Wolf wrote on the influence of *Daniel Deronda* in the entry on "Zionism" in the *Encyclopaedia Britannica, 1911* edition.

Sir Charles Warren, *The Land of Promise: or, Turkey's Guarantee* was published in 1875 in London, while Sir Isaiah Berlin wrote an incisive study of the *Life and Opinions of Moses Hess,* whom I quote from Barnet Litvinoff's work, already cited, along with Herzl and Weizmann. Maxim Gorky's *Bystander* was first published in English in 1930, while there is a stimulating chapter on the 1905 Revolution in Russia in Otto Friedrich, *The End of the World: A History* (New York, 1982). G. N. Giladi, *Discord in Zion: Conflict between Ashkenazi & Sephardi Jews in Israel* (London, 1990) takes a strong line on the Sephardi side. Asquith spoke on the Ottoman Empire on 9 November 1914, while the leader in the *Jewish Chronicle* appeared four days later. Asquith wrote to his confidante Venetia Stanley on 13 March 1915. Chaim Weizmann wrote of his story in *Trial and Error* (London, 1949). The war correspondent who accompanied the Egyptian Expeditionary Force was W. T. Massey, who wrote of his experiences in *The Desert Campaigns* (London, 1918) and *How Jerusalem Was Won: Being the Record of Allenby's Campaign in Palestine* (London, 1919). David L. Bullock, *Allenby's War: The Palestine-Arabian Campaigns, 1916–1918* (London, 1988) is good on strategy. Major-General Sir George Macdonogh was the director of British intelligence in 1916: He is quoted in Ronald Sanders's work, already cited, while Balfour's "Memorandum Respecting Syria, Palestine and Mesopotamia" is quoted in Karen Armstrong's *Holy War,* already cited.

FOURTEEN   INTOLERABLE MANDATE

The most informative account of this period is by Dov Joseph, who served as the military governor of Jerusalem for the new State of Israel and wrote of his experiences in *The Faithful City: The Siege of Jerusalem, 1948* (The Hogarth Press, London, 1962). I have quoted from his own text and used his quotations from Sir Alan Cunningham to Ben-Gurion, from the Israeli provisional government's reply to Count Bernadotte, and from Dr. Weizmann's speech at Jerusalem in 1948. Emmanuel Litvinoff, *Road to Jerusalem: Zionism's Imprint on*

History, work cited, is admirably impartial on the issue, and he quotes David Ben-Gurion's evidence to Sir Harold MacMichael and on the outbreak of the Second World War and to the United Nations Special Committee. I have further used his text for Ben-Gurion's "Declaration of Independence." Weizmann's memoirs on his conversation with Feisal have already been mentioned: Philip Noel Baker was the British delegate at the Paris peace conference and is quoted in Yigal Lossin, *Pillar of Fire: The Rebirth of Israel—A Visual History* (Jerusalem, 1983). Ronald Storrs is quoted in *The High Walls of Jerusalem,* already cited, as are the White Papers of 1922 and 1939 and the Peel Commission of 1937. Jabotinsky's views appear in Karen Armstrong's *Holy War,* already cited, as do Weizmann's on the partition plan. The former British commander of the Arab Legion puts the Jordanian point of view on Israel and its history in John Bagot Glubb, *Peace in the Holy Land* (London, 1971). Folke Bernadotte's *To Jerusalem* was published in 1951 in London.

FIFTEEN   IRREVOCABLE CAPITAL

For material for this chapter, I am indebted to the important *Four Arab-Israeli Wars and the Peace Process* by Sydney D. Bailey, published in London in 1990: He quotes David Ben-Gurion, General Moshe Dayan, Abba Eban, General Burns, Gamal Nasser, Anwar Sadat, and Muhammad Heikal, while he also defines the three Nos of the 1967 Khartoum Summit. Karen Armstrong, *Holy War,* already cited, tells of Moshe Dayan's militant archaeology and of Anwar Sadat's speech to the Knesset, while the UNRWA quotation comes from its report, 1 July 1963–30 June 1964. On the Suez Crisis, Hugh Thomas, *The Suez Affair* (rev. ed., London, 1970) and David Carlton, *Britain and the Suez Crisis* (London, 1988) are informative, while Moshe Dayan, *Diary of the Sinai Campaign* (London, 1966) is essential reading. Chaim Herzog, *The Arab-Israeli Wars: War and Peace in the Middle East* (rev. ed., New York, 1984) is important. Professor Saadia Tourel made the observation of Kissinger as conductor of the orchestra, while the Egyptian foreign minister who resigned was Ismail Fahmy.

President Carter's speech on biblical Israel was delivered on 1 May 1978, and on American and Israeli pioneers to the Knesset the following year: Both are quoted in the significant book by Regina Sharif, *Non-Jewish Zionism: Its Roots in Western History* (London, 1983). David Willey describes Pope John Paul II's importance in destroying Marxism in *God's Politician* (London, 1992). Amin Maalouf wrote of the enduring importance of *The Crusades Through Arab Eyes,* work already cited. *Newsweek* reported Saddam Hussein's remarks on his withdrawal from Kuwait in 1992, also those of Richard Cheney and Yitzhak Rabin on the PLO accords and the followers of Meir Kahane. The Kuwaiti roving ambassador spoke on the B.B.C. News on 25 February 1991, while the citizens of Baghdad commented on 27 February 1991. The leader in the London *Sunday Times* on the consequences of the Gulf War was published on 5 September 1993. Karen Armstrong again quotes the prayer of the Kibbutz Dati in *Holy War,* and she comments on the similarity of Jewish and Muslim extremists. Teddy Kollek's autobiography was written with his son Amos and published in 1990 in London, while his remarks on Jerusalem come from his John Galway Foster Memorial Lecture on 1 November 1994 in London. News of Ehud Olmert's election and attitude as mayor of Jerusalem and of King Fahd's definition of a *jihad* was printed in the London *Times,* 3 November 1993: 20 and 24 May 1994. Also on 15 July 1994, the *Times* quoted Shimon Peres in Jerusalem. The sympathetic rabbi was Shlomo Aviner, quoted in *Newsweek,* 10 February 1992. President Dudayev of Chechenia was quoted on his *jihad* by the *Times,* 12 August 1994. Gilles Kepel, *The Revenge of God: The Resurgence of Islam, Christianity and Judaism in the Modern World* (London, 1994) is valuable on recent religious fundamentalism.

ENVOI

Avishai Margalit, "The Myth of Jerusalem," *The New York Review of Books,* 19 December 1991, is admirable on the cemeteries of Jerusalem. His book with Moshe Halbertal, *Idolatry* (tr. Naomi Goldblum, Harvard University Press, 1994) is also important on its subject, and it is quoted, as is Kanan Makiya's important *Cruelty and Silence: War, Tyranny, Uprising and the Arab World* (Norton, New York, 1993). Bernard Lewis wrote his quoted article, "Muslims, Christians and Jews: The Dream of Coexistence," *The New York Review of Books,* 26 March 1992. Anti-Semitism is treated admirably in Léon Poliakov, *Histoire de antisémitisme: de Voltaire à Wagner* (Paris, 1968). The poem of William Blake is quoted from his collected works. Amos Elon, *Jerusalem: City of Mirrors* (New York, 1989) is prophetic on his solution of a peace with the removal of rigid boundaries of sovereignty in Jerusalem.

INDEX